Sourcebook
for English Papers

1001 Ideas for Term Papers, Projects, Reports, and Speeches

Walter James Miller
Professor of English
New York University

An ARCO Book
Published by Prentice Hall Press
New York, New York 10023

An ARCO Book
Published by Prentice Hall Press
A Division of Simon & Schuster, Inc.
Gulf + Western Building
One Gulf + Western Plaza
New York, New York 10023

PRENTICE HALL PRESS is a trademark of Simon & Schuster, Inc.

Manufactured in the United States of America

1 2 3 4 5 6 7 8 9 10

Library of Congress Cataloging-in-Publication Data

Miller, Walter James, 1918–
   Sourcebook for English papers.

   "An Arco book."
   Bibliography: p.
   Includes index.
   Summary: Offers suggestions for research topics,
both literary and nonliterary, when doing papers
for English class.
   1. Report writing.   2. English language—
Composition and exercises.   3. English language—
Rhetoric.   [1. Report writing.   2. English
language—Composition and exercises.   3. English
language—Rhetoric]   I. Title.
PE1478.M54   1987   808'.042   87-6938

ISBN 0–668–06609–1

CONTENTS

1

Introduction: Why and How to Use This Book

Whenever your English teacher assigns a paper—or an oral report—you see three big challenges looming ahead of you:

1. You have to find a writable Idea (or a speakable one).

By this you mean more than just an Idea that *can* be discussed. You mean an Idea that excites you enough to power you through the next two problems:

2. You have to wield that Idea as a kind or organizing tool—a combination shovel and sieve!—when you trigger that landslide called research-in-progress.
3. Then you have to compose your findings into a new, special pattern of Ideas all developed from that original notion.

Once again, as you face these challenges, you realize this strange fact: Most books about English term papers, etc., help you mainly with (2) how to research, and (3) how to present, your materials. Yet don't you often need just as much help with (1) how to find *viable Ideas*?

This book provides that help. Here we pursue a dual purpose: not only to excite you about specific Ideas you can use right now, but also to show you ways to discover such Ideas on your own in the future.

Remember this too: Even if your English teacher gives you the format, and a general topic—say, a book report on Ernest Hemingway's *A Farewell to Arms,* or an oral report on AIDS—you still have to find an "angle," a "slant," an aspect, a subtopic, an approach, an *emphasis* that becomes *your* idea for *your* work.

Here we shall discuss *Ideas for English Term Papers, Projects, Reports, and Speeches,* in two broad categories: (1) Ideas for Literary Subjects, and (2) Ideas for Other, Nonliterary Subjects.

BROAD IDEAS ON LITERARY SUBJECTS

We shall start off with general Ideas that you can apply to all literature, i.e., to any work of fiction, drama (stage, film, TV), poetry, or nonfiction. Hence our discussions of your own involvement with literature ("Wow! Did I See a Good Movie!" and "Your Own Critical Judgment"), of "Master Themes in World Literature," and of the basic techniques that any author might use, might well suggest to you maybe *millions of Ideas* more than you and all your classmates could ever use.

For example, perusing these general Ideas and applying them to the author you're working on, you might see at once that it's *scene-summary-scene* you should focus on in F. Scott Fitzgerald, it's *tonal effects* you ought to explore in Samuel Taylor Coleridge, it's *symbolism* that really piques your curiosity in Virginia Woolf's *To the Lighthouse.*

And such choices may now be open to you for the first time because this book gives you full understanding of precisely what we mean by such ideas as *tonal patterns, symbolism, free verse, nonfiction formats, Freytag's Pyramid structure in drama,* etc.

Incidentally, in several cases these full explanations offer you a new and original approach—e.g., how a play's or story's structure can be ascertained by a "Three Moods" approach, or "Mood as a Factor in Understanding Poetry." In other cases these full explanations are simply succinct summaries of long-standing concepts, widely used in the literary profession: the different styles of essay, the old and the new conceptions of biography, the "Three Unities," etc. Or they are summaries of new developments in literature like "gut" journalism.

SPECIFIC IDEAS ON LITERARY SUBJECTS

So then, either you yourself apply and adapt some of our general Ideas to the specific author you're studying, *or* you find your topic by browsing through our crowded bazaar of specific Ideas, such as:

What is the Nature of God in Alice Walker's *The Color Purple?* How do authors use telephone calls or tape recorders as a means of revealing character? If you felt uneasy over *Ivanhoe,* why not report on William Makepeace Thackeray's parody of it? Did you know that James Fenimore Cooper wrote *The Pilot* to put down (show up!) Walter Scott's *The Pirate?* What influence have great psychologists—William James, Sigmund Freud, Carl Jung, Erich Fromm, R. D. Laing—had on literature?

What two entirely different approaches to the short story were developed by Russian and American authors? How do writers explain Mona Lisa's smile? How has Darwin influenced drama about the Vietnam war? How has the Bible influenced Gabriel García Márquez's *One Hundred Years of Solitude?* How does Lorraine Hansberry stage her characters' unconscious experience? Who killed radio drama in the U.S.?

In most cases, this book explains the implications of the topic, suggests directions in which you can take it, cautions you about opposing views you must reckon with, and often indicates even the publication to use as your launchpad.

IDEAS FOR NON-LITERARY SUBJECTS

First we shall let you in on the secret of picking such Ideas "out of the air." Many of you will be able to stop right there, because the secret works if you relax and give it a chance. Most of you will still go on to skim through the hundreds of samples that *I* have picked out of the air until some sentence directly inspires you or indirectly leads you, by free association, to a related Idea you can use, such as:

Did the "blues" originate entirely in the U.S. or can its roots be found in Africa? Why, after five other major nations have had a woman as head of state, does the U.S. still have only men? In what ways is Gainsborough's painting *Blue Boy* a direct slap at the Establishment? Why were black Air Corps officers in World War II called "The Lonely Eagles"? How are we learning to *live*— not just *visit* but *live*—*under water?* What happened to the title of Rembrandt's *Night Watch* after they washed it? Why did the Negro 9th Cavalry have to rescue the (lily white) Rough Riders at San Juan (Kettle) Hill—and why did the Roughs still get all the credit for the battle? Why do your tastes in music change so often? What is the radon danger in your home? your classroom?

LOCATING THE TWO TYPES OF IDEAS

Chapters 2 through 5 are devoted mainly to Ideas for discussing the themes and techniques of fiction, drama, and poetry. Chapter 6 is a blend of Ideas about the classics of nonfiction discussed (a) for their value as literature and/or (b) for their contributions to other fields as well: e.g., psychology, engineering, fishing.

In Chapter 6 you will find an extended discussion of the *various structures authors use for nonfiction. No matter what topic you choose to write about, you should consult this passage (pp. 176–178) before you outline your own oral report or term paper.*

Chapter 7 takes up Ideas about music, art, science, history, and current affairs, Ideas that take you to sources that are informational and expository, with little or no literary pretensions. Actually, some such Ideas can be gleaned from any section (glance through the Index): Ideas about reforms in the meat-packing industry, about slavery, about Jesus of Nazareth may be found in Chapter 2's sections on "Fact and Fiction" in the novels of Upton Sinclair, Harriet Beecher Stowe, George Moore.

Chapter 8 supplies you with a list of books to consult when you get beyond the hunt for Ideas and into research and composition.

Chapter 9 is the all-important Index. This book is so organized that everybody who uses it must consult the Index from time to time. For example, to avoid needless repetition, the dates of persons, books, paintings, etc., are usually given only once, in the Index (unless they are actually needed to establish a point of order in the text). You are often directed to the Index to pick up related Ideas, definitions, etc. And just glancing through the Index in itself may lead you to better Ideas, to new connections, to a reunion with Ideas you had forgotten.

SYMBOLS AS GUIDES

To help you decide which Ideas will most interest you, we characterize them in part with a system of symbols based on those used in *10,000 Ideas for Term Papers, Projects and Reports* (Arco, 1984).

- Indicates an Idea that presents only average difficulty.
- Tags an Idea that may appeal more to someone with previous knowledge in the field.
- ★ Denotes an Idea that can be researched in most libraries.
- ▲ Such an Idea might take you to a larger library, or require that you arrange an interlibrary loan. (Why not find out all about such a loan?)
- ☐ Indicates you might have to view a film, video, TV show, or slides, and/or you might have to screen a film, video, or slides as part of your presentation.
- ♫ Means you might have to listen to recorded music, drama, or poetry (in a library?) as part of your research and/or maybe to play recorded speech or music as part of your presentation.

DIFFERENT WAYS TO USE THIS BOOK

At different times you and your friends might use different approaches to the resources of this book.

1. The Desperate, Panic-Stricken Approach. You go straight to the Index hoping to find out exactly where we offer Ideas on the Puerto Rican poet and dramatist Miguel Piñero. Maybe you score. Right on. But there's also the likelihood that your best Ideas on Piñero might hit you if you read our general sections on *dialogue* or on *free verse*.

2. The Calm Approach. You read in full whatever general sections are devoted to the field you'll be working in: fiction, drama, poetry, music, etc. You locate them by scanning the Table of Contents and checking key words/names in the Index. As we've seen, the chances are good you'll make the best connection by applying a general idea (say, on the structure of fiction) to the author you're studying (Cynthia Ozick, maybe, or Don DeLillo). Then you scan the ''Specific Ideas'' in your field, slowing down to contemplate the most attractive ones. Even here, though, you may make best use of these resources if you establish your own connections: Take an Idea we offer about Paul Simon and apply it instead to Bruce Springsteen.

3. The wisest, most economical, longest-range, biggest-payoff approach. Realizing that this book will not only suggest Ideas you can use *today* but also show you ways to generate Ideas on your own *tomorrow*, you devote a rainy day to reading all the general sections and sampling-skimming-sampling all the specific Ideas. *Then you annotate the margins with related Ideas you yourself dream up as a result of free associations and other connections you make as you* *read us.* Now then, you are a coauthor of this book, and you proudly put it in an honored position on your bookshelf to look into it again and again in your student years.

Let's go. As Walt Whitman would say, Haven't we stood here like trees in the ground long enough?

2

Ideas for Literary Subjects

"WOW! DID I SEE A GOOD MOVIE!"

You freeze. Your English teacher has just told your class you have to write a term paper . . . or make an oral report . . . on some author and her books. On literature!

You *deep* freeze. "What should I write about? I never come up with any good ideas on literature!"

Oh yes you do. You do it informally quite often. It's only the *formal* assignment that makes you freeze and forget a process you've been through many times. Like this:

"Wow!" you say to your friend. "Did I see a good movie on the 'Late Late Show.' "

"What was it about?" she asks.

You start telling her about this man who's sleeping in a strange house during a violent snowstorm. He hears a tapping on the window. It looks as if the wind is knocking a branch against the pane. When he opens the window he's touched by a cold clammy hand and hears a frail voice. . . .

Yes, you're talking freely now about literature. For a writer wrote the screenplay. And in this case he adapted it from a classic English novel. You and your friend have already broached two of the main ideas, or questions, we consider whenever we discuss any literary work:

1. What's it about?
2. How did you like it?

7

At some point you're also going to tell your friend how the man who is touched by a ghost finds out what happened in this haunted house.

"Well, when he gets back to his own place, he asks his housekeeper. She tells him that was the ghost of Cathy trying to get back into her old room at Wuthering Heights. Once Cathy was in love with a poor orphan named Heathcliff. But she married a rich squire. When Heathcliff comes back years later. . . ."

And now you're telling your friend *how* the author handled the time problem in unraveling her story. Through flashbacks.

Again, at some point your friend and you might muse over the situation that drove Cathy mad and killed her. Her intellect, her social reasoning, made her marry into the rich, cultured, refined Linton family. But her passions, her wild love of life, still identified with the poor, earthy servant, Heathcliff.

"And he took cruel revenge on her. . . ."

So far, then, you two have already talked about (1) the subject, the central problems, the *themes* of the film play: frustrated love, revenge; (2) the people involved, their nature, their conflicts, what motivates them, in short, *characterization*; (3) some of the *techniques* the author uses to unfold her story, e.g., flashbacks; and (4) your own *critical judgment*: It was "a good movie," and that's what you're trying to illustrate, to prove, to your friend.

And each of these four topics of your conversation is at least the beginning of an *idea* for a full discussion of any work of literature.

YOUR OWN CRITICAL JUDGMENT

Let's first expand on that last topic: *your own critical judgment*. One reason you deep-froze is that it's *easy* to say "Wow! Did I see a good movie!" but *hard* to explain *why* you think it was good—or boring, saddening, provocative, whatever the case may have been. But explaining your own reaction will be easier if you keep in mind these *self-respecting ideas:*

You watched *Wuthering Heights* because—like all TV fans, baseball fanatics, readers, *et al.*—you wallow in vicarious experience. That is, you seek second-hand adventures: you let some actress, shortstop, or ET substitute for *you!* Although you are bound to your own space and time, you can still "live" for a while in the lives of others: e.g., you can "be" Heathcliff or Cathy in England in 1801. Through TV plays, record-setting RBIs, exciting s-f, you can face new problems and win new insights without taking the same risks you'd face if the problems were really—not vicariously—yours.

Respecting your own needs, then, you're already equipped with some basic expectations, some simple criteria by which you can judge a literary work you have to report on—especially if you can choose your own work. You need only ask yourself:

Has the playwright, novelist, poet, essayist, whoever, created a *climate* in which I can become involved—involved emotionally and intellectually? Have I been able, in that climate, that situation, to gain any new pleasures, new experience, new insights?

The next question is: How can I analyze that experience, rewarding or disappointing as it may be, so I can explain it to the teacher and/or the class? So we're back to that author's *themes* and *techniques* and the part they played in offering you some vicarious experience.

MASTER THEMES IN WORLD LITERATURE

You entertained your friend with details about the "gypsy" orphan Heathcliff and his wild love for Cathy. Although Emily Brontë invested her story with all the rich local color of northern England, with all the rural customs of Yorkshire in 1801, we can say that, in one sense, all her particulars simply add some new variations to some timeless and universal themes: love, social ambition, the search for happiness, revenge. And all the probings of the newcomer to Wuthering Heights into the mystery of the ghost can also be subsumed under such themes: the quest for knowledge, curiosity about the human condition. As a matter of fact, the more you watch TV movies and read paperback novels, the more you realize that all literature can be classified under the headings of some dozen or so major themes. This knowledge can be a great help to you in "dreaming up" ideas for English.

First you establish what the themes of a work or an author are. Keep always in mind that maybe the author, or the characters, will *declare* the themes; but more than likely, you yourself will have to *infer* the meaning, the message, from the action, the setting, the characterization, and the outcome. Do not hesitate to try out your own interpretations. And of course you can consult the critics too.

Once you have established the themes, you are ready to use them in a discussion. At this point, let us consider very simple examples. If you decide that "the nature of young love" is one of the themes of *Wuthering Heights,* the phrase might remind you of the play *Romeo and Juliet.* Should you do a paper on "Young Love as a Theme in Brontë and Shakespeare"? Or does the phrase "young love" suggest a contrast with cynical love, so that you might consider a paper on "Love in the Novels of Emily Brontë and Stendhal"?

Here are some of the universal master themes to which all authors, from the Brontë sisters to Don DeLillo, continually return. Do any of these themes figure in the work(s) you are preparing to report on? If so, consider how you can apply the ideas explored here to a discussion of your author's work.

Illusion and Reality

Every work of literature is concerned, to some extent, with the difference between illusion and reality. Any person's history—and all humanity's history—can be measured in terms of discoveries of what's authentic behind what's apparent. Ophelia discovers how mistaken she was to think Hamlet could really love her; science discovers that the sun does not revolve around the earth. And all characters, and their authors, differ largely in the way their own individual illusions, their blind spots, cloud their vision of the truth. And *plot, whether in a novel, a short story, or a TV movie, is really a series of efforts to close the gap between partial knowledge and full truth.*

Looking at literature this way gives you a handle on any author's work: What illusions does s/he deal with? Why does reality evade her characters? What does this author regard as the reality in the situation s/he is probing? Does the author perchance believe (as Eugene O'Neill seems to suggest in *The Iceman Cometh*) that humanity *needs* illusions? protects itself from *dis*illusionment? Material here for scores of papers! • ★

Why Humanity Suffers

Every author provides answers, explicit or implicit, to this question. The early chapters of *The Book of Genesis* blame man's suffering on womankind. In *The Book of Job*, Job's friends tell him he has met disaster because he has sinned; actually he suffers because God is testing him. Alexander Pope's *Essay on Man* explains that people suffer when they step out of their place in the scheme of things. Upton Sinclair's *The Jungle* says that immigrants living in Chicago around 1900 suffer because of the greed of their employers. Naturalist writers generally indicate that man's fate is a result of biological and social forces. Some of Eugene O'Neill's characters in *The Iceman Cometh* suffer when their illusions are stripped away. What reasons does your author find? Research into the critics' discussions of these causes, add your own reactions, and you have a paper of whatever scope you wish: e.g., "Why Humanity Suffers: Beckett's Answer in *Waiting for Godot*" (or, "in His Early Plays"); or, "Why Mankind Suffers: The Answers in Shakespeare's *King Lear* and Beckett's *Endgame*." • ★

Relations between the Sexes

The Book of Genesis says that woman must be controlled by man; John Milton makes this the main theme of *Paradise Lost* and of *Samson Agonistes*. Usually in Western literature the belief in male supremacy is not stated at all but is taken for granted. But even before the feminist revolution of the 1960s there were writers who spoke up for equality of the sexes. Euripides in *Medea*, John Webster in *The Duchess of Malfi*, William Congreve in *The Way of the World*, all included the position of woman in society as one of their main themes. Almost every long poem, play, or novel is susceptible to this inquiry: What do the author and his or her characters *assume* is the proper role of women in society? Recent literature for equality—like Germaine Greer's *The Female Eunuch*—can serve you as a catalogue of women's grievances and ambitions. • ★

Relations between the Races

Many classics consider the psychological (as well as economic, social, or physical) effects of racial "superiority" on both the racist and his victim. This is typical of the kind of topic with which you have greater success if you do a *comparative study*: e.g., "The Psychology of Racism in Richard Wright's *Native Son*, Margaret Mitchell's *Gone with the Wind*, and William Faulkner's *The Bear* (or *Intruder in the Dust*)." The critical literature is enormous, allowing you to choose from numerous aspects of the subject those that suit you and the conditions of your assignment. • ★

Patriotism and Nationalism

When is patriotism, or love of one's country, an ennobling force, a justified cause, and when is it a cover for evil, "the last refuge of a scoundrel" (Dr. Samuel Johnson)? When is the nationalist a hero, when a dupe? From Voltaire's *Candide* and Jules Verne's *Family without a Name* to the myriad novels and plays about twentieth-century wars—Joseph Heller's *Catch-22*, Kurt Vonnegut's *Slaughterhouse-Five*, Norman Mailer's *The Naked and the Dead*—literature provides a broad spectrum of reactions to these two major "ideas." • ★

Why Men Make War

Homer portrays Achilles as a truculent man who preferred a short life of war to a long life of peace. The poet W. H. Auden wrote, on the outbreak of World War II,

> Intellectual disgrace
> Stares from every human face

For millennia, poets, playwrights, and novelists have studied the psychology of warmakers and their victims. Your problem as a writer of a term paper on this question is how, from thousands of works, to select a cluster that will produce good discussion and good results. • ★

The Nature of Love

In plays like Shakespeare's *Antony and Cleopatra* and Henrik Ibsen's *A Doll's House*, in novels like Jane Austen's *Pride and Prejudice* and Doris Lessing's *The Golden Notebook*, in nonfiction like Erich Fromm's *The Art of Loving* and Germaine Greer's *The Female Eunuch*, writers have tried continually to define the varieties of the love passion and the nature of true love. Sociologists and psychologists often use such plays and novels as the basis for their own discussions, providing writers of term papers with more combinations of creative and critical materials than they really need. • ★

The Nature of Good and Evil

For novelist Nathaniel Hawthorne, evil is the "violation of the human heart." For poet Dante Alighieri, adulterous love is less evil than forgery if the man and woman truly love each other. The English playwright Oscar Wilde is imprisoned for homosexuality while in Plato's dialogues homosexual love is often presented in a noble light. You can take up the question of the nature of good and evil in the works of any author or, for a more provocative study, in selected works of two or more writers compared. • ★

• average difficulty	○ previous knowledge	★ most libraries
▲ larger library	☐ visual component	☊ audio component

The Individual and Society

A question inherent in most literature is: "What are the responsibilities of the individual and society to each other?" You could consider, and compare, radically different treatments in novels like Edward Bellamy's *Looking Backward*, John Steinbeck's *The Grapes of Wrath*, Upton Sinclair's *The Jungle*, George Orwell's *1984*; in plays like Sophocles' *Antigone*, Shakespeare's *Henry V*, and Arthur Miller's *The Crucible*; and in classics of political science like Plato's *Republic* and Alexander Hamilton's, James Madison's, and John Jay's *The Federalist*. Most challenging, perhaps, would be an effort to find the relations implicit, taken for granted, in works of literature not regarded as predominantly political, like Mark Twain's *Huckleberry Finn* or F. Scott Fitzgerald's *The Great Gatsby*. • ★

Relations between Generations

This is probably a sensitive question among your peers and you. Fictional explorations of the subject include Thomas Mann's *Buddenbrooks*, Samuel Butler's *The Way of All Flesh*, D. H. Lawrence's *Sons and Lovers* and "The Rocking Horse Winner," and Don DeLillo's *White Noise*; dramatic explorations include Sophocles' *Oedipus Rex* and *Antigone*; Shakespeare's *King Lear* and *Henry IV*, Parts I and II; Arthur Miller's *All My Sons, Death of a Salesman, The Price*; Samuel Beckett's *Endgame*; Harold Pinter's *The Homecoming*. • ★

The Quest

In many works the hero(in)es set out in search of something vital to their lives. In the case of King Arthur's knights, it may be, specifically, the Holy Grail, or, generally, whatever adventure befalls them that day. Often, as in W. Somerset Maugham's *Of Human Bondage*, the hero is seeking the meaning of life, a viable philosophy. In Henry Fielding's *Tom Jones*, he is seeking a measure of his own worth. Considering the nature and purpose of the Quest is a fruitful enterprise; sometimes the hero discovers it was not the end (the *what* or the *why*) but the means (the *how*) that was most important. Can the work of literature you are reporting on be made more meaningful if you see it as an account of a Quest? • ★

Justice

In many works of literature, the Quest is for Justice. This theme can include any or all of the following ideas already mentioned as separate themes: the proper relations between Good and Evil; between the individual and society; between the sexes, the generations, the races. Nora's struggle in Ibsen's *A Doll's House*, a struggle to find her rightful place as a woman, wife, mother, and person, is a quest for Justice. Tom Joad's struggle to improve the lot of the migratory workers in John Steinbeck's *The Grapes of Wrath* is an effort to see that justice is invoked for the poor as well as for the rich. ● ★

The Meaning of Life

Implicit in all literature, by the very fact that different characters choose different pursuits, is the search for the meaning of existence. From the medieval tale "My Lady's Tumbler" to Samuel Beckett's drama *Waiting for Godot* and Germaine Greer's treatise *The Female Eunuch*, the ultimate quest is this one. ● ★

The Nature of Family Life

What is the role of the family in shaping the individual? How does each member of the family influence the personality of the others? Does an authoritarian family setup condition people for fascism, as Wilhelm Reich believes? Why are families so different in novels like Samuel Butler's *The Way of All Flesh*, Virginia Woolf's *To the Lighthouse*, Thomas Wolfe's *Look Homeward, Angel*, Don DeLillo's *White Noise*? ● ★

The Nature of Friendship

What is a true friend? Why are friendships so different in Shakespeare's play *Hamlet*, Jules Verne's novel *Twenty Thousand Leagues under the Sea*, and Doris Lessing's novel *The Golden Notebook*? ● ★

What Is the Ultimate Reality?

Dante's *Divine Comedy* depicts a long but feasible search for God, which is the ultimate reality to Dante. Aristotle's *Metaphysics* identifies that ultimate power as the Unmoved Mover, an impersonal power he refuses to call God. Lucretius' philosophical poem *On the Nature of Things* finds that Democritus was right: the basic reality is the atom. In most literary works, however, the ultimate reality is not the object of a quest but is rather some force either taken for granted or ignored by the hero and other characters. If you are interested in the role of an ultimate reality in the lives of some fictional characters, you could compare works in which it's an important, vivid question, like William Langland's poem *Vision of Piers Plowman* or Cynthia Ozick's *The Pagan Rabbi*, with works in which the central characters manage to function without ever thinking about it, like Doris Lessing's *The Golden Notebook* and Jules Verne's *From the Earth to the Moon.* • ★

See the INDEX for further discussions of Theme.

| • average difficulty | ○ previous knowledge | ★ most libraries |
| ▲ larger library | □ visual component | ♫ audio component |

3

Ideas about Fiction

GENERAL IDEAS APPLICABLE TO ANY FICTION

Your discussions of literature, as we have seen, revolve around three topics: its themes, its techniques, and critical judgments of its effectiveness. And you will find that any theme can be common to all types of literature. The poet, the playwright, and the novelist may all write on the absurdity of war, or on the nature of jealous love, or on the dangers of getting a swelled head. Where poetry, drama, and fiction will differ, then, is in their media and their techniques. First let us consider the techniques of the fiction writer, who works in prose through the medium of the printed page to reach the individual reader.

You can analyze any novel or short story in terms of its plot, characterization, setting, point of view, prose style and tone and, of course, the way these elements contribute to the themes. You could deal with just one of these elements, e.g.

"Point of View in Three Novels by Henry James"

or with some combination of them:

"How Setting Contributes to Theme in Poe's Fiction"

You could compare and contrast these components as used by two or more authors:

"The Death-Wish Theme in the War Novels of
Mailer, Heller, and Vonnegut"

And of course you can break down any of the various components into its subcomponents, as we shall suggest in the clusters of Ideas that follow. The only limit to your formulation of any topic is, of course, the acid test: Is this study/analysis/comparison likely to produce any worthwhile conclusions? Do I have to narrow it down or expand it to meet the needs of my assignment?

Here then are some master ideas about technique that you can apply to any work of fiction.

Characterization in the Fiction of_____

If development of character in the fiction you are studying is the most interesting feature of the author's work, consider: What problems does he or she create to test or reveal character? What conflicts, internal and external, do the characters suffer? How (well) does he or she supply motivation for their behavior? How does he or she involve the reader emotionally? What makes the characters distinctively different and memorable? How do they change or grow? What is the significance of the change? What does the reader learn about human psychology as a result of sympathizing with these characters? • ★

(**Wider scope:** Include more works or more authors plus critical studies • ★)

Structure in the Fiction of_____

If you are fascinated by the way an author unravels his/her narrative, consider the difference between *story* (the chronological order in which events actually have occurred) and *plot* (the non-chronological order in which the author has revealed those events). How does your author create *suspense,* or reader's concern about characters' fate? How does he or she handle *exposition*: i.e., provide us with necessary background information? Can you locate that point where the main character becomes "locked in" to a definite *conflict*? How does his/her problem worsen, or seem to improve, his/her fortunes ebb and flow? Does he or she face one or several *crises* before the main *climactic situation?* Perhaps you'll make some good connections with your novelist's techniques by doing some basic research on plot in a handbook of literary terms (or a work like *How to Write Book Reports* by Walter James Miller and Elizabeth Morse-Cluley). For example, become handy with terms like *rising and falling action, final reaction, denouement.*

Once aware of the techniques of narration available to the fiction writer, judge your author's success. For example, does your novel get off to a slow and discouraging start because the author dumps too much background (exposition) on you before he or she launches the main action? What is the overall significance of the structure? Why does Joseph Conrad present so many stories within a story? Why does the line of action *spiral* in Joseph Heller's *Catch-22?* • ★ (**Wider scope:** Consult histories of the novel and critical studies. ▲)

Scene-Summary-Scene in the Fiction of_____

How do novelists create—in just a few hundred pages—the illusion of a long life, or even of a family's history, as in Thomas Mann's *Buddenbrooks* or Samuel Butler's *The Way of All Flesh?* One secret: they alternate between *scenes* and *summaries*. A scene is a full dramatization of a situation, with detailed treatment of action, of setting, of dialogue, of one or more characters' thoughts. On the other hand, a *summary* swiftly condenses many situations, occurring over a longer period of time, into a few compact, general statements. A summary usually provides transition between two scenes. Naturally, scenes are more interesting than straight narration or exposition in summary fashion. If you find a certain novel boring, consider the possibility that there are too few scenes, too many summaries. For an interesting study of narrative techniques, compare any two novelists of the same period (F. Scott Fitzgerald with Ernest Hemingway, for instance) for their use of alternating scene and summary. • ★

A Study of Setting in the Fiction of_____

Does the author contrive artistic ways of "looking" at the environment—for example, through the eyes of different characters? Does the setting help the reader to accept the fictitious world as real, that is, to suspend disbelief? How does setting contribute to mood? suspense? help shape, test, reveal character? Does it take on significant symbolic value? Does Nature take on the importance of a villainous antagonist, as does the sea in some stories by Joseph Conrad? As you and/or the critics see it, how does setting help formulate the overall meaning? • ★

Literary Point of View in the Fiction of_____

A major artistic question in the study of fiction is: From whose point of view is the action observed? From the author's (as in Nathaniel Hawthorne's *The House of the Seven Gables*)? From the heroine's (as in Daniel Defoe's *Roxana*)? From a minor character's (as in Herman Melville's *Moby Dick*)? From a child's (as in Henry James' *What Maisie Knew*)? Does the author shift the point of view from, say, the heroine's to the hero's (as in Rosalyn Drexler's *To Smithereens*)? What advantages does your author gain from the point of view he or she uses? How does the point of view affect the order in which events are revealed (i.e., the plot)? What does the point of view reveal about the characters observed and observing? about the author's message? Check INDEX for other ideas about Point of View. • ★

Style and Tone in the Fiction of_____

In its broadest sense, a writer's *style* is his/her overall manner or approach, including plotting, characterization, use of point of view, and so on. But if those aspects are considered separately, then *style* has the limited meaning of the author's way with words: his/her characteristic diction, sentence rhythms and syntactical maneuvers, dialogue, and use of metaphors and symbols. *Tone* is the overall attitude of the author: Is he or she urbane? sarcastic? sympathetic? Style and tone are the easiest components of writing to react to, the hardest to describe and analyze. Perhaps you should not attempt a *style-and-tone study* unless you have at least sampled the critical literature. And even then, a beginner can best describe an author's style by comparing it with another author's, as in: "Syntax in Hemingway and Faulkner." ○ ▲

The Function of Metaphor in the Fiction of_____

A metaphor is a figure of speech in which two unlike things are likened. One function of such a comparison is to explain the unknown in terms of the known. Thus in *Slaughterhouse-Five* Kurt Vonnegut describes a dying colonel's breathing: "Every time he inhaled his lungs rattled like greasy paper bags." He describes prisoners crowded on the floor of a cattle-car as "nestled like spoons." The narrator in Joseph Conrad's *Lord Jim* comments that Cornelius' "slow laborious walk resembled the creeping of a repulsive beetle, the legs alone moving with horrid industry while the body glided evenly." Such analogies force us to make rapid and unexpected connections. The shocks in comprehension that they cause help the author to control our emotional responses. If you find yourself thrilling to an author's use of rich and upsetting metaphor, write a paper (or make an oral report) analyzing his/her most effective figures of speech. (You might want to consult a standard dictionary of literary terms for fuller definitions and more examples of metaphor, simile, synecdoche, metonymy, symbol.) From what areas of human knowledge does your author take his metaphors, and why? For example, in *Hamlet* Shakespeare achieves his effects largely by using metaphors of disease, adding up to the overall impression that "Something is rotten in the state of Denmark"; in *Othello* he uses much animal imagery, keeping us reminded of the bestial forces in men. ○ ★

Symbolism in the Fiction of_____

One aspect of style rather easily isolated is symbolism. But you must be sensitive to the resonating meanings of a symbol: that is, something that stands for something else, usually something larger than itself. Most often a symbol is a material thing that stands for something immaterial. When Upton Sinclair's characters in *The Jungle* watch hogs being led to the slaughter, are they watching an action symbolic of their own lives? When the hero bathes in a country stream, is he washing away his city life, being baptized into a new life? What are the many symbolic values of the lighthouse in Virginia Woolf's *To the Lighthouse*? Symbols add to the emotional depth of art; in writing about them, you are adding another level to your discussion of the meaning of a work. Some experience in reading in-depth criticism is advisable, e.g., Harry Slochower's *Mythopoesis*, William York Tindall's *The Literary Symbol*. ○ ▲

Irony in the Fiction of_____

Much of the suspense and tension in good literature consists, as we have noted, in the author's exploring the difference between appearance and reality. Devices used toward this end are considered under the general heading of *irony*. An author is using *dramatic irony* when he or she allows his/her audience to know something that certain characters do not yet know. Thus Homer's audience knows that Odysseus has entered his own home disguised as an old beggar. But the suitors besieging his wife, Penelope, and indeed Penelope herself, are not aware of his real identity. The audience, then, can observe how these characters act in their ignorance of the real situation. We find a more recent example in Don DeLillo's *White Noise*. The wife is unaware that her daughter and husband know of her drug use; we watch how she acts as she thinks her secret is safe.

We say the author is using *verbal irony* when he, or a character, says one thing but means another, or when a character says more than he or she realizes, or says something apparently true now but soon to be proved false. Thus in Upton Sinclair's *The Jungle*, Jurgis, watching hogs being led unknowingly toward "a horrid fate," says "I'm glad I'm not a hog." We soon see that the packers exploit Jurgis and other immigrants almost as though they *are* hogs.

Literature without irony is undramatic, uninstructive about life itself. After all, we all act in real life in partial ignorance of the real situations we are groping through. If you are seeking the real reason behind an author's success or failure, you may find it by analyzing his/her ability to set up *ironic situations.* ○ ★

Themes in the Fiction of_____

By the themes of a literary work we mean, as you have surely inferred by now, its central ideas, thesis, message, moral, overall meaning. Some themes can be made explicit in the characters' speeches or in the author's own remarks, but other themes—like those communicated by mood, tone, symbol, setting, action—can remain implicit.

Hence, in writing about an author's themes, you undertake to combine the explicit with the implicit meanings. Your research might reveal that different critics find different meanings; your paper or oral report might have to discuss several such interpretations, including your own. ● ★

So far, then, you have two lists of IDEAS applicable to any fiction:

1. The MASTER THEMES common to all literature, and
2. The MASTER IDEAS ABOUT TECHNIQUES of fiction.

Here are a few other, miscellaneous topics that you can apply to many works of fiction.

Autobiographical Elements in the Fiction of_____

Reading Don DeLillo's novel *End Zone,* you can't help wondering how he learned so much about how it *feels* to play football. Reference works like *Current Biography* or *Contemporary Authors* will both pique your curiosity further and slake it. But reading Stephen Crane's *The Red Badge of Courage* and checking *his* life in the *Dictionary of American Biography* will surprise you: he had seen no combat when he wrote that novel. *Such matters become important in your study of the creative process.* How much of their material (setting? problems? types of people?) do authors draw from their own experience? How much from research? How has the material been transformed? What meaning has the novelist found in his/her own experience? Was Kurt Vonnegut motivated in part, when working on *Slaughterhouse-Five,* by a personal need to comprehend his own World War II service? • ★

The Novel versus the Film Version

When a screenwriter translates a novel into a movie, he or she sometimes condenses the action to make it more dramatic or invents new scenes to get the audio-video equivalents of certain literary passages. Consider the changes made by Hollywood in Nathaniel Hawthorne's *The House of the Seven Gables,* Jane Austen's *Pride and Prejudice,* William Styron's *Sophie's Choice,* Sol Yurick's *The Warriors,* Joseph Heller's *Catch-22,* Kurt Vonnegut's *Slaughterhouse-Five,* Margaret Mitchell's *Gone with the Wind,* or any other novel made into a feature film. Are the changes justified (and why?) by the need to translate from one medium to another? Are the changes faithful at least to the *spirit* of the novel? For example, what does the film version of Emily Brontë's *Wuthering Heights* gain and lose by omitting the story of the second generation, the younger Cathy, Linton, and Hareton? the film version of *The House of the Seven Gables* by changing the anarchist into an abolitionist? • ▲ □

Female Characters, Male Authors

A reliable subject for a paper/oral report on any male author: his treatment of women. Do he—and his male characters—consistently view women as inferior, entitled only to limited roles in society, needing male protection and domination? Does he have any female characters who are the equals of the males in intelligence, nobility, capacity to lead, to innovate? Does he represent the position of women as determined by nature or by society? • ★

(**Wider scope:** Compare two male authors—or one male and one female author—of the same period, for their treatment of women as human beings. • ★)

SPECIFIC IDEAS ABOUT THE NOVEL

Theme of "Awakening" in the Modern Novel

Psychiatrist R. D. Laing says in *The Politics of Experience* that many people are so brainwashed by outer forces (family, school, TV, etc.) that they never will "wake up" or "find themselves." Such an awakening to the truth about the world around us, and our place in it, provides you with subjects galore in many highly different works, such as Alice Walker's *The Color Purple*, Ray Bradbury's *Fahrenheit 451,* and Kate Chopin's *The Awakening*. Trace the growth of the leading character in each such work: the motivation for the character's change, the problems it causes, the happy or tragic fates that result from each character's awakening. How authentic do these character changes seem to be when measured against Laing's professional psychological studies? What do you and/or the critics see as the impact of these "awakenings" on the average reader? ○ ▲

The Plots and Subplots of *The Color Purple*

Alice Walker's novel teems with life. How much of this is a function of the complexity of her plot (really, two main plots and several subplots!)? and of her huge cast of characters? Draw up a genealogical chart of the several generations involved, with their cross-relationships. The chart will be as wide as it is deep! Note the large number of distinct plots (Celie's life in America, Nettie's in Africa) and subplots (Shug's many loves, Harpo's, Sofia's complicated life, Connie's, etc.). How is each one resolved? To what extent is the turning point (Celie's inheritance) a "bolt out of the blue," an artificial device to rescue the characters, a *deus ex machina* resolution? What did the critics say about the plot(s) when the novel first appeared? ● ★

Walker and Bennett: Use of Parallel Plots

In his novel *The Old Wives' Tale,* Arnold Bennett depicts the lives of two English sisters who are separated when one goes to live in Paris for several decades. Compare Alice Walker's use of a similar plot structure in *The Color Purple*: Two Black American sisters are separated and one lives for decades in Africa. What advantages does each author reap by the use of parallel plots? ● ★

Vonnegut, Bennett, Walker: Use of Parallel Plots

In his *Breakfast of Champions* Kurt Vonnegut uses a simpler version of the parallel plot: Two main characters *not* related—not even known to each other beforehand—are moving toward a collision. Compare the structure of his novel with that of Walker's and Bennett's mentioned above. What entirely different benefits do these novelists reap by the use of parallel plots? What are the psychological and esthetic advantages of the parallel plot? ● ★

Epistolary Form of the Novel

Novelists sometimes develop a story in a series of letters. The epistolary form allows the novelist to reveal the main character's private feelings while developing the action; forces the reader to visualize the action from the point of view of a character reflecting on events and trying to recreate them for a specific person; and provides a natural way to shift the point of view as characters answer each other's letters. Compare and contrast the results obtained through use of this device in any two, three, or all of the following classics: Samuel Richardson's *Pamela* (1740) and *Clarissa Harlowe* (1748); Johann Wolfgang von Goethe's *The Sorrows of Young Werther* (*Die Leiden des jungen Werthers,* 1774); and Alice Walker's *The Color Purple* (1982). • ★

(**Wider scope:** From histories of the novel, especially of the epistolary novel, compile a list of epistolary writers who might have exerted a strong influence on Richardson, Goethe, or Walker. Read one or more of these writers and compare their work with that by one of the distinguished three. • ▲)

Woman's Place: *The Awakening* and *The Color Purple* Compared

In Kate Chopin's novel *The Awakening,* a nineteenth-century white American woman rebels against the traditional concepts of a woman's place; in Alice Walker's *The Color Purple,* the heroine has additional traditions to contend with as a *black* woman in a twentieth-century racist society. Explore the similarities and differences (including the nature of their different fates) in the careers of Edna and Celie. What have critics for feminist publications had to say about these novels? critics for black literary journals? for *The New York Review of Books?* • ▲

Symbolism: *The Awakening* and *The Color Purple*

Trace the psychological significance of colors in Walker's novel, and of a walk through grass and swimming in the sea in Chopin's. Explain how these and other things take on profound symbolic significance for the leading characters. How does the symbolic system in each work affect the reader's emotional

---

• average difficulty	○ previous knowledge	★ most libraries
▲ larger library	☐ visual component	Ω audio component

experience of the books? Were these effects, on first reading, conscious or subliminal? Elaborate on how symbolism operates on both the intellectual and the unconscious levels of reader experience. Compare Walker and Chopin as symbolical writers. (See INDEX for other ideas on Symbolism.) • ★

Patriarchy: *The Awakening* and *The Color Purple*

Explore and explain the mind-set of the male characters, their assumptions toward women, and the rights of each sex, in Walker's and Chopin's novels. • ★

The Nature of God in *The Color Purple*

Compare and contrast Celie's concepts of God with Shug's, Albert's, Nettie's, and other characters'. How do the male characters use the Bible to justify their attitudes toward women? What do critics for religious periodicals and theological journals have to say about *The Color Purple*? • ▲

Black Americans' African Roots: Fictional and Nonfictional Treatments

Alex Haley's non-fiction book *Roots* and Alice Walker's novel *The Color Purple* both trace Black Americans' relationship to their African origins. Compare and contrast their findings, their techniques, their impact. How do the two works reinforce each other? How have critics for historical journals rated the historical accuracy of these books? • ▲

The Black American Goes to Africa

In both Malcolm X's *Autobiography* and Alice Walker's novel *The Color Purple,* an American Negro goes to Africa and then returns to his/her native land. How does religion figure in each one's sojourn in Africa? To what extent, in what ways, do Walker and Malcolm X differ in their conclusions? • ★

Alice Walker: In Faulkner's Company

The Nation magazine said that *The Color Purple* "places Walker in the company of Faulkner." Compare *The Color Purple* with any William Faulkner novel (e.g., *Intruder in the Dust*). In what respects are the two authors similar? dissimilar? • ★

(**Wider scope:** Read the *Nation* review and other reviews of Walker, and reviews that appeared in response to the Faulkner novel you've read. Which reviewers could foresee the impact and career of the work under review? How were the novelists' respective innovations received? • ▲)

Carolyn Chute: A New Faulkner?

After Carolyn Chute's novel *The Beans of Egypt, Maine* was published, critics compared her to William Faulkner. Read *The Beans* and at least one Faulkner novel, and reviews of both books. Is the comparison based on similarities in style? tone? characterization? subject matter? point of view? themes? To what extent has Chute been influenced by Faulkner? ○ ▲

Carolyn Chute: A New Caldwell?

Critics have also compared Carolyn Chute's work with Erskine Caldwell's. Read *The Beans* and at least one Caldwell novel, and reviews of both. Is the association based on their styles? tone? characterizations? subject matter? point of view? social attitudes and criticism? Discuss and quote passages that substantiate your points. Do you and/or the critics believe that Caldwell has been an active influence on Chute's work? • ▲

Carolyn Chute's "Art out of Life"

The New York Times called Carolyn Chute's *The Beans of Egypt, Maine* "a triumph of art out of life, art over life." Read her novel, the *Times* and other reviews, and biographical articles about her (e.g., in *Current Biography, Writer's Digest*). In what ways is the novel based on her own experience? on her observations of real people? on her desire to make her characters' plight known to the world? Does her novel make a good case for fiction as social protest? • ▲

Themes in García Márquez' Classic

What philosophical and psychological conclusions can be drawn from Gabriel García Márquez' *One Hundred Years of Solitude*? Starting with the way he titles his story, explain the techniques he uses to state, advance, and explore his themes. How have the critics formulated his message? ○ ▲

Feminine and Masculine Values in García Márquez' *Solitude*

Compare and contrast the beliefs, attitudes, ideas, and significance of the men and the women in Gabriel García Márquez' *One Hundred Years of Solitude*. What do these differences contribute to García Márquez' themes? What have the critics seen as the difference between the sexes in this novel? How has the feminist press reacted? ● ▲

The "Second Opportunity" in García Márquez and Bradbury

The idea of a people getting a second chance to prove themselves figures in both Gabriel García Márquez' *One Hundred Years of Solitude* and Ray Bradbury's *The Martian Chronicles*. Compare the two novelists' ideas on the need for, and the likelihood of, a second opportunity. How have the critics responded to this problem? ● ▲

García Márquez' Narrative Techniques

Most twentieth-century authors apparently feel that scenes should predominate over narration in long novels. But Gabriel García Márquez has managed to make *One Hundred Years of Solitude* an international success even though he uses far less dramatization and much more straight narration (i.e., story without dialogue) than is considered appropriate. What do you and/or the critics see in García Márquez' techniques that makes the reader accept long passage after long passage unrelieved by dramatization? ○ ▲

(**Wider scope:** Compare García Márquez' degree of dramatization with that of two or more of the following authors: John Updike (*Rabbit, Run*; *Rabbit Redux*; *Rabbit Is Rich*); Joseph Heller (*Catch-22*, *Something Happened*, *Good as Gold*, *God Knows*); Kurt Vonnegut (*Slaughterhouse-Five*, *Breakfast of Champions*, *Galápagos*); Samuel Beckett (*How It Is*). What do you and/or the critics conclude about the need for extensive dramatization in fiction? ○ ▲)

Fictional Modes in García Márquez'
One Hundred Years of Solitude

How and why does Garbriel García Márquez depart from realism in *One Hundred Years of Solitude*? Which of the nonrealistic episodes represent private fantasy, and which would be termed mass illusions? Why does García Márquez report on the real and the nonreal as though both were real? What is the relation between these departures from realism and the technique known as surrealism? What do you and/or the critics see as the value of García Márquez' blending of the objective and the subjective? • ▲

Surrealist Techniques: Heller and García Márquez

Establish a working definition of surrealism by consulting a handbook of literary terms and a history of modern art, at least. In what ways do both Joseph Heller, in *Catch-22,* and Gabriel García Márquez, in *One Hundred Years of Solitude,* use surrealistic techniques? How do these methods advance their characterization? their themes? Why is it better that they alternate surrealism and realism instead of using either one exclusively? What do you and/or the critics conclude about the effectiveness of Heller's and García Márquez' surrealism? ○ ▲

Symbolism in García Márquez

What are the symbolic values of fish in religion and literature? Consult the one-volume edition of Sir James Frazer's *The Golden Bough,* Jessie L. Weston's *From Ritual to Romance,* and William York Tindall's *The Literary Symbol.* Consider the effect of García Márquez' use of *little* (and *gold*) fish in *One Hundred Years of Solitude*. What other things, places, events take on symbolic value in the novel? How do you and/or the critics and scholars interpret García Márquez' overall symbolism? ○ ▲

The Bible and García Márquez

How does the fecundity of Aureliano Segundo's cattle in *One Hundred Years of Solitude* resemble the fecundity of Jacob's in *The Book of Genesis*? How does the arrival of Meme Buendía's son parallel that of Moses in *Genesis*? Compare the advanced age that some of García Márquez' characters reach with that of the patriarchs in *Genesis*. What do you and/or the critics see as the function and impact of these Biblical parallels? • ▲

The Spiraling Plot in Heller and García Márquez

In both *Catch-22* and *One Hundred Years of Solitude,* the author will mention an event (e.g., in Heller, the death of Snowden; in García Márquez, facing the firing squad) and then spiral away from it for many pages, then barely mention it again, then spiral, etc. How does this technique of foreshadowing, this use of echoes, help create mystery and suspense? mood? a sense of simultaneity of past, present, and future experience? What was your and/or the critics' initial response to this spiraling? How have critics explained the similarity in Heller's and García Márquez' structure (if they've noticed it at all)? • ▲

Use of Tag-Names in Modern Fiction

In your analysis of fiction, remember that some authors use tag-names for characters. Outstanding examples: In Gabriel García Márquez' *One Hundred Years of Solitude,* consider the meaning of the family name Buendía and the given names of Rebeca, Petra Cotes, Babilonia, Santa Sofia, and others. In Joseph Heller's *Catch-22,* check on the significance of the names of Lieutenants Nately, Orr, Scheisskopf, and Snowden; Captain Black; Major —— de Coverley; and Luciana and Dori Duz. For the way Heller's tag-names fit into his system of second meanings, consult the present author's "Descent into Heller: Mythic Imagery in *Catch-22,*" *Journal of Mental Imagery,* 1982(145–156)6; his "Joseph Heller's Fiction," in Richard Kostelanetz, ed., *American Writing Today,* volume 1; and his Monarch Note, *Joseph Heller's "Catch-22."* • ★

Sergio Ramírez' Narrative Technique

In his novel *To Bury Our Fathers,* Sergio Ramírez opens with "The Main Lines of the Story." This consists of six one-paragraph summaries of as many sub-plots. Each summary is headed by a drawing that serves as a kind of logo or sign for that subject. Then Ramírez advances one situation briefly, headed by its sign, then another, alternating as the relationships become clear and the drama mounts. Why has Ramírez structured his story this way? How does it suit his themes—life under the Somoza dictatorship in Nicaragua, the growth of the anti-Somoza and Sandinista movements? How does Ramírez create states of mind, memory, reminiscence? What is the effect of his emphasis on colors? How does he use myth? Stressing whichever of these aspects impresses you most, report on what you and/or the critics see as "The Unique Fictional Approach of Sergio Ramírez." • ▲

Ramírez' *Fathers* and Heller's *Catch-22* Compared for Their Structures

Heller's plot spirals around certain subjects, getting closer each time. Would you and/or the critics say that Ramírez' plot develops in a similar fashion? • ▲

Ramírez and García Márquez: Their Techniques Contrasted

See above Ideas and INDEX for García Márquez. • ▲

Irony in *Fahrenheit 451*

The word "fireman" has an ironically different meaning in Ray Bradbury's novel from its meaning in common usage. Find other examples of irony in *Fahrenheit 451*. How does Bradbury's irony reinforce his suspense? his themes? • ★

(**Wider scope:** Report on his use of irony in at least two other novels and on the critical reaction to it. • ▲)

Gaddis' Symbolism in *Carpenter's Gothic*

Even the title of William Gaddis' novel points to a symbol used in the text: It's a style of architecture representing a certain quality in the American way of life. Note too how "The Great Rift," a geological formation—where, science believes, humanity began—is symbolic of many rifts in the characters' lives (and bodies) and in the state of national intelligence (in both senses of the word!). Check out the symbolic value to Gaddis of the stopped clock, the littered kitchen table, Halloween, moving patterns of shadows. In your and/or the critics' judgment, how successful is this system of symbolism? • ▲

Gaddis' Characterization through Telephone Calls

A major portion of the dialogue in William Gaddis' *Carpenter's Gothic* consists of telephone conversations. Since we hear only one end of these dialogues, they help build suspense. Show how they also create irony (at our end of the conversations, we know things the speaker at the other end doesn't) and reveal character. What do you and/or the critics see as the artistic value of this device? • ★

Vietnam Vets in Fiction by Gaddis and Mason

In Bobbie Ann Mason's *In Country* as in *Carpenter's Gothic* by William Gaddis, Vietnam veterans seem out of touch with humanity and its values. How do the two novelists explain this? On what causes do they agree? disagree? differ entirely? What do you and/or the critics think of their explanations? • ▲

Black Humor

What is it? Who are some of the major black humorists in contemporary fiction? Why did the term "black humor" not come into general use until the 1960s? Why did Kurt Vonnegut dislike being labeled a black humorist? Start with handbooks of literary terms (e.g., Karl Beckson and Arthur Ganz, *Literary Terms: A Dictionary*), anthologies of black humor edited by Bruce Jay Friedman and by Douglas M. Davis, the Monarch Note on Vonnegut's *Slaughterhouse-Five*. • ▲

(**Wider scope:** Trace the history of black humor from medieval drama in England, through the Elizabethan period—e.g., in Shakespeare's *Romeo and Juliet*—and down to contemporary Anglo-American literature. Then treat in some detail of only the highlights, maybe of just two periods, more realistically, of only one major author from each period. ○ ▲)

A Funny Dirty Little War and *Catch-22* Compared

Italo Calvino, late Italian master of the short story, praised Osvaldo Soriano's *A Funny Dirty Little War* for its "black humor, dizzying action, crisp, keen dialogue . . ." Compare Soriano's work and Joseph Heller's *Catch-22*, with emphasis on Calvino's three categories. What do you and/or the critics see as the themes in each work? • ▲

(**Narrower scope:** Limit your comparison to just one of Calvino's categories. • ▲)

World War I in Fiction

French, German, Czech, and American combat veterans of World War I produced some of the greatest novels of the twentieth century. Compare any two or more of the works listed here for (1) their overall message about the war and about war in general and (2) the techniques they used to dramatize their message. What do you and/or the critics and literary historians see as the effectiveness of these works?

Jaroslav Hašek, *The Good Soldier Schweik* (use the complete translation published by Thomas Y. Crowell); Arnold Zweig, *The Case of Sergeant Grischa*; Erich Maria Remarque, *All Quiet on the Western Front*; Ernest Hemingway, *A Farewell to Arms*; Louis-Ferdinand Céline, *Journey to the End of Night*. • ▲

Céline's Influence on Heller, Vonnegut

Both Joseph Heller and Kurt Vonnegut have said, in interviews available in periodicals, that Louis-Ferdinand Céline has been a powerful influence on their writing. Using Céline's novel *Journey to the End of Night*, trace (with or without the guidance of the critics) Céline's influence on Heller's *Catch-22* and Vonnegut's *Slaughterhouse-Five*. For orientation (bibliography, biography, criticsm), consult the Monarch Notes on Heller and Vonnegut; don't overlook Vonnegut's famous speech at Wheaton College for his remarks on Céline (printed in *Palm Sunday*). • ▲

Hašek's Influence on Heller's *Catch-22*

In "War and the Comic Muse" (*Comparative Literature* XX, Summer 1968), J. P. Stern details what he considers the "direct influence of Hašek's work (*The Good Soldier Schweik*) on Heller's (*Catch-22*)." Heller himself claims Stern has exaggerated the connection. Consulting other critics or not (according to the scope of your assignment), decide who's right: Stern or Heller. • ▲

Nature Imagery in Emily Brontë

In *Wuthering Heights,* Catherine describes herself, and contrasts Heathcliff and Linton, through vivid nature imagery (moonbeam; lightning; foliage; eternal rocks, etc.). Study the text for the way her emotions, and the emotions of some other characters, drive them to use intense metaphor, mainly nature imagery. What does the imagery reveal about the characters using it? What does lack of imagery in a character's speech indicate? Compare Catherine's, Linton's, and Nellie's speech especially. What do you and/or the critics and scholars (see *PMLA*—or *Publications of the Modern Language Association*—especially) conclude about Brontë's use of imagery to characterize? • ★

Nature Imagery in Conrad

Following the clues given above, do a similar study of nature imagery in one or more novels of Joseph Conrad (*Lord Jim, Heart of Darkness, The Nigger of the "Narcissus,"* etc.). • ★

Nature Imagery in Brontë and Conrad

Compare the two authors' use of imagery (as detailed above). Which author sees nature as more friendly to mankind; who sees nature as more malevolent toward humanity? In your opinion, and/or in the opinion of selected critics, how do Brontë's and Conrad's use of nature imagery reflect their respective characterizations? themes? • ▲

Brontë and Conrad: A Study in Narrative Techniques

Emily Brontë's *Wuthering Heights* is related to us by Mr. Lockwood, who gets most of the story from his housekeeper, who pieces it together from personal conversations, eavesdropping, hearsay, letters, and (probably) her own imagination. Joseph Conrad's *Lord Jim* is also a collage of first-, second-, and third-hand evidence. In both works, we have—at best—information that comes to us refracted through several media. We have then an "impressionistic" view of reality.

What is the psychological effect of this narrative method on the reader? What are the authors saying about human perception of personality? and even of events? • ★

(**Wider scope:** Consult the critics and scholars on these questions; have any of them made this specific comparison before it was suggested here? • ▲)

Brontë's Influence on Conrad

Joseph Conrad's narrative technique in *Lord Jim* (1901) (see above) is considered an important breakthrough in modern psychological/subjectivist/impressionist fiction. Was he influenced by Emily Brontë's *Wuthering Heights*? With or without the aid of the critics, compare the two authors' approaches, including their apparent conceptions of the purpose and function of fiction. Should Brontë be given credit for the "breakthrough"? Have the literary histories and biographies of Conrad given it to her? • ▲

Two Different Ways Novelists Handle Time

Some works of fiction—like Daniel Defoe's *Robinson Crusoe* and Jules Verne's *The Mysterious Island*—are narrated in chronological order, from the beginning to the end of the story. Others—like Homer's *Odyssey* or Don DeLillo's *America*—start *in medias res* (in the middle of things), with earlier action recalled in flashbacks. Consider in detail one or more examples of each technique. With or without the help of the critics (check the library catalogues for studies in the craft of fiction, in the nature of narrative, and for reviews of your examples), explain the advantages and disadvantages of each approach, especially as they are revealed in your examples. • ★

Wuthering Heights: The Function of Fiction

Emily Brontë's novel sparked a critical controversy about the proper function and purpose of fiction. Should characters like Heathcliff be created? Should the novel acknowledge real, raw passions such as those that flare in the love between Catherine and Heathcliff? Or should the novel create a more rational world, point toward an ideal life, toward what is desirable rather than what is? In various critical reactions to Brontë's work you find the timeless questions about the role of art in society. Get your bearings with the Norton Critical Edition, with Ruth Blackburn's sourcebook *The Brontë Sisters,* with Wilbur Scott's *Five Approaches of Literary Criticism.* • ▲

• average difficulty	○ previous knowledge	★ most libraries
▲ larger library	☐ visual component	☊ audio component

The Two Catherines in *Wuthering Heights*

Compare and contrast the Catherine who loves Heathcliff with her daughter, the Catherine who marries Hareton. *Show how the differences between the ways the two women conduct their lives may point to the author's main message.* • ★

Contrast of Characters in *Death Comes for the Archbishop*

What do we learn about human relations from Willa Cather's contrast of the archbishop and his priest-assistant? • ★

Meaning of Contrast of Characters in (any novel)

Are there two characters in the novel you are studying who could be compared with meaningful results? What does the author mean us to infer from the differences between them? • ★

Austen and Brontë Compared

Compare and contrast Jane Austen's *Pride and Prejudice* with Emily Brontë's *Wuthering Heights*. In which novel is passion more prevalent, in which is reason emphasized? Consider the differences in style, tone, use of setting, message, theme. • ★

(**Wider scope:** With the aid of histories of literature, fiction, the novel, show how the differences between the two novels actually reflect the differences between the Age of Reason [neoclassicism] and the Age of Romanticism. • ▲)

Critical Controversy over *Native Son*

Ever since 1940, writers have argued over Richard Wright's portrayal of the black man in *Native Son*. Establish your own reactions to the novel before you consider the following authors' views (preferably in the order in which they addressed the question): James Baldwin, Irving Howe, Ralph Ellison, Norman Mailer, Eldridge Cleaver. • ▲

(**Wider scope:** Include reviews of the novel when it appeared. • ▲)

Wright's *Native Son,* Baldwin's *Another Country*

Richard Wright's novel is conceived and rendered in the Zolaist-Dreiser tradition of "naturalism," with emphasis on sociological influences; James Baldwin's in the Henry James-Virginia Woolf tradition of "subjectivism," with emphasis on psychological processes. With or without the help of the critics and literary historians, compare and contrast the novels in terms of their aims, values, style, and tone, their motivation and other techniques of narration and characterization. What does each story offer that the other lacks? ● ▲

Richard Wright and Feodor Dostoevsky

Compare and contrast Wright's *Native Son* with Dostoevsky's *Crime and Punishment.* What do you and/or the critics have to say about the novelists' characterization and motivation; plot; the trial scenes; theme and message? ● ▲

Conditioning of Criminals

Consider Graham Greene's *Brighton Rock* as a sympathetic (and religious and theological) treatment of the criminal mentality. What does the novel add to your views criminological and penological? ● ★

(**Wider scope:** How have reviewers for psychological, criminological, penological, and literary journals regarded the novel? ● ▲)

A Modern King Arthur

Read Sir Thomas Malory's fifteenth-century *Morte d'Arthur* in which he collected and unified the Arthurian legends. (There is a version of Malory in modern idiom by Keith Baines and another by John Steinbeck.) Then compare any of the following treatments with Malory's: Alfred Tennyson's *The Idylls of the King*; T. H. White's *The Once and Future King*; Richard Wagner's libretto for his opera *Tristan und Isolde*; John Erskine's *Galahad*; Richard Monaco's *Parsival, or A Knight's Tale* and *The Grail War*. With or without guidance from critics and literary historians, consider these questions: What is so valuable in the original that it deserves so many modern renditions? How does the modern interpretation differ? What does it add to our understanding? ● ▲

King Arthur: Fact and Fiction

Some scholars (e.g., Norma Love Goodrich) believe that the Arthurian legends are based on a real figure who lived in the early Middle Ages. How does their historical figure differ from, and correspond to, the King Arthur of Thomas Malory's *Morte d'Arthur*? • ▲

(**Wider scope:** Apply a like question to Malory's Queen Guinevere and/or Lancelot. From reviews of Goodrich, especially in the scholarly journals, get clues as to scholars who disagree with Goodrich; include them in your study. • ▲)

Fact and Fiction in Sinclair's *The Jungle*

How much of this 1906 classic "muckraking" novel about the meat-packing industry is based on actual events, people, and situations, how much on Upton Sinclair's inventiveness? Are his fictional inventions justified by the facts? Are they artistically necessary? What do his inventions add to our understanding that factual reportage might not provide?

The critical and historical literature on this subject is enormous. For general orientation and a bibliography suitable for college or high school students, see the Monarch Note, *Upton Sinclair's "The Jungle": A Critical Commentary*. For advanced research, see Ronald Gottesman's *Upton Sinclair: An Annotated Checklist*. ○ ▲

(**Narrower scope:** Take just one aspect of Sinclair's exposé, e.g., the incidents based on conditions in the Armour plants and others; the corruption of the courts; the real estate business' exploitation of immigrants; the rigging of elections; the activity of the labor unions, Socialist Party, etc. ○ ▲)

Fact and Fiction in (any social-problem novel)

Use the same approach to any novel that, like *The Jungle*, treats of sociopolitical conditions *at the time of publication*. Examples: Voltaire's *Candide*, Charles Dickens' *Oliver Twist* or *Hard Times*, Mark Twain's *Huckleberry Finn* (yes, it's a novel of social protest!), Edward Bellamy's *Looking Backward*, John Steinbeck's *The Grapes of Wrath*, Richard Wright's *Native Son*, Truman Capote's *In Cold Blood*, E. L. Doctorow's *The Book of Daniel*. ○ ▲

(**Narrower scope:** As with *The Jungle*, you will probably realize, soon after you commence your research, that you should limit your study to one aspect of the novelist's overall complaint. ○ ▲)

Fact and Fiction in *The Brook Kerith*

Here you deal with historical fiction, i.e., fiction about actual events that occurred a good time *before the publication of the novel*. George Moore takes known, objective facts about the lives of Jesus of Nazareth and Joseph of Arimathea and adds imaginary episodes to give us *his* version of what he thinks *might* have happened. What is the effect of his combining Christian and non-Christian sources? How valid is his alternative exploration? Get started with the 1969 Liveright edition of the novel with a "Foreword" by the present author; with I. A. Richards' review of that edition in *The New York Review of Books*; with biographies of George Moore. ○ ▲

   (**Narrower scope:** Select one aspect of Moore's treatment of, e.g., the crucifixion; Joseph's part in Moore's version; the monasteries in the Syrian hills—were they Essene?; Moore's episodes based on non-Christian sources. ○ ▲)

Fact and Fiction in (any historical novel)

Apply what's pertinent in the last three Ideas above to any historical fiction, such as Walter Scott's *Ivanhoe*, Howard Fast's *Conceived in Liberty*, Gore Vidal's *Lincoln* or *Burr*, Paxton Davis' *Three Days*, Edward Bellamy's *The Duke of Stockbridge*, Anthony Valerio's *Valentino and the Great Italians*. Compare the fictional story with any standard historical account or biography. How much liberty has the novelist taken with the facts? Have his inventions captured an *essential* truth that enhances and clarifies the historical truth? ○ ▲

   (**Narrower scope:** Compare just one aspect of the novel with its historical counterpart, e.g., the historical Robert E. Lee with Davis' portrait; the historical "duke" of Stockbridge, Massachusetts, with Bellamy's conception; or some historical battle in Shays' Rebellion as Bellamy uses it for his purposes. ○ ▲)

The Rosenberg Trial as Seen by Two Novelists

Establish the fact that the "conspiracy" trial of Julius and Ethel Rosenberg is the acknowledged model for both E. L. Doctorow's *The Book of Daniel*

Robert Coover's *The Public Burning*. How does each novel depart from the historical facts? To what end, for what reason? Show how each author's distinct purpose determines his plot, characterization, setting, point of view, style, tone. What is the value of such fictional treatments? *This is not one of those topics which you might attempt without the aid of the critics and scholars.* ○ ▲

(**Narrower scope:** Consider just *one* character that appears in both the historical and fictional accounts. ○ ▲)

Stephen Crane: Experience and Imagination

Veterans of the Civil War marveled that Crane, who had never been in combat, could so perfectly capture the smell and sound of battle in *The Red Badge of Courage*. But some of his works—like "The Open Boat"—are based on his own direct, first-hand experience. Using as many of his works as you need to suit the scope of your assignment, measure their action, setting, and people against Crane's biography. Did he do much research? *You* certainly will for this topic or any part of it. ● ★

Hemingway as Soldier-Writer

How much of Ernest Hemingway's fiction is based on his actual experience and/or first-hand observation in World War I? in the Spanish Civil War? in World War II? ● ▲

(**Narrower scope:** After reading a standard biography of Hemingway, limit your paper to treating of one war or maybe even one battle, e.g., the Battle of Caporetto. ● ▲)

Hemingway as Sportsman-Writer

Hunter, fisherman, boxer—Ernest Hemingway participated in many different sports and was a close student of several others. How much of his writing is based on his own first-hand experience as sportsman? How much on his observation of others? How authentic do professional sportsmen consider his writing to be? What is the consensus among bullfight experts about his *Death in the Afternoon*? among fisherpersons about *The Old Man and the Sea*? among hunters about *The Green Hills of Africa*? ○ ▲

(**Narrower scope:** Read a standard biography, then choose just one of his sports and one or more of his fictional treatments thereof. ○ ▲)

Maugham and Stone on Gauguin and Van Gogh

Consider Irving Stone's novel *Lust for Life* and/or W. Somerset Maugham's *The Moon and Sixpence* in comparison with any standard biography of the subject(s): Vincent Van Gogh and Paul Gauguin, respectively. With or without the aid of the critics and scholars, take up such questions as these: How has the novelist reinterpreted the biography? Are the fictional inventions justified by the facts? Has the novelist heightened or distorted our understanding of the historical Van Gogh or Gauguin? ○ ▲

(**Narrower scope:** Compare Stone's treatment of one of the other painters in *Lust for Life* with that by his biographer. ○ ▲)

Social Protest Novels Compared and Contrasted

Take a realistic novel based strictly on historical fact (e.g., Upton Sinclair's *The Jungle*) and one that uses historical event as a point of departure for fantasy, burlesque, satire (e.g., Robert Coover's *The Public Burning*). Show how plot, characterization, setting, author's voice, tone, are all influenced by the author's artistic and political purposes. This is a study in literary methods. Invoke the aid of the critics, especially those who treat the novels in the light of history. ● ▲

How the Fiction Writer Can Influence History

Rarely does a work of fiction have a measureable effect on history. Outstanding examples can be counted on the fingers of one hand: Harriet Beecher Stowe's *Uncle Tom's Cabin* helped turn American sentiment against slavery; Nikolai Gogol's *Dead Souls* turned Russian sentiment against serfdom; Ivan Turgenev's *A Sportsman's Notebook* (or *Sketchbook,* in some translations) helped induce the Tsar to abolish serfdom; Upton Sinclair's *The Jungle* helped Theodore Roosevelt to pressure Congress into passing landmark laws to regulate the meat-packing industry. Using one or more of these or other examples, and consulting critics and literary historians, consider: *What has the novelist done with factual materials to make them so politically effective?* Has the fictional treatment distorted or just emphasized the facts? Are the fictional inventions justified by the real situation? Are they necessary for artistic success? What has this artistic treatment added to our understanding that nonfiction coverage might not provide? ○ ▲

How Big Business Influences Literature

Narrow or widen the scope by treating one, both, and/or other examples: George Moore's battle with the English circulating libraries to get his novels to the public; the conspiracy against the "muckrakers" by Big Business advertisers, and Upton Sinclair's difficulties with major publishers, after the sensational success of his *The Jungle*. Standard biographies of Moore and Sinclair will get you started. ● ▲

The Working Class in Fiction and Film

Read Chuck Wachtel's *Joe the Engineer*, which won a PEN/Hemingway Citation for a First Novel (1983). How many novels have you read, movies and TV plays have you seen, that treat of the working class as Wachtel does? Which social classes are most often represented in American fiction and screen drama? Which class is, in reality, the largest? How can you explain the disparity in representation? How does the situation square with our notions of a pluralistic society and equality of opportunity? ● ▲ □

Working-Class Novels: A Comparison

Compare Chuck Wachtel's *Joe the Engineer* (1983) with John Steinbeck's *The Grapes of Wrath* (1939) and Upton Sinclair's *The Jungle* (1906). Consider the rarity of American fiction about the working class, the changing needs and problems of the American worker, the psychology of the working people. Get oriented with Alfred Kazin, *On Native Grounds: An Interpretation of American Prose Literature*; Walter B. Rideout, *The Radical Novel in the United States*; *The Autobiography of Upton Sinclair*; Harvey Swados, *A Radical's America*; Carl Van Doren, *Contemporary American Novelists* (revised edition). Why not interview Chuck Wachtel, by telephone if not in person? Write to him through his publisher; if your library does not have *Joe the Engineer* and/or a library card for it, check *Books in Print* for 1983–1984. Compare the kinds of reviews the three authors elicited. To what extent do they reveal the changing political moods of those periods? ● ▲

● average difficulty	○ previous knowledge	★ most libraries
▲ larger library	□ visual component	♫ audio component

Growth of Bellamy's Social Consciousness

Edward Bellamy set forth an entirely new system of social and economic justice in his world-wide best-selling novel, *Looking Backward* (1888) and in its sequel, *Equality* (1897). But his concern with social problems began with his very first novel, *The Duke of Stockbridge*. The hero is one of the leaders of Shays' Rebellion (1786), in which western Massachusetts farmers, most of them veterans of the Revolutionary War, tried to free themselves from economic exploitation by eastern (Boston) businessmen. Reading all of Bellamy's fiction in its chronological order, trace the development of his social vision. • ▲

(**Wider scope:** Include Bellamy's nonfiction in your study. • ▲)

Shays' Rebellion: History and Fiction

Captain Daniel Shays, who fought in the American Revolution (he was awarded a sword by his commander, the Marquis de la Fayette), led an insurrection of western Massachusetts farmers against the eastern (Boston) business community which they felt was exploiting them economically and socially (1786). There are several historical accounts (catalogued under "Shays's Rebellion") and two novels about this civil war: *The Duke of Stockbridge* by Edward Bellamy (see above) and *The Regulators* by William Deganhard. Compare the historical and fictional treatments (in the former include Thomas Jefferson's famous statement about the advisability of such rebellions). Why did Bellamy ignore the "duke's" real marital status? Why is Shays not a central figure in either novel? • ★

(**Narrower scope:** Limit your comparison of historical and fictional accounts to those of Captain Shays himself, or to those of another major figure in the actual rebellion, the "duke." • ★)

Jules Verne as Social Prophet

Best known in the U.S. as a writer of prophetic science fiction, Jules Verne is equally well known in Europe as a social satirist and social prophet. To explore this side of Verne, take your pick of one or more of his 60-odd novels by considering the discussion of them in Jean Chesneaux' *The Political and Social Ideas of Jules Verne* and the present author's two-volume *The Annotated Jules Verne*. Consult also Brian Aldiss' *The Billion Year Spree*. Why is this side of Verne hardly known in the U.S.? ○ ▲

Jules Verne's Influence on William Golding

In his book *The Hot Gates and Other Occasional Pieces,* William Golding reveals an intimate knowledge of the works of Jules Verne. Among Verne's 60-odd novels is *Two Years Holiday,* a story about rivalries and politics among schoolboys who are marooned on a desert island. Golding's own classic novel, *Lord of the Flies,* treats a similar subject. How much was Golding influenced by Verne? Who has the better grasp of adolescent psychology, Verne or Golding? Explain in detail why you (and/or the critics) think that Golding's (or Verne's) novel is the better work of literature. • ▲

Matrilineal Culture in Western Literature

In some cultures, one's descent is traced through one's maternal ancestors rather than through the paternal ones. Show how matrilineal descent figures in such fictional works as Homer's *Iliad* and *Odyssey* and in the Arthurian romances. Get your bearings with Norma Love Goodrich's *Ancient Myths, Medieval Myths,* and *King Arthur.* • ▲

(**Narrower scope:** Analyze only one Homeric epic and/or one Arthurian romance. • ▲)

E. L. Doctorow and the Political Novel

In a 1985 essay in *The New York Times,* novelist E. L. Doctorow laments the fact that American critics regard a political novel as "impure" and that, to avoid the stigma, American novelists usually eschew political themes. After considering Doctorow's definitions and goals, read his own fiction, at least *The Book of Daniel.* How did American critics respond to Doctorow's own "political" novel? How did the British critics review *The Book of Daniel*? How have other American writers and critics responded to Doctorow's call for a more political fiction? The public relations department of Doctorow's publisher will have a complete clipping file on this matter. So too, probably, will the larger libraries, since in January 1986 Doctorow debated other American and European writers on this subject at the International PEN Congress held in New York. PEN American Center (568 Broadway, New York, NY 10012) has a clipping file of thousands of articles on the PEN Congress proceedings; *The New York Times Index* should be most helpful. • ▲

Doctorow's Model: The European Novel

In his *Times* essay (see above), E. L. Doctorow points out that there is no stigma attached to "political" novels in Europe. Read some or all of the European novels he mentions. Write an essay on the type of novel Doctorow is urging for America. • ▲

Fiction as Protest against Racism

Compare and contrast the literary methods used by certain novelists in their protests against white imperialism. Include Jules Verne's *Twenty Thousand Leagues under the Sea* (the chapters about British treatment of the British Indians), Alan Paton's *Cry, the Beloved Country*, Joseph Conrad's *Heart of Darkness*, and Alice Walker's *The Color Purple*, all of which deal with white oppression of Africans. • ★

Pearl S. Buck as a Naturalist Writer

Before writing *The Good Earth*, Mrs. Buck came under the spell of Theodore Dreiser, one of the giants of the naturalist (Zolaist) movement in literature. In the naturalist tradition, the writer concentrates on the forces of heredity and environment that shape individual character. What techniques do Buck's characters use to survive in the struggle for existence? (Zolaism is based on Darwinism.) How do changes in their environment affect them? How much "free will" can/does a naturalist's character exercise in the face of circumstance? • ★

Dreiser's Influence on Buck

Using the questions posed above, compare Pearl S. Buck's *The Good Earth* with a typical Theodore Dreiser work ("The Old Neighborhood," *Sister Carrie, An American Tragedy*). Discuss the similarity of Buck's novel to Dreiser's work and the difference, mainly the difference in *style*. • ▲

Darwinian Luck in Pearl S. Buck

As a naturalist—in her tracing of causation if not in her style and tone—Pearl S. Buck establishes luck as a major factor in man's fate. In *The Good Earth*, how do good and bad luck determine the character development of O-lan? of Wang Lung? of the neighbors who rob Wang Lung? Considering the role of luck in his career, to what extent is Wang Lung *really* superior to his neighbors? What are the social implications of naturalism? How have the critics and the historians of fiction dealt with Buck's naturalistic characterizations? • ★

Darwinian Coincidence In Hardy's Fiction

Review the role of accident, chance, coincidence, "luck" in Darwin's Theory of Evolution. Focus on several memorable examples. Then consider at least five co-incidences in Thomas Hardy's *Tess of the D'Urbervilles*. Has Hardy been faithful to—or exceeded the requirements of—the Darwinian view of circumstance? • ★

Coincidence in the Novels of Hardy and Goldsmith

To broaden the study suggested above, consider also at least five coincidences in Oliver Goldsmith's *The Vicar of Wakefield*, written before Darwin was born. How many of these coincidences would be accepted as ordinary in real life? Where in these two novels do you suspect the author of relying on coincidence simply to serve the needs of his plot? Speaking philosophically, who was more justified, more in tune with his times, in his use of coincidence, Goldsmith or Hardy? • ★

Moore's *Esther Waters:* An Answer to Hardy's *Tess?*

George Moore is supposed to have written his novel *Esther Waters* as an answer to Thomas Hardy's *Tess of the D'Urbervilles*. Compare and contrast the two novels in terms of action and motivation. In what scenes does Moore seem to be contradicting Hardy? Is one of them wrong, or is there room for both points of view? If you need orientation from the critics, consult William York Tindall's *Forces in Modern British Literature*, then histories of the English novel, finally pertinent studies of Hardy and Moore. • ▲

Darwinism in Recent Novels by Malamud, Vonnegut, Gaddis

In the 1980s three leading American writers produced novels about humanity's fate if it ignores the lessons of Darwinism. In a history of science (or a basic

• average difficulty	○ previous knowledge	★ most libraries
▲ larger library	☐ visual component	♫ audio component

biology text) find a full working statement of Darwin's Theory of Evolution. Compare and contrast Bernard Malamud's *God's Grace,* Kurt Vonnegut's *Galápagos,* and William Gaddis' *Carpenter's Gothic* for: plot, mode (satiric? realistic? other?), treatment, *character development under pressure,* and—make everything converge on this—the author's message about Darwinism. • ★

(**Wider scope:** Check book review digests for reviews of these novels in the biological and scientific journals as well as those in *The New York Times Book Review, The New York Review of Books,* and other intellectual periodicals. • ▲)

(**Wider still:** Study Darwin's *Origin of Species* at first hand; include reviews of the novels by theological journals. ○ ▲)

(**Narrower scope:** Limit your study to the scientific relevance of one of the novels and/or the religious and theological implications. ○ ▲)

Zola's Influence on (an American naturalistic novelist)

Establish the premises of "Zolaism" or "naturalism" as a literary approach. Choose an American writer usually labeled "naturalistic" or "Zolaist" (e.g., Frank Norris, Upton Sinclair, Theodore Dreiser, James T. Farrell, Richard Wright, John Steinbeck). To what extent does he or she adhere to Zolaist principles? depart from them? for what discernible reason (critics will be of help especially here)? With what success? • ▲

(**Wider scope:** Read Zola's original statement of naturalist aims in *The Experimental Novel;* and/or read a Zola novel, e.g., *The Dram Shop, Germinal, Nana;* use both in your discussion of Zola's impact on the American writer. • ▲)

Critical Reaction to Zolaism in American Fiction

How did American critics, accustomed to romanticism and the polite realism of William Dean Howells, react to the importation of Zolaism into American fiction? By 1906 the French source of American naturalism was clearly identified in such *New York Times Book Review* headlines as:

JURGIS RUDKUS AND "THE JUNGLE"
A 'Dispassionate Examination' of Upton Sinclair's
Application of Zola's Methods to a Chicago Environment

Do an in-depth study of newspaper and magazine reviews of one classic of American naturalism. • ▲

Zola's Influence on George Moore

Read (1) Emile Zola's *The Experimental Novel,* (2) those sections of George Moore's *Confessions of a Young Man* that deal with his conversion to Zolaism, (3) Zola's novel *The Dram Shop,* (4) Moore's novel *A Mummer's Wife.* Just how "Zolaist" is the Moore novel? Don't overlook the effect on the heroine of the change in her environment. The 1966 edition of *A Mummer's Wife* (by Liveright) has a helpful "Foreword." • ▲

(**Wider scope:** Include Moore's earlier attempt at Zolaism: *A Modern Lover.* • ▲)

Willa Cather vs. Naturalism

Willa Cather wrote what she called "unfurnished novels," in which she emphasized poetic mood rather than social scene. In short, she was opposed to the "naturalistic" school of writers. Compare one or more of her novels with one or more by a major American naturalist (see above). How did the critics respond to her anti-naturalism? • ▲

"The Troughs of Zolaism" 100 Years After

Read (1) those sections of Alfred Tennyson's "Locksley Hall Sixty Years After" in which he indicts Zolaist writers for "wallowing" in the "sewer"; (2) Emile Zola's *The Dram Shop* and/or *Germinal;* (3) George Moore's *A Mummer's Wife* (which provoked Tennyson's attack). How valid do Tennyson's charges sound more than "one hundred years after"? What conclusions do you draw about the changing nature of art, mores, taste? • ★

The Five-Generation Novel

Many naturalists and realists believe that to succeed, a novel about the influence of heredity and environment must span at least five generations of family history. Consider Thomas Mann's *Buddenbrooks,* Samuel Butler's *The Way of all Flesh,* and Gabriel García Márquez' *One Hundred Years of Solitude.* To what extent do their themes, their message, depend on the multi-generational survey? (N. B. If you need this closer identification, remember that Mann is a naturalist,

Butler a realist, García Márquez a realist-surrealist. What effects do these differences have on the family-history approach to character?) If you read the critics, scholars, literary historians *after* you read the three novels, they will help you gain perspective on the overall question. • ▲

Censorship of American Novels

Write to PEN American Center (568 Broadway, New York, NY 10012) and ask for literature about the banning of certain novels from American schools and libraries. Check *The New York Times Index* for accounts of book-banning. Write to newspapers in the towns involved for copies of their accounts and editorials on the subject. Read three or more of the proscribed works (e.g., Richard Wright's *Native Son,* Kurt Vonnegut's *Slaughterhouse-Five,* Mark Twain's *Huckleberry Finn*). Review the parts of the U.S. Constitution mentioned in some of the literature. Write an objective account of the controversy, the events, and the issues. • ★

After completing the research paper on the book-banning, and letting the issues marinate in your mind, write your own editorial on the controversy (for a school newspaper? check the wordage they prefer) *or* write a piece for the op/ed page of your local newspaper. •

Religious Fundamentalism in Fiction of the 80s

Two prominent novelists consider possible consequences of the fundamentalist movement in America. William Gaddis' *Carpenter's Gothic* predicts international troubles; Margaret Atwood's *The Handmaid's Tale* foresees total suppression of women within one or two generations. With or without help from the critics, compare and contrast these two works for their (1) themes and messages and (2) the totally different techniques they use to get their points across. • ★

Atwood's and Orwell's Futuristic Novels Compared

E. L. Doctorow has hailed Margaret Atwood's *The Handmaid's Tale* as ''a companion volume to [George] Orwell's *1984.*'' Taking your cue from him, read both novels and explain in which ways they are ''companions.'' To what extent have the critics regarded these futuristic novels as justifiable warnings? • ★

The Scarlet Letter and *Billy Budd*

Herman Melville was influenced by Nathaniel Hawthorne, especially in his treatment of evil. Can you see this influence in Melville's *Billy Budd*? Compare it with Hawthorne's *The Scarlet Letter*. How does Claggart resemble Chillingworth? and Melville's hero, Hawthorne's? How do the settings of the two stories compare as suitable stages for the conflict of morality and law? *Don't turn to the critics and literary historians until you've formulated some answers of your own; in that way you'll be better able to keep your own reactions separate from theirs and to report perspicaciously on both.* • ★

Claggart Measured against Other Villains

For a better understanding of the nature of evil as seen by writers, compare Herman Melville's Claggart (*Billy Budd*) with Nathaniel Hawthorne's Chillingworth (*The Scarlet Letter*) and/or Shakespeare's Iago (*Othello*) and/or Satan in the Garden of Eden story (*The Book of Genesis*) and/or in John Milton's *Paradise Lost*. Try to get each author's "feel" for evil before you read the critics' versions. • ★

Utopian Novels Compared

In his 1516 novel *Utopia* (a pun on two Greek words meaning "no place" and "good place") Sir Thomas More described an ideal society. Since then scores of utopian works have appeared: e.g., Samuel Butler's *Erewhon* (anagram for nowhere), Edward Bellamy's *Looking Backward*, B. F. Skinner's *Walden II*. Implicit in any utopian work is a criticism of the author's own society. Study three or more utopias. How do they compare with present society? with each other? What conditions do they aim to correct? What ideas do they have in common? What do you and/or the critics think of their feasibility? Get your bearings by consulting a standard survey of utopias, e.g., Lewis Mumford's *The Story of Utopias* or C. A. Doxiadis' *Between Dystopia and Utopia*. • ▲

Dystopian Novels Compared

A type of novel that sees in our future not ideal improvement but descent into totalitarianism, perversion of science, enslavement of humans by humans, or other nightmares is now called a *dystopia* ("bad place"). Examples: George

Orwell's *1984*, Aldous Huxley's *Brave New World*, Margaret Atwood's *The Handmaid's Tale*. Compare three or more dystopias. What do they see as extrapolations from today's trends? To what extent do you and/or the critics see these novels as justifiable warnings? (See Doxiadis citation above.) • ★

Rebecca as a Judge of Character

Reread Walter Scott's *Ivanhoe* and consider Rebecca's estimates of the characters of Rowena, Ivanhoe, and the Templar. How accurate is she, in your opinion? What is it about her situation that gives her special advantages as an observer of other people? • ★

The Outsider as Critic

In William Faulkner's *Intruder in the Dust*, a lawyer declares that only women, children, and blacks can tell you what's really going on in a society dominated by white male adults. Study Faulkner's novel as substantiation of this view. Adapt and extend his reasoning to include such outsiders as the Jewess in Scott's *Ivanhoe* (above) and the boy Huck and black man Jim in Mark Twain's *Huckleberry Finn*. • ★

Attitudes toward U.S. Citizens in Foreign Literatures

Discuss the attitudes displayed toward the U.S. and its people in such works as Gabriel García Márquez' *One Hundred Years of Solitude*, W. Somerset Maugham's *Our Betters*, Doris Lessing's *The Golden Notebook*, Jules Verne's *From the Earth to the Moon*, Charles Dickens' *American Notes* and *Martin Chuzzlewit*. What do foreigners seem most to like, and most to dislike, in the U.S. and its citizenry? What literary techniques do they use to make their appreciation/criticism effective? Perhaps you could begin your paper with this quote from Robert Burns:

> Oh wad some power the giftie gie us
> To see oursels as others see us! • ★

Thackeray's Burlesque on *Ivanhoe*

If you find Walter Scott's *Ivanhoe* difficult to take seriously, you might be a sympathetic reader of W. M. Thackeray's burlesque, *Rebecca and Rowena*. What is it in Scott that seems to have upset Thackeray? his plot? characterization? style? With or without the aid of the critics, conclude with a detailed judgment: Is Thackeray's burlesque fair, unfair, or a blend of rights and wrongs? • ▲

Irony in Thackeray

William Makepeace Thackeray is noted for his use of irony in his fiction: that is, for stating one thing but meaning another. Show how, in one or more of Thackeray's novels (e.g., *Vanity Fair, Henry Esmond, Pendennis*) his ironic devices contribute to his characterization, suspense, and overall message. • ▲

Irony in Two Periods of Literature

Compare Thackeray's irony (see above) with irony in William Gaddis' *Carpenter's Gothic* or Don DeLillo's *White Noise*. Why is Thackeray's irony easier (for us) to understand than that used by our contemporary novelists? Check out the reviews of Gaddis' and DeLillo's books just to make sure you didn't *miss* some of their irony! • ▲

Secrets of Dickens' Style

How does Charles Dickens achieve his rich, lively, plunging pell-mell style? Three clues to get you started: He greatly varies the length and structural patterns of his sentences; he packages his paragraphs very neatly, often with topic sentences and wind-up sentences; he appeals not only to our visual sense but also to our senses of touch, smell, taste, and—strongly—to our sense of sound. Try these ideas out on *Oliver Twist,* for example, and as you become practiced in analyzing his sentences, discover other stylistic devices on your own. (Should you seek the aid of a manual of rhetoric to become familiar with such terms as periodic sentence; loose sentence; topic sentence; principle of mass; parallelism?) ○ ★

Twain's Satire on Cooper

Is Mark Twain justified in his fault-finding essay "The Literary Offenses of Fenimore Cooper"? How does the contrast between Cooper and Twain illustrate (in part) the rapid growth of a native American style (see below)? ○ ▲

Growth of an American Style

In the early days of the Republic, American writers wrote, not surprisingly, like Englishmen. Compare, for example, the style of James Fenimore Cooper (*The Pilot*) with that of Sir Walter Scott (*The Pirate*). But by the late 1800s writers like Mark Twain had developed a distinctly American style (e.g., as in *Huckleberry Finn*). And by the mid-1900s writers like Ernest Hemingway (*A Farewell to Arms*), James Agee ("A Mother's Tale"), and William Faulkner (*The Bear*) had accomplished native innovations in style. Read the works cited and describe the growth of this American style. Critics, scholars, and literary historians stand by waiting to help—but read the primary sources first to enjoy your own reactions and conclusions and to keep them separate in your final critique. ○ ▲

Walter Scott Teaches Historians

Novelists like Victor Hugo and Alexandre Dumas regarded Walter Scott as "The Father of Historical Fiction." But even historians learned from Scott, especially how to *dramatize non*fiction. Read a Scott novel or two and then a book by historian William H. Prescott. In his colorful, vivid account of the *Conquest of Mexico* or *Conquest of Peru*, how much do you (and/or the critics) see of Scott's influence? ○ ▲

The Robinson Crusoe Theme in Fiction

Trace the theme of the shipwrecked survivor from its historical origin in the experiences of Alexander Selkirk (1704–09) to its fictional treatment in Daniel Defoe's *Robinson Crusoe*, Johann David Wyss' *Swiss Family Robinson*, Jules Verne's *The Mysterious Island* and *Two Years Holiday*, and William Golding's *Lord of the Flies*. How does each succeeding author add to the concept? How do the four authors differ in their treatment, message, emphasis, appeal, and in their literary skills? What is the permanent attraction in this theme? ● ★

H. G. Wells and Orson Welles: Two Tests That We Failed

In H. G. Wells' autobiography you read that he conceived of an invasion from Mars as a test "of the present ability of our race to meet a great crisis bravely or intelligently." Consider his *The War of the Worlds* in this light. How well do Wells' characters fare in this test? What really saves them?

● average difficulty	○ previous knowledge	★ most libraries
▲ larger library	□ visual component	♫ audio component

On the night of October 30, 1938, when Orson Welles broadcast a radio drama based on Wells' novel, millions of Americans panicked, many piling possessions into cars and driving fiercely away from the ''hot cylinder'' that had ''landed'' in New Jersey.

Check *The New York Times Index* for 1938 for full details on the Welles ''Mercury Theatre of the Air'' broadcast. Will the headline for this item serve as the title of your paper? • ★

Voltaire Versus Pope

Consider, in detail, Voltaire's novel *Candide* as an attack on the philosophy of Optimism as it is expounded in Alexander Pope's *Essay on Man* (especially Epistle I). A good scholarly edition of Pope will orient you to the philosophical issues involved. ○ ▲

William Wordsworth as Critic of Voltaire

Find that passage in Wordsworth's *The Excursion* in which he describes Voltaire's *Candide* as the ''dull product of a scoffer's pen.'' What passages could be considered dull? Which are certainly not dull? To what extent can you justify Wordsworth's criticism? Can you explain it as a result of differences in temperament (e.g., was Wordsworth humorless?) or of differences between the Age of Reason (Voltaire) and the Age of Romanticism (Wordsworth)? Was Voltaire justified in scoffing at the Optimists (and their slogan ''This is the best of all possible worlds'')? Read the primary sources first; turn to the critics and literary historians only when you have specific questions for them to answer. ○ ▲

Women in Dumas' World

Focus on the fate of the women in Alexander Dumas' *The Three Musketeers:* Kitty, Milady, Mme. Coquenard, Mme. Bonacieux, the Queen, *et al.* Consider comments on women made by the male characters, especially M. de Tréville and Athos. Are women and men being judged by different moral and legal standards? • ★

Samuel Butler and the Role of Women

In Samuel Butler's *The Way of All Flesh,* Christina and Charlotte follow the well-established nineteenth-century path for women. Ellen and Alethea choose an unorthodox course. What were the rewards and risks in each case? What made the unorthodoxy possible, the orthodoxy necessary? Why and to what extent were women tempted by circumstances to become devious in their dealings with men? • ★

(**Wider scope:** Contrast the women in Butler's classic with those in a twentieth-century novel like Doris Lessing's *The Golden Notebook.* • ★)

Scott and Cooper at Sea

James Fenimore Cooper felt that Walter Scott's novel *The Pirate* betrayed Scott's ignorance of sea life. It was partly to "show up" Scott that Cooper, drawing on his own intimate knowledge of deck and rigging, wrote *The Pilot.* In standard dictionaries of biography, check the sea credentials of both authors. Compare and contrast the novels. Why is it that it's Cooper's novel that's credited with founding a new popular genre—the sea tale? After you've thought about these matters, check with the critics and literary historians to see if you've missed any major points. • ▲

Philosophy Majors: A Field Day with Beckett

In his fiction, poetry, and film-writing, Samuel Beckett makes direct references to Heraclitus, Descartes, Geulincx, Malebranche, Berkeley. In all his works, he uses concepts and images from the writings (and the lives) of these and other thinkers (St. Augustine, Wittgenstein, et al.). Get your bearings from the present author's bibliography and "Beckett's Philosophical Relations" in his Monarch Note on *Samuel Beckett's "Waiting for Godot" and Other Works.* Choose your favorite philosopher(s) and discuss the novelist's treatment. For example, you could explain how the Greek philosopher Heraclitus (and his beliefs) figure in Beckett's novel *How It Is;* or discuss Beckett's novel *Watt* as a commentary on the philosophy of Wittgenstein. ○ ▲

Points of View in the Novel

Are you ready to make your own study of the question of point of view in fiction? You could read one novel for each of these main points of view that an author can employ:

1. Author-Omniscient. The author tells the story in the third person: *he, she, they.* Godlike, the author can be inside/outside any or all characters, thus providing the reader with more objective information than any single character can possess. E.g., Gabriel García Márquez, *One Hundred Years of Solitude;* William Makepeace Thackeray, *Vanity Fair.*

2. Third-Person Observer. The author tells the story in the third person— *he, she, they*—but mainly from the point of view of one character; this limits the reader's knowledge mainly to what one person knows. E.g., Kate Chopin, *The Awakening;* Upton Sinclair, *The Jungle.*

3. First-Person Narrator. The author tells the story strictly in the voice of one character, in the first person—*I*—hence, subjectively, severely limiting the reader's knowledge to that person's experience, mood, curiosity, intelligence, etc. E.g., Margaret Atwood, *The Handmaid's Tale;* Joseph Conrad, *Heart of Darkness.*

What advantages and disadvantages does each author experience in his/her particular choice of point of view? How has this choice affected suspense? dramatic irony? reader identification with characters? the way the plot unfolds? • ★

James on Point of View

In the prefaces he wrote for the collected edition of his works (published separately as *The Art of the Novel*), Henry James discussed his techniques, including his variations on point of view. Select three of his prefaces, representing different points of view, and in each case discuss (1) the effects James himself achieves in the related novels and (2) the effects a later novelist achieves in using a similar point of view. ○ ▲

Four Progenitors of Psychological Fiction

Curious about "stream of consciousness" fiction but stumped by James Joyce and William Faulkner? Do yourself and your fellow students a favor: Research and write a survey of how it all began, understanding the movement from its beginnings. You'll find the concept of a "stream of thought" in William (brother of Henry) James' *Principles of Psychology* (1890); of "psychological time" and thought as "a flow of images" in Henri Bergson's *Time and Free Will* (1889); of free association and the unconscious in Sigmund Freud's *The Interpretation of Dreams* (1900); and you'll find the earliest, easiest-to-grasp experiment with stream of consciousness in Edouard Dujardin's novel *We'll to the Woods No More* (1897). It's legitimate for you to work up to Bergson and Freud through reputable encyclopedia articles, textbooks, histories of philosophy, psychology, and psychoanalysis. Write your paper as an information report, a background study, for young readers approaching stream-of-consciousness literature for the first time. ● ▲

Dujardin's Influence on Moore and Joyce

An easy introduction to stream-of-consciousness fiction is, as we've noted, Edouard Dujardin's *We'll to the Woods No More,* which is the novel that inspired both George Moore and James Joyce to explore this technique. Trace its development from Dujardin's simple experiment to Moore's "continuous transition" in *The Brook Kerith,* his novel about Jesus, through to James Joyce's *Ulysses,* the first popular classic of the new medium. Quote and analyze one or two passages from each of the three to show the rapid maturation of the method. Helps along the way: articles on "stream of consciousness" in dictionaries of literary terms; the "Foreword" to the 1969 Liveright edition of *Kerith;* and I. A. Richards' splendid review of that edition in the *New York Review of Books.* ○ ▲

Freud's Influence on Joyce

At the time that Joyce wrote *Ulysses,* Freud had postulated two major components in the human psyche: the ego and the id (or unconscious). In a standard encyclopedia, a textbook of basic psychology, or a history of psychoanalysis, establish working descriptions of the ego, the id, the subconscious, the process of free association, and Freud's dream symbols. Then read *Ulysses* first to establish the story, themes, techniques (see next Idea). Then review the text to find brief examples of Joyce's use of each Freudian concept listed above. Write (or outline for oral delivery) a report on "How a Knowledge of Freud Contributes to Our Understanding of Joyce's *Ulysses.*" ● ▲

Oedipus Complex in Freud and Lawrence

Establish a working definition of the Oedipus Complex as described by Sigmund Freud (and, if you're that much interested in psychology, as described by Erich Fromm and Harry Sullivan). Then consider D. H. Lawrence's study of mother-son relations in his novel *Sons and Lovers;* compare it with Freud's doctrine (and with Fromm's and Sullivan's?). ● ▲

● average difficulty	○ previous knowledge	★ most libraries
▲ larger library	☐ visual component	♫ audio component

(**Wider scope:** Include in your study Sophocles' play *Oedipus the King* and/or Lawrence's "The Rocking Horse Winner," and definitely include Fromm's and Sullivan's versions of the Oedipal situation. • ▲)

The Function of Metaphor in *The Martian Chronicles*

Show how Ray Bradbury's use of figures of speech—especially *irony, metaphor,* and *simile*—helps us visualize Mars and the Martians. (Should you review the meaning of these three terms first? See INDEX.) • ★

Symbolism in *Moby-Dick*

For each of the characters in Herman Melville's *Moby-Dick,* the white whale has a different meaning. And in all probability it signifies something different for every reader too. For D. H. Lawrence, the whale stood for "the deepest blood-being of the white race. . . . And he is hunted by the maniacal fanaticism of our white mental consciousness." For William York Tindall, it is possible that the whale is "a phallic being endangered by the mind." Presumably Tindall sees the whale as a Freudian symbol of sexuality and Ahab its hunter as an embodiment of the superego opposed to sexuality. Considering one or several of these notions (some of the characters' ideas too?), discuss the function of symbolism as demonstrated in *Moby-Dick.* • ▲

(**Wider scope:** Read the sections on *Moby-Dick* in Tindall's *The Literary Symbol,* Lawrence's *Studies in Classic American Literature,* and W. H. Auden's *The Enchafed Flood.* Show that, although by its very nature a symbol will signify something different to every reader, *these meanings overlap.* How does the overlapping validate our study of symbolism? • ▲)

Woolf and Faulkner: A Contrast in Subjectivism

James Joyce's *Ulysses* (see above) provided both the English Virginia Woolf and the American William Faulkner with new technical means of exploring the psyche. But each developed the Dujardin-Joyce approach in a new and original manner. Contrast Woolf's *To the Lighthouse* with Faulkner's *The Bear.* Consider how they differ vastly in their syntax, cadences, use of symbols, and psychological subject matter, yet both manage to represent the *quality* of the private mental life. Consult the critics and literary historians only after your own thinking has crystallized; keep your original ideas separate from theirs in your paper/oral report. • ▲

Carl Jung's Influence on Hermann Hesse

During World War I, the German novelist Hermann Hesse was psychoanalyzed by a disciple of Jung and then by Jung himself. Almost immediately thereafter, Hesse wrote his novel *Demian*. Using a history of psychoanalysis or a popular guide to Jungian thought, establish working definitions of these concepts: the Persona; the Shadow; the collective ("racial") unconscious; the animus and anima; other "archetypes"; individuation; the Self; Jung's theory of how/why an author creates his characters as he does. Then read *Demian* and report on "The Relationship between Psychology and Literature as Exemplified in the Story of Emil Sinclair." ○ ▲

(**Wider scope:** Trace the concepts listed above to the original passages in Jung's works; and/or read the critical and psychological literature on *Demian*. ○ ▲)

Mythic Underpinning in Joyce's *Ulysses*

Since depth psychology and anthropology reestablished the importance of myth in man's psyche, major writers have used classical myths as patterns for their plots and characterizations. Joyce's *Ulysses,* for example, is based on Homer's *Odyssey:* Mr. Bloom is the "modern" Odysseus or Ulysses, Mrs. Bloom the "modern" Penelope, and Stephen a "modern" Telemachus in search for a father. Read a prose translation of the *Odyssey* (Samuel Butler's?), then *Ulysses*. What clues do you get that link a Joycean scene with a Homeric episode? What does Joyce mean by having his three main characters so different from Homer's? Compare, for example, the meaning of the theme of the Search for the Father in Homer and in Joyce. After you have exhausted your own insights, consult a standard critique of each author. William York Tindall's is a good handbook for beginners in Joyce's world. ○ ▲

Mythic Underpinning in Heller's *Catch-22*

Your thesis: Joseph Heller underscores his story with covert mythic images that attract and gratify the reader, usually on an unconscious level. Examine at least these parts of the story to prove your point:

Luciana chapter: What are the parallels with pagan and Christian festivals of light; with the story of Saint Lucia?

Bordello scene: How does the setting resemble Wagner's Venusberg in *Tannhäuser?* What's the point of the resemblance?

Yossarian's thigh wound: How does it link him with the Fisher King? Arthurian legendry? T. S. Eliot's *The Waste Land?*

Yossarian and Milo in the tree: Adam and Satan?

Major —— de Coverley: Jehovah? Relation to Sir Roger de Coverley in Joseph Addison's *Spectator* papers?

Yossarian's Descent into Hell: Parallels with Dante (starting in Chapter 39)?

What does Heller intend his readers to get from these mythic parallels— consciously? subliminally? What do they add to your enjoyment of the story?

When you've exhausted your own insights, use as your guidebooks: "Descent into Heller: Mythic Imagery in *Catch-22*," *Journal of Mental Imagery,* 1982 (145–156) 6; the Monarch Note on Heller; and selected works from the Note's bibliography. ○ ▲

Zora Hurston's Themes in Fiction and Nonfiction

Zora Neale Hurston was a black anthropologist who interpreted black folktales in such collections as *Mules and Men* and *Tell My Horse;* she also wrote two novels, *Jonah's Gourd Vine* and *Their Eyes Were Watching God.* What thematic relationships do you (and/or the critics) see between her nonfictional (critical) and fictional writings? ● ▲

Mythic Underpinning in Updike and Shorris

Two novels that rely on mythic underpinning are John Updike's *The Centaur* and Earl Shorris' *The Fifth Sun: A Novel of Pancho Villa.* For Updike, review the stories of the half-man-half-horse creatures in ancient Greek mythology; for Shorris, check on the Aztec myths of creation and the gods. Compare and contrast the two novels for their modern extensions and interpretations of ancient legends. What would the reader who ignores the mythic underpinning be missing? ● ▲

Recent Novels Based on Aztec Legendry

Jamake Highwater's novel *The Sun, He Dies* is set in the final days of the Aztec empire. Earl Shorris's *The Fifth Sun: A Novel of Pancho Villa* uses the same

Aztec legends as underpinning for a story set in modern North America. What do these two recent works add to our understanding of Indian traditions, ways of life, ways of looking at reality different from the dominant culture's way today? of an Indian basis for modern Mexican life? of American (including United States) history?

A stylistic comparison: Discuss the way Highwater and Shorris use two entirely different styles to suit their different approaches to the Aztec material. What have the critics noticed that you missed in your first readings? • ▲

R. D. Laing's Influence on Doris Lessing

Read R. D. Laing's *The Politics of Experience* and then Doris Lessing's *Briefing for a Descent into Hell*. How does Lessing's science-fiction novel make use of Laing's psychiatric principles? (Can you find a sentence in Laing she borrows verbatim? This is clue enough that she expects us to make this comparison!) What has Laing's book added to the novelist's understanding of humanity, and Lessing's novel added to our understanding of both Laing and humanity-at-large? And what do the critics add to your understanding of both the psychiatrist and the novelist? • ▲

Impressionism in Fiction: Conrad and Momaday

When writers describe the outer world not objectively but the way it impresses itself on a character's mind, and the way it blends in with her/his memories and associations, we say they are using *impressionistic techniques*. Compare (the Native American) N. Scott Momaday's *House Made of Dawn* with (the Polish-English) Joseph Conrad's *Lord Jim*. How do they compare in their use of impressionistic rhythms and sentence structures? of point of view? of techniques of characterization? of imagery and symbolism? in their treatment of the theme of alienation? Based on these major examples, how appropriate and successful is literary impressionism as a means of recreating states of mind? Only after your own answers to these questions are crystallized should you turn to the critics to discover what you've ignored and maybe for a difference of opinion or two. • ▲

Impressionism in Three Arts

The impressionist artist, e.g., Claude Monet, paints objects not as they exist in the objective world but as they impress themselves on the subjective state of humans. The impressionist in music, e.g., Claude Debussy, is less interested in contours of melody than in suggestive harmonies and "colorful" tonalities. And in fiction, the impressionist—Henry James, Joseph Conrad, N. Scott Momaday—is interested in outer reality mainly as it may blend with subjective impressions, memories, associations in the mind of a character.

Choose one work from each art—say Monet's *The River*, Debussy's *La Mer*, and either James Joyce's *Portrait of the Artist as a Young Man* or Momaday's *House Made of Dawn*—to demonstrate how Impressionism combines, in varying degrees, the objective and the subjective. Consult the critics at least to establish a full understanding of what the word *Impressionism* signifies in each art, but also for other critical points you may have missed. ○ ▲

Expressionism in Kafka

One psychological mode used by the modern writer shows how the outer world impresses itself on—or is received by—a character's mind: *Impressionism*. Another mode shows how the outer world is distorted by a character's state of mind, how that character's inner experience is projected onto the other world: *Expressionism*. Thus in reading fiction by Franz Kafka we can never be sure whether we are inside a character's fantasies or witnessing objective reality. Consider Kafka's *The Trial*, and/or *The Castle*, for their success in recreating certain states of mind. When your own impressions have crystallized, consult the critics; in your writing (or speaking) keep your original ideas separate from theirs. ○ ▲

Expressionism in *Catch-22*

Which scenes in Joseph Heller's novel are, according to the definition given above, *expressionistic?* How does use of this technique fit the needs of Heller's story? How did the critics react to this planting of expressionistic episodes in seriocomic realism? ● ▲

Expressionism in Four Arts

The term *Expressionism* has been used to label the painting of Oskar Kokoschka and Max Beckmann; the drama *The Hairy Ape* of Eugene O'Neill and *The Dream Play* of August Strindberg; certain musical compositions by Anton Webern and Alban Berg; and (see above) fictions like *The Trial*, *The Castle*, and "Metamorphosis" by Kafka. What do these works have in common? Why are some critics unhappy with the term "Expressionism"? Why was it applied to one art after another? While recognizing the critics' displeasure, try to see the psychological connections among these four types of expression that have, more or less, established the common term for them. ○ ▲

Your Identification with a Fictional Character

Unless the novelist succeeds in evoking your sympathy for at least one of his characters, you will become bored with his work, maybe finish it only under compulsion of an assignment. Which fictional characters do you recall having identified with? The young Catherine in *Wuthering Heights*? The painter in *The Moon and Sixpence*? O'lan in *The Good Earth*? Celie in *The Color Purple*? Here's a subject for a written or oral report that should set yourself and your classmates abuzz:

What does it reveal about yourself that you identified with *that* character? What did it teach you about yourself and your relations with others? about the function of literature? and your literary preferences? Did it blind you to other considerations in the novel? Check back with what we said about vicarious experience on pp. 8–9 before you draft this one. •

The Novel as a "Message" Medium

In *Brighton Rock, The End of the Affair,* and other novels, Graham Greene clearly intends to leave us with certain religious conclusions or at least with questions. Upton Sinclair made no bones about it: He intended *The Jungle* to arouse sympathy for "wage slaves" and he was disappointed when, groping for his reader's "heart," he reached only his "stomach." That is, Sinclair had wanted broad social and pro-labor legislation but got instead only pure-food laws. Kurt Vonnegut once said that he wrote *Jailbird* to show America why it needed a new left wing in politics and how it had lost the old left wing. He wrote *Galápagos* in response to his view that "Darwinism is in trouble." In *Joe the Engineer,* Chuck Wachtel treats the psychological and social plight of the blue-collar worker. In *Catch-22,* Joseph Heller mounts an all-out attack on American professions and institutions, military and civilian. In *The Naked and the Dead* Norman Mailer characterizes American military commanders as virtually fascists. In *White Noise,* Don DeLillo sees Americans as fatally passive, in deep despair. In *The Golden Notebook,* Doris Lessing explores the compartmentalization of modern life and works out some now-famous ideas about women.

Using any three or more of the novels mentioned, write about "The Ideological Intention of the Novelist." Does it ever affect his/her work as art? Does it deepen or dull *your* interest? *What would these novels be without that intention?* • ★

Two Stages of Fiction about Nuclear War

In the late 1950s, and again from 1978 on, novelists have taken up the theme of nuclear war. How do the earlier novels differ from the later ones? Why was there a two-decade period when novelists mainly ignored the subject? For the Fifties, consider: Nevil Shute, *On the Beach;* Hans Hellmut Kurst, *The Seventh Day;* and Pat Frank, *Alas, Babylon.* For '78 and after, consider: General Sir John Hackett, *The Third World War;* Whitley Strieber and James Kunetka, *Warday;* Louise Lawrence, *The Children of the Dust.* For the interim of 1959–1978, consider the effect of *detente* on writers' and readers' choice of subject matter. Why, then, have they returned to this subject? • ▲

(**Wider scope:** Include in the '78-on period of writers' concern the productions of *The Day After* on ABC-TV and *Threads* on BBC television. If you cannot view reruns, try to get copies of the scripts from the networks or, as a last resort, report on these works through the reactions of the critics. • ▲ ☐)

Success of the "Idea Novel"

Earlier we noted that Stowe, Turgenev, and Sinclair were among the very few fiction writers to have had any influence on the course of history. Check the critical reviews at the time of publication of those Lessing, Vonnegut, Greene, Heller, Mailer, and DeLillo works cited above. Did they seem to have any *immediate* ideological impact, judging from the critical reactions? Then check critical studies of these authors for their *long-range* effect. (E.g., after a while *Catch-22* became a catchword in many languages.) Finally, check the histories of literature to review the influence of Stowe, Turgenev, Sinclair. How do today's writers compare in ideological impact with the three classics? • ▲

Personal Experience with Novel Themes

After considering the above remarks about "Message" and "Idea" in the novel, and reviewing our earlier entry on "Themes in the Fiction of ____" (p. 22), write, or outline for oral delivery, a report on "How Long Does It Last—

The Influence of the Novel on Me?'' *Do not reread or even skim through the novels you remember as being the most influential on your own growth.* Just list two or three of them and try to figure out why you remember them at all—for their atmosphere? their mood? their heroines? their ideas on love, war, motherhood, feminism, future scientific or political developments? How do you explain these novels' lasting impact on you? Now that you've crystallized *that* experience, what are you going to do about it? •★

GENERAL IDEAS APPLICABLE TO ANY SHORT STORY

You will find that our survey of master themes (pp. 9–15) will help you discover an ''angle'' for discussing a short story just as well as it does for a novel. And our checklist of techniques used by the novelist (pp. 17–22) will serve you here again, but *with this crucial distinction:* the short story writer obviously cannot use them on anything like the scale the novelist enjoys.

The short story writer, so the tradition goes, limits his/her wordage to what you can digest comfortably in one sitting. This means that he or she can't achieve anything like the full *characterization* we experience in the novel (or even in the *novella,* or short novel). Rather the short story writer usually concentrates on just one aspect of the personality of his/her main character(s). Reading O. Henry's ''The Gift of the Magi'' we discover the mutual altruism of a young wife and her husband. Most often the short story writer confines himself to just one change in just one character, as does James Joyce in his ''Araby.''

The brevity of the short story affects its *structure* too. The author has no time or space for a long *rising action.* Usually he begins *close to the climax,* as does Ambrose Bierce in his ''An Occurrence at Owl Creek Bridge.'' Necessary background is provided *after* the main conflict is already launched.

Economy, compactness, swift suggestiveness, then, instead of massive, detailed treatment, are the toolmarks of short story authors. And during the past century or so that they have been perfecting their techniques, short story writers have tended to use either of two main approaches. We might as well make those the first of our:

• average difficulty	○ previous knowledge	★ most libraries
▲ larger library	☐ visual component	♫ audio component

SPECIFIC IDEAS ABOUT THE SHORT STORY

Two Main Approaches to Short Story Writing

In his famous review, "Hawthorne's Tales," the American Edgar Allan Poe prescribed one approach to writing a short story: The writer invents incidents which, when plotted to a suspenseful climax, achieve one sweeping "unique or single *effect.*" But on the other side of the world, the Russian Ivan Turgenev was using a different approach: He began by depicting characters whose needs would trigger events that would further reveal their makeup. Of course, as Henry James pointed out, incidents and characterizations ultimately prove to be identical: Events test character, character creates events. Still, most stories do lean more to action or more to characterization.

Read at least two short stories by Poe and two by Turgenev. Show how these works illustrate their respective approaches. What is the effect on the reader in each case? ● ★

Poe's Theory and Practice

Read Poe's "Hawthorne's Tales" (*Graham's Magazine*, 1842). Concentrate on the "single *effect*" passage. Then read at least three of Poe's stories. With sufficient reference to the technical details and effects they produce, show that the theory Poe promulgated was, by and large, the theory he practiced. What do the literary historians see as Poe's influence on the genre? ● ▲

(If *Graham's* is not available in your library, take out an edition of Poe's collected works or an anthology of classics of criticism, like Edmund Wilson's *The Shock of Recognition.*)

Garshin, Turgenev, Poe

Vsevolod Mikhailovich Garshin dedicated his short story "The Red Flower" *To the Memory of Ivan Sergeevich Turgenev*. Compare "The Red Flower" with a Turgenev story and a Poe story. To what extent does Garshin favor Turgenev's approach, or Poe's, or a third approach? If you need material to prove your point (or to expand your scope), add a second story by each author. ● ▲

Turgenev and the Tsar

Turgenev's *Sportsman's Notebook* (or *Sketchbook,* as it can also be translated) was credited, as noted earlier, with influencing history. Study the "sketches" in this book for their revealing story detail and characterization. Which characters are depicted as more human, the serfs or their owners? What reactions, do you imagine, would especially have influenced the Tsar to free the serfs? • ★

(**Wider scope:** But when the *Notebook* first appeared, Turgenev was banished from St. Petersburg to his country estate for 18 months. Check biographies and histories of fiction for a paper on "Turgenev's Changing Fortunes vis-à-vis the Russian Government and Public Opinion." • ▲)

The Surprise Ending in O. Henry and Maupassant

After Poe's initial concern with a theory of the genre, some short story writers developed the technique of the *surprise ending*. Instead of a gradual change or revelation, they produced a sudden and complete reversal of expectation. Compare O. Henry's technique in "The Gift of the Magi" with Guy de Maupassant's in "The Diamond Necklace." Include a consideration of the surprise ending as a form of dramatic irony. • ★

The Smash Surprise vs. the Quiet Surprise

O. Henry's and Maupassant's endings are likely to be smash surprises. More common in today's story resolution is what we may call the quiet surprise. In "The Hint of an Explanation," Graham Greene waits until the very end to let us see that the narrator's train-rider acquaintance wears the collar of a priest. This is not the crucial part of the resolution, but it strengthens it. Compare O. Henry, Maupassant, and Greene stories for their different degrees of sensational revelations. • ★

Zolaism in Short Stories of_____

Émile Zola's philosophy of fiction, as we have seen, requires that the author study characters as products of heredity and environment, of circumstance and experience. Zola believed the writer must approach his material scientifically, that is, objectively, scrapping all preconceptions, sentimental attachments, and moral judgments. He must simply observe and record data on his human specimens. He must scrap *the conventional plot,* which Zola sees as a tendentious tampering with the data of life to achieve a moral effect—as, for example, when a story ends with virtue rewarded, evil punished, rationality triumphant. Instead of fashioning such a plot, Zola opines, the scientific writer must trace the chain of causation: each step in the action must be the effect of a clearly demonstrated cause. Belief, triumph, defeat, fate must appear as inevitable workings-out of the laws of biology.

What do you see as Zola's influence on the short stories of Theodore Dreiser (e.g., "The Old Neighborhood"), Ernest Hemingway (e.g., "Soldier's Home"), John Steinbeck (e.g., "Flight"), or other naturalist writers? • ▲

(**Wider scope:** Read Zola's *The Experimental Novel* and/or historians of fiction for a deeper appreciation of Zola's impact on the short story. • ▲)

Psychological Time and Ambrose Bierce

As part of their growing interest in the inner life of their characters, modern writers have explored the difference between "clock time" and "psychological time." Clock time, based on astronomy, is objective, rigid, external, equal for all of us. Psychological time is subjective, personal, internal, variable: in minutes of clock time we may experience "years" of growth. According to Henri Bergson, in his *Time and Free Will,* psychological time is the only real measurement of experience.

Ambrose Bierce's "An Occurrence at Owl Creek Bridge" provides you with an easy introduction to Bergsonian fiction. Report on how the author blends external events with the main character's inner life, how the outer and inner events differ in duration, how this approach increases the scope and verisimilitude of fiction. • ★

(**Wider scope:** Read Bergson and/or compare Bierce's use of psychological time with Virginia Woolf's in her *To the Lighthouse.* • ▲)

Virginia Woolf and Arnold Bennett

Read Woolf's essay "Mr. Bennett and Mrs. Brown" in which she compares Mrs. Brown as the realistic writer Bennett would describe her with Mrs. Brown as a psychological writer like Woolf would depict her. Extend your study to one or more short fictions each by Woolf and Bennett. Which author presents us with a "fuller" representation of life? What can be said in defense of Bennett's approach? • ▲

Impressionism in Woolf's Short Fiction

The subjectivist author is often interested in the outer event mainly as it impresses itself upon a character's mind. In Virginia Woolf's "The Mark on the

Wall'' the ''real'' subject is not the objective fact but the subjective responses it triggers off. Using this story and as many other Woolf stories as you need for the scope of your assignment, report on ''The Nature of Reality for Virginia Woolf.'' • ★

(**Wider scope:** After you've formulated your own ideas about this topic, compare your reactions with the critics'. • ▲)

Impressionism in Conrad

Life comprises not only a series of impressions. To the psychological writer, it is often a series of impressions of impressions. Demonstrate this by reporting on ''The Lagoon'' by Joseph Conrad. (N. B.: Arsat's brother is known to the traveler only as Arsat describes him; Arsat is known to us only as the traveler sees *him;* the traveler is known to us only as Conrad sees HIM. Just as the traveler has his own associations with the events in Arsat's house and history, so you—the reader—have your associations. Impressionism is a study of the way reality is filtered, reflected, refracted through many media. Check INDEX for Impressionism.) • ★

(**Wider scope:** Include ''The Secret Sharer'' and/or other Conrad stories, and/or compare your own impressions of impressionism with those of selected critics and historians of fiction. • ▲)

Joyce's ''Araby'' as Psychological Fiction

Consider the relative importance of outer event and inner psychological process—and their interaction—in ''Araby.'' Joyce uses in this story his device of the ''epiphany.'' An epiphany has occurred when any trivial object or action provides a sensitive observer with a ''shining forth'' of truth. William York Tindall locates ''a typical epiphany'' in the ''inane conversation of a young lady with two young gentlemen . . . [it] shows forth emptiness and provides the sinking sensation.'' Why does that conversation have such significance for the main character at that particular point in his life? What other epiphanies do you see in this story? • ★

(**Wider scope:** Consult Tindall's books, read the Joyce stories he discusses, report on ''A Critic's Epiphanies about Joyce's Epiphanies.'' • ▲)

Epiphany in Joyce and in the Bible

Study the Christian Feast of the Epiphany (January 6—''Twelfth Day'' or ''Little Christmas'') from which Joyce took the name for his characters' insights. Study his use of it in several of his short stories. How does fiction stressing psychological processes like this add to our knowledge of the human condition? What do the critics see as the value of Joyce's use of the word *epiphany?* ○ ▲

Stream of Consciousness: Different Approaches

Stream of consciousness, as we've seen in our Ideas about the novel, consists of those images, feelings, thoughts that flow through a character's mind in apparently haphazard order. Different authors use different techniques to represent the stream. Compare Virginia Woolf's and William Faulkner's methods in one or more short stories by each. What do you and/or the critics see as the differences in *quality* in these authors' depiction of the stream? ○ ▲

Stream of Consciousness and Interior Monologue

Some critics use the term *interior monologue* interchangeably with the term *stream of consciousness*. Other critics insist on a sharp distinction between the two expressions. Check their usage in at least two handbooks of literary terms and in two critical studies of psychological fiction. Read one or more short stories by each of three authors cited and report in full on the fine differences in technique and effect. ○ ▲

Expressionism in the Short Story

When a writer constructs a story based on the way the outside world *impresses* itself on a character's psyche, the writer is said to be using *impressionistic* technique. When he constructs a story based on the way reality is *distorted* by a character's state of mind, or the way his inner reality is *projected* onto the outer world, the writer is said to be using *expressionistic* technique. Report on Franz Kafka's ''Metamorphosis'' and/or other of his short stories as expressionistic fiction. See INDEX for Expressionism. ● ★

(**Wider scope:** Contrast the effects gained by expressionism and impressionism by comparing stories by Kafka with stories by Conrad or Woolf. What do you and/or the critics see as the main differences? ○ ▲)

Short Stories in the Bible

The term *short story* can be used in two senses. In its broader sense, it refers to any brief narrative and so includes fables, fairy tales, parables, and folktales. In its narrower sense (the sense in which we've been using the term here), the term refers only to the modern artistically-wrought short fiction, replete with plot (as opposed to story), characterization, conflict, suspense, complication, crisis, climax, resolution, etc. This carefully contrived story, which dates from the days of Poe and Turgenev, is intended for a secular audience who buy fiction as fiction.

How then do we classify the Books of Ruth, Jonah, Esther in the Bible? Written for a religious audience, these stories are devised to deliver a religious moral. How do these "Books" compare, in structure and the other elements mentioned above, with the modern story? • ▲

(**Wider scope:** For fuller understanding of the Bible stories, you may want to read critical commentaries on the Bible as literature, especially to be sure of the moral intended in each case. ○ ▲)

Verne's "Forgotten Masterpiece"

At the time of his death, Jules Verne was working on "The Eternal Adam," a short story that one of his biographers, Peter Costello, calls "one of Verne's almost forgotten masterpieces." In what ways is this story a denial, a reversal, of the optimism (and of the religious views) of the earlier Verne, the optimism by which he is better known? How does "The Eternal Adam" bear out the idea of "eternal recurrence" promulgated by the philosopher Friedrich Nietzsche? What literary qualities in the story justify Costello's calling it a masterpiece? What do you and/or other critics think of both the theme and the techniques? (The story appears in English translation in Verne's *Yesterday and Tomorrow*.) ○ ▲

Verne's First and Last Short Stories about Science

Compare Verne's first use of science in his short story "Master Zacharias" with his final view of science in "The Eternal Adam," the story he was working on just before his death. How have his views changed? Why do the critics disagree on the significance of these stories? Especially consult Peter Costello, *Jules Verne: Inventor of Science Fiction;* Jean Jules-Verne, *Jules Verne;* Jean Chesneaux, *The Political and Social Ideas of Jules Verne.* • ▲

Robert Coover and Fairy Tales

Read the stories of Little Red Riding Hood and Jack the Giant Killer (in unabridged, unexpurgated editions). Then read Robert Coover's short story,

"The Door." What does Coover provide that the "fairy tales" lack? And vice versa? How do the narrative techniques in the tales and the short story differ? What do you and/or the critics see as Coover's aim in retelling these tales? • ▲

(**Wider scope:** Read psychological interpretations of the tales by Erich Fromm, Bruno Bettelheim, others. Has Coover been influenced by them? • ▲)

Two Puerto Rican Stories Compared

Emilio Diaz Valcarel's story "Damian Sanchez, G.I." is about a Puerto Rican–American serving in the Korean War. Piri Thomas' novel *Down These Mean Streets* is about life in Spanish Harlem. The two places have this in common: In both the Puerto Rican is the victim of cruel racism. Compare the two authors' techniques for revealing this condition and their characters' responses to it. • ▲

Borges' Influence on Donald Barthelme

Jorge Luis Borges, Argentine poet and inventor of new forms of short fiction, has had an enormous influence on U.S. writers, especially on short story writers. Narrow your study down to Donald Barthelme's early fictions as compared to Borges' *ficciones* already in print when Barthelme began to write. What do you and/or the critics see as Barthelme's debt to the genius of Buenos Aires? • ▲

N. Scott Momaday and Joseph Conrad

The Native American (i.e., "Indian") writer N. Scott Momaday, like the Polish-English writer Joseph Conrad, uses an impressionistic style replete with luxuriously long and involuted sentences. Compare one or more short stories by each of them for their rhythms, their success in recreating the quality of life and circumstances, their message. • ▲

(**Wider scope:** How have professional critics compared Momaday and Conrad? • ▲)

Mario Suarez and Nick Vaca: Two *Barrio* Writers Compared

Both Mario Suarez and Nick Vaca write stories about the *barrio* (a Mexican-American section of a city), and both explore the differences between the dominant Anglo-Saxon people and the Mexican-Americans. But Suarez and Vaca differ vastly in their techniques. Suarez' stories like "Señor Garza" and "Las Comadres" consist mainly of vignettes of people and places. Vaca's stories like "The Purchase" and "Martin" are highly dramatic. Compare their techniques in detail: their use of dialogue, description, metaphor, irony, point of view, as well as their themes. • ▲

The Four Million and O. Henry

O. Henry said that he wrote not for "the four hundred" (as the New York aristocrats were called in his day) but for "the four million." Read at least ten short stories by O. Henry that show a definite sympathy for the common man and woman. How does he treat the more affluent people involved in his stories? • ★

(**Wider scope:** Read the biographical dictionaries and other biographical studies on O. Henry. How did his own experiences compare with those of the four hundred and the four million? Which of the events, characters, settings in his stories could have been based on his own experiences? • ★)

"Blues" Symbolism in James Baldwin

One of the great short stories of our time is James Baldwin's "Sonny's Blues." Discuss Baldwin's storytelling not only in terms of themes, conflict, style, setting, but especially in terms of his use of the "blues" as a symbol of the black man's salvation, his transcendence over suffering. You might want to consult a history of music for a definition, description, and examples of the blues.• ★ ♫

Samuel Beckett and Dante Alighieri

Beckett based his first fictional hero, Belacqua Shuah (in the short story collection *More Pricks than Kicks*) on a character in Dante's *Purgatory* (Canto IV). Compare the two treatments of Belacqua. What does Beckett gain by using Dante's prototype? How has Beckett modernized and/or developed the Dante character? • ▲

Music as a Literary Challenge

It is extremely difficult to describe a sustained performance of music, to create in words a representation of the developing sounds of voice and instruments.

Compare and contrast Turgenev's technique in "The Singing Contest" (in *A Sportsman's Notebook*) with Baldwin's in "Sonny's Blues" (in *Going to Meet the Man*). Consider the authors' resort to rhythm in their prose, sensuous detail, use of simile and metaphor, their descriptions of the effect of the music on the listeners. • ▲

(**Wider scope:** Compare Turgenev and Baldwin with Ralph Bates, especially for his descriptions of guitar-playing in his classic novel *The Olive Field*. • ▲)

Ironic Reversal in the Short Story

A simple structural device that the short story writer often uses is this: He brings several people together and lets us either (1) know their reputation or (2) form our own impressions of their characters; then he subjects them to some common disaster. The disaster may reveal that some people are different from what we had assumed. Compare plot, characterization, point of view, style, tone, and theme in Bret Harte's "The Outcasts of Poker Flat" with Thomas Mann's "The Railroad Accident." • ★

Exposition in the Short Story

Passages in a story that supply background information about the characters and their situation constitute the *exposition*. At what point in the story do you find these passages in Guy de Maupassant's "The Diamond Necklace" and in F. Scott Fitzgerald's "The Freshest Boy"? Which arrangement is more dramatic? Why do you say so? • ★

(**Wider scope:** Consider other stories with the same questions in mind, again balancing nineteenth-century stories against twentieth-century examples. What do the time contrasts show about the growing artistry of the short story writer? about changing tastes, changing demands for our attention? • ★)

Time Patterns in the Short Story

Some stories—like James Baldwin's "Sonny's Blues," Guy de Maupassant's "The Diamond Necklace," F. Scott Fitzgerald's "The Freshest Boy"—consist of several scenes, scattered over time and linked by transitional summaries, all rising to a climactic situation and its resolution. Others—like Joseph Conrad's "The Lagoon," Ambrose Bierce's "An Occurrence at Owl Creek Bridge," James Stephens' "Desire"—begin *in medias res* (in the middle of things), actually very close to the climax, and are narrated in one continuous time period. The trick in this second type is that either the author or a character recalls relevant past action as flashbacks. Consider the advantages of each type of time pattern and, in each example you use, the probable reasons the author chose that type. (You might also check your conclusions against those reached by authors of books on the art and craft of fiction writing.) • ▲

Scene-Summary-Scene in F. Scott Fitzgerald

Fitzgerald is a master of the structural technique described earlier (see INDEX) as "scene-summary-scene." Demonstrate this by discussing his narration in at least "The Freshest Boy," and, better yet, in two or three of his short stories. What effects does he produce by the alternation of the two types of narrative? • ★

(**Wider scope:** How do the critics, literary historians, historians of fiction, authors of books on the craft of fiction, rate Fitzgerald's technique? • ▲)

Uses of Setting in Short Fiction

Working in a form that demands economy of language, short-story writers can afford to explore setting only as it contributes to their total effect. Show in three or more of the following cases how the author limits his/her use of setting to its function in the story:

- A black writer sees a city as a symbol of racial prejudice (Paule Marshall, "Brazil") and a house as symbolic of isolation (her "Barbados");
- A naturalistic writer wants to show the influence of environment on character (John Steinbeck, "Flight"; James Agee, "A Mother's Tale");
- A horror-story writer, a theorist of short fiction, needs a suitable place where his protagonist can subject his victim, a lover of fine wines, to a slow death (Edgar Allan Poe, "The Cask of Amontillado");
- A romantic realist, one of whose main themes is our need to come to terms with time and place, writes about an impressionistic high school student who is much aware of atmosphere (F. Scott Fitzgerald, "The Freshest Boy");
- A subjectivist writer creates a character who often reveals his changing state of mind by his reactions to things around him (James Joyce, "Araby" or another story from *Dubliners*);
- Another subjectivist contrasts the poverty of the real world with the richness of the dream land (James Stephens, "Desire");

• A third subjectivist wishes to contrast objective reality with the way it appears to a character under stress (Ambrose Bierce, "An Occurrence at Owl Creek Bridge"). • ▲

Point of View in the Short Story

The author can, as we have seen (see INDEX), tell his story from one of several different points of view ("camera angles"). Choose at least one story to represent each of the main points of view listed below. In your opinion, why has the author preferred that "line of sight" over the others? What advantages does he reap by using that viewpoint?

1. The Author-Omniscient (able to be anywhere, inside or outside all characters, speaking in the third person): e.g., Ernest Hemingway, "The Killers"; Rudyard Kipling, "Rikki-Tikki-Tavi"; D. H. Lawrence, "The Rocking Horse Winner."

2. The Author as Limited Narrator (limited to the point of view of one character expressed in the third person): e.g., Robert Louis Stevenson, "Markheim"; Joseph Conrad, "The Lagoon"; F. Scott Fitzgerald, "The Freshest Boy."

3. A Character as Narrator (limited to point of view of one character, him- or herself speaking in the first person): e.g., O. Henry, "The Ransom of Red Chief"; Ring Lardner, "Haircut"; James Joyce, "Araby"; Edgar Allan Poe, "The Imp of the Perverse," "The Telltale Heart"; Joseph Conrad, "The Secret Sharer." • ★

(**Wider scope:** If you become especially interested in the point-of-view problem in the writing and criticism of short fiction, you may want to consider a breakdown of the three main points of view into seven or more approaches. For a full discussion, consult Walter James Miller and Elizabeth Morse-Cluley, *How to Write Book Reports;* Cleanth Brooks and Robert Penn Warren, *Understanding Fiction*; and/or any of numerous handbooks on the writing of fiction.

The critical question in doing an analysis of the author's point of view is this: What advantages in storytelling does he gain by seeing the action from that angle? For example, how does the point of view influence the unfolding of the plot, the degree of suspense, irony, etc.? ○ ▲)

A. Conan Doyle's Models for Sherlock Holmes

Doyle once said, "If any man is Holmes, I confess it is myself." How literally are we to take that remark? How much of the fictional detective resembles his creator, how much represents his creator's ideals, how much is modeled on Doyle's associates (like Dr. Joseph Bell)? Compare the detective in the short stories (at least five) with the Doyle portrayed in the biographical studies. • ▲

Sherlock Holmes and Poe's Dupin

Even as a boy, A. Conan Doyle admired Auguste Dupin, the master detective created by Edgar Allan Poe, "Father of the Detective Story." How was Doyle influenced by Poe and Dupin in his creation of Sherlock Holmes? Read at least two detective stories by each author; compare your own conclusions with those of the critics. • ▲

Doyle's Sherlock Holmes and Gaboriau's Lecoq

A. Conan Doyle also admired Lecoq, the detective created by Emile Gaboriau. Read three stories by each author. How much of Gaboriau's techniques and Lecoq's personality traits do you see in Sherlock Holmes? Compare your conclusions with those of the critics. • ▲

(**Wider scope:** Combine the last three topics: "The Ancestors of Sherlock Holmes." • ▲)

Mona Lisa's Smile: A Fictional Interpretation

H. W. Janson, in his *History of Art,* wonders why, of all the smiles ever painted, *Mona Lisa*'s should have been "singled out as mysterious." Anthony Valerio offers an original explanation in "Mona Lisa," one of his short fictions in his *Valentino and the Great Italians.* Compare Valerio's interpretation with: Janson's; that of other art historians; Jules Verne's (see INDEX). • ▲

Metaphor in the Short Story

Descriptions that explore similarities between dissimilar things help the reader to imagine the situation and to experience greater emotional resonance. This technique helps make it possible for James Thurber, for example, to cram a dog's life into four pages in his classic "Snapshot of a Dog." Rex's brindle eye "made him look like a clown." He could hold a baseball in one cheek "as if it were a chew of tobacco." And "the torrent buffeted him about like a log in a freshet." In this and/or other successful stories, show how the author uses unexpected comparisons, each one a shock or at least a surprise, to make the reader "look" more intently and to make the story more exciting. (See INDEX for *Metaphor*.) • ★

The Martian Metaphors

Show how Ray Bradbury, in his story "The Off Seasons," creates much of the atmosphere of a strange planet, with strange creatures moving in strange vehicles, through his adept use of metaphor and simile. ("The Off Season" is one of some twenty-odd stories that make up the book *The Martian Chronicles*.) • ★

Techniques of Characterization in the Short Story

Consider the various ways in which an author can "characterize" the people in his stories. He can (1) offer us his own descriptions and judgments (e.g., Guy de Maupassant, "The Diamond Necklace"; Bret Harte, "The Outcasts of Poker Flat"; O. Henry, "The Gift of the Magi"); or (2) let us know what the characters think of each other (e.g., James Stephens, "Desire"; John Steinbeck, "Flight"): or (3) let us know what the character thinks of himself (e.g., Conrad Aiken, "Impulse"; Robert Louis Stevenson, "Markheim"; F. Scott Fitzgerald, "The Freshest Boy"): or (4) *show* us, rather than *tell* us, how the character reacts to, and changes in the face of, circumstances (Harte, "The Outcasts"; Ernest Hemingway, "The Killers"; D. H. Lawrence, "The Rocking Horse Winner").

How does the author you are studying use each of these techniques? How does he combine them; for what effects? How much of your conception of each character is based on each type of information? Compare any two or three short story writers for the degree of their reliance on each of the techniques. What conclusions do you and/or the critics draw from these breakdowns? • ★

Minor Characters in the Short Story

Write or talk about how every character in a short story has his/her function in the overall effect, often as a reflector for the main character. For example, in Daphne du Maurier's "The Birds," consider how the attitudes of Mr. Trigg and the radio announcer serve to emphasize the resourcefulness of the central figure, Nat. In Bret Harte's "The Outcasts of Poker Flat," consider how the drunkard's taking a selfish way out enhances by contrast the gambler's generous and noble way. • ★

Motivation of Characters in the Short Story

One of the miracles the short story writer has to perform in the brief space allowed him is this: He must provide credible motivation for what his characters do. How does John Gartner, in "Peewee Half," convince us that a 125-pound, slight-of-build boy really *wants* to play college football? In his "The Diamond Necklace," how does Guy de Maupassant meet this obvious question that surely pops up in the reader's mind: Why doesn't Mme. Loisel tell Mme. Forestier about the loss of the necklace right after she discovered it? In "Flight," how does John Steinbeck convince us that ". . . the knife went almost by itself. It flew . . . before Pepe knew it"? Notice how an author tries to prepare you to accept the characters' behavior as *natural for them*. Show how this succeeds or fails. • ★

Dialogue as Characterization in the Short Story

Given only a few thousand words to work in, the short story writer must make every word count. Every speech by a character must help reveal his/her personality. In O. Henry's "The Ransom of Red Chief," the first-person narrator, Sam, speaks of "somnolent sleepiness" and "external outward surface." In addition to adding to the humor, these redundancies characterize Sam as feckless, a waster of energy, a man of pretentious activity instead of genuine action. In Ernest Hemingway's "The Killers," two strangers in a lunchroom quickly reveal themselves as cynical, sadistic, evil, simply through what they say. The character differences among the three lunchroom employees are later developed almost entirely in the different ways they speak about the gangsters and their prey. In D. H. Lawrence's "The Rocking Horse Winner," notice how a terse three-word answer the mother gives her son—"Quite moderately nice"—sums up her character and convinces us of what the boy and his father are up against. Using these or any other literary short story, show how the author defines his characters largely in terms of their vocabulary, the pace of their sentences, the figures of speech they use, their tone of voice, and other qualities of their dialogue. • ★

Your Identification with a Short-Story Character

Yes, even in the brief compass of the short story, the author strives to elicit your sympathy for—maybe even your identification with—the character(s). Good subject here for essays or oral reports! Which characters have you strongly identified with in your reading of short stories? The 125-pound college student in John Gartner's "Peewee Half"? His coach? The high school student in despair in F. Scott Fitzgerald's "The Freshest Boy"? Or the actress? The traveler listening to the priest in Graham Greene's "The Hint of an Explanation"? Perhaps the rabbi in Isaac Bashevis Singer's "The Gentleman from Cracow"?

Analyze the reasons for your identification. What did it teach you about yourself? about literature? about your literary preferences? • ★

The Short Story as a "Message Medium"

In "The Hint of an Explanation," Graham Greene clearly intends to leave us with some religious conclusions or at least with religious questions. He does it so artistically that we don't think of it as preaching, but of course it is. In a story like O. Henry's "The Gift of the Magi," the author hits us over the head with his message: to the real story he adds a preachy paragraph telling us what to think about his characters and *our* lives. Later writers, like Greene, are likely to be more subtle, to get their message across implicitly rather than so blatantly. From Daphne du Maurier's "The Birds" we can infer a message common to science fiction: Men and women are too smug; they take the survival of their species for granted. Reading Emilio Diaz Valcarel's "Damian Sanchez, G.I.," we become ashamed all over again of the way America has treated its minorities; and Shirley Jackson's "The Lottery" makes us ashamed of our perennial need for a scapegoat. What do we respond to as the theme of John Steinbeck's "Flight," Cynthia Ozick's "The Pagan Rabbi," Bret Harte's "The Outcasts of Poker Flat," Ernest Hemingway's "Soldier's Home," Theodore Dreiser's "The Old Neighborhood"? Using any three or more of these stories, write (or prepare an oral report) about "The Ideological Intention of the Short Story Writer." Does it affect her/his works as art? Does it dull or deepen *your* interest? • ★

Success of the "Idea" Story

We noted earlier that Ivan Turgenev's short stories in *A Sportsman's Sketchbook* are among the very few works to have had any influence at all on the actual course of history. Check the critical reviews at the time of publication of the stories listed above (publication in book form, that is, which may be much later than original publication in a periodical). Were the critics affected by the *ideas* of Valcarel, Jackson, Greene, *et al.*? Note that "The Lottery" reached a wide audience when it was adapted for TV. Check the critical reviews for that too.

Finally, consult critical studies and literary histories for the long-range effect of any of the stories listed above. How do today's short story writers compare in ideological impact with Turgenev? How do you explain the comparison? ○ ▲

"How Long Does It Last . . ."

After considering the above remarks about "Message" and "Idea" in the short story, and reviewing our earlier entries on "Themes" (see INDEX), write, or outline for oral delivery, a report on "How Long Does It Last—The Impact of the Short Story on Me." *Don't look up any stories you've read or even your notes on them.* Play it strictly from your unaided memory, your lasting impressions. List at least three stories you remember well—for what reasons? Their atmosphere? their emphasis on the reality of states of mind? their ideas on God, love, hate, feminism, future scientific developments? their hero(in)es? How do you explain the lasting impression these stories have made on you, of all the short stories you've ever read? ●

● average difficulty	○ previous knowledge	★ most libraries
▲ larger library	☐ visual component	♫ audio component

4

Ideas about Drama

GENERAL IDEAS APPLICABLE TO ANY DRAMA

You will find that our survey of major themes in literature (pp. 9–15) will help you discover an "angle" for reporting on drama just as it does for fiction. But our checklist of the technical concerns of the fiction writer—characterization; plot; setting; point of view; style and tone, including metaphor, symbolism, irony; and formulation of theme (pp. 17–22)—must in some respects be changed radically when we think of them as the concerns of the dramatist. Let's begin with those elements that especially distinguish drama from fiction.

Spectacle in the Drama of_____

In fiction, language does it all, providing not only dialogue but descriptions of place (setting), things (properties), what the characters wear (costumes), and how they move about (narration). But in *drama,* which is the Greek word for *action,* the story is not *narrated* but *acted out.* Thus setting, "props," and movement of people can all be presented *nonverbally, visually.* True, during some periods of dramatic history, *spectacle* is definitely *subordinate* to language. Shakespeare is famous for the way his characters can describe for us a setting that isn't "really" there. But in modern drama, spectacle becomes a *coordinate* factor.

Samuel Beckett is likely to communicate as much with the sight of a person stuck in a trash can, or of a tramp fussing with his boots, as he does with what those people say. In television or film drama, spectacle can be the main element for minutes at a time, often the only sounds being not words but noises.

You can profitably narrow down your paper/oral report on any play to WHAT THE PLAYWRIGHT COMMUNICATES THROUGH SPECTACLE. If you wish to compare different dramatists' use of spectacle (setting, props, costume), report on two or more of the following: Sophocles' *Oedipus Rex;* Shakespeare's *Hamlet,* or *The Tempest,* or *Henry V,* or *Othello;* William Congreve's *The Way of the World;* Oscar Wilde's *The Importance of Being Earnest;* John Millington Synge's *Riders to the Sea;* Samuel Beckett's *Waiting for Godot* or *Endgame.* To show the advantages in use of spectacle that TV and film writers enjoy—like "establishing shot," close-up, cross-cutting, POV and reverse POV—include Paddy Chayevsky's *The Mother* and Peter Shaffer's *Amadeus.* (POV, of course, means point of view.) • ▲ ☐

(**Wider scope:** Use enough of the examples cited here to illustrate "The Changing Role of Spectacle in the Drama of the Western World." • ▲ ☐)

(**Wider still:** Include histories of drama, critical studies, biographies to show critical reactions to use of spectacle: e.g., critics' response to Synge's use of a dripping wet canvas sail in *Riders to the Sea.* Criticize the critics. • ▲)

Pantomime in the Drama of _____

Pantomime, or "dumb show," dramatization without language, originated in Rome in the time of the Emperor Augustus. Shakespeare uses it in the dumb show or prologue that "imports the argument of the play" that Hamlet stages for the court (Act III, Scene II). Buster Keaton and Laurel and Hardy exploited mime on a large scale in their film classics; Samuel Beckett's *Film* (starring Keaton) and his *Acts without Words* are exclusively pantomimic. What are the functions of pantomime? its artistic advantages over dialogue? Why does it have an almost continual history in the last nineteen centuries? To what extent is pantomime *literary* (see Beckett's stage directions)? • ▲ ☐

Sound Effects in the Drama of _____

The fiction writer lavishes much talent on *description* of sound, descriptions to be *read silently.* The playwright of course presents the actual sound to be *heard* (as of an alarm clock going off) or some simulation called a "sound effect" (like, in radio drama, the crumpling of cellophane to sound like eggs frying in a pan). In a modern drama nonverbal sounds signify so much that the playwright chooses them with deliberate care. In Synge's *Riders to the Sea,* the water splashing from the canvas shroud brings the Sea as Killer right into the house. In Beckett's *Waiting for Godot,* the cracking of Pozzo's whip to drive Lucky forward dramatizes their relationship as much as any speech they deliver. In Anton Chekhov's *The Cherry Orchard,* the tragic ending is enhanced as we hear "the muffled sound of an axe hitting a tree."

Dripping water, the cracking of a whip, the blow of an axe are all realistic sounds that can add symbolism to verisimilitude. But in drama a sound can be purely abstract, or subjective, or *purely* symbolic. Twice in *The Cherry Orchard* we hear a sound "apparently coming from the sky, like the sound of a string snapping." The characters speculate: Was that the sound of a heron? an owl? a bucket dropped into a well? The first time the celestial string sounds it helps create an ominous *mood;* the second time, it helps indicate that a way of life has been ruptured.

If you are especially interested in the artistic engineering of sound effects, do a report on "How and What the Dramatist Communicates through Sound Effects." If you wish to compare different dramatists' use of these nonverbal effects, report on two or more of these: Christopher Marlowe, *Doctor Faustus;* the Chekhov, Synge, or Beckett plays cited above; Norman Corwin's radio drama, *On a Note of Triumph* (available on LP and in book format); Chayevsky's TV play, *The Mother.* • ▲ ☐

(**Narrower scope:** Radio drama of course depends largely on sound effects to indicate *action,* e.g., footsteps, and *place,* e.g., fog-horns. Write about several radio classics to show "How the Radio Dramatist Stages His Play in the Ear and the 'Mind's Eye'." Include Archibald MacLeish's *Panic* or *The Fall of the City,* Alfred Kreymborg's *The Planets,* Corwin's *Triumph.* • ▲)

Point of View in Drama by _____

In fiction, the author may talk to us directly, as a voice separate from his characters, very much *present* as the author, omniscient (see INDEX). Thus O. Henry offers his own comments on the action in his story "The Gift of the Magi." But in drama, the author seems to be *absent* (off somewhere paring his nails, as James Joyce put it). He speaks only through his characters, and presumably they express a contrariety of impressions, notions, ideas. As a result, the audience feels closer to the action, unaware of the author as intermediary.

The illusion of authorial objectivity is further enhanced by the fact that we may hear many different, live voices. Of course, like fiction, drama tends to feature a hero(ine) or a few "major" characters, and in that sense the point of view is usually, implicitly, theirs, and we tend to identify, or at least sympathize, mainly with them. So, in discussing drama, you'll find it profitable to *stress point of view only if the playwright has done something out of the ordinary.* Four Ideas about extraordinary point of view in drama:

1. If the dramatist uses a narrator on stage (e.g., Thornton Wilder, *Our Town;* Tennessee Williams, *The Glass Menagerie*) or on screen (e.g., Francis Ford Coppola, *Apocalypse Now*), take up the question of why he chose to represent the action so explicitly from that person's point of view. • ★ ☐

2. Report on Akira Kurosawa's film play, *Rashomon,* in which he screens four different versions of the same event (robbery and rape), each from the point of view of one of the people present. Was this the best way of making his point? Which is—? • ▲ ☐

3. Consider Tom Stoppard's modern classic, *Rosenkrantz and Guildenstern Are Dead,* in which he restages the action of Shakespeare's *Hamlet* not from Hamlet's point of view but from that of the two courtiers he offhandedly consigned to death. What has Stoppard taught us about point of view, about "the other side of the story," and about the consequences of different treatment of "major" and "minor" characters? • ▲

4. Consider Gerhardt Hauptmann's *The Weavers,* which has a cast of more than 40 characters. The whole group, rather than any "major" character, is the real hero—the "mass hero." What happens to the audience's involvement, our usual dramatic experience? Whose point of view do we tend to adopt? With whom do we identify? What are the psychological and social effects? • ▲

Traditional Plot in Drama by _____

When we discuss the *structure* of fiction or drama, we make a technical distinction between *original story* and *artistic plot.* In this sense, *story* is chronological account: it moves in only one direction, forward. Authors find it better to change story into *plot,* or an arrangement of events that moves in two directions: backward to uncover past causes and situations, forward to discover future outcome and effects. *Plot* will usually start *in medias res,* in the middle of the *story,* with a situation that provokes *flashbacks, exposition, suspense.*

The playwright chooses from the story a series of incidents that put his characters into *conflict,* force them to change either their own character or their life circumstances or both, and reward them and the audience with greater *insight* into matters human and social.

Conflict may be three-fold: person against person, one person's group and ideals against another's, and person against her/himself. No profound change in character is possible unless the person engaged in conflict with outer forces is also caught in a conflict with his/her inner forces.

If the dramatist intends to produce a comedy, he designs a plot in which the characters change from bad to good; to produce a tragedy, a plot in which fortunes change from good to bad. Most modern plays, however, blend both comic and tragic elements and so are called either *tragicomedy* or simply *drama*.

If you have enjoyed the plot of a play, that is, its structure, and you would like to report on that aspect of the work, you should first subject it to an analysis of its components, locating them as follows:

- *Exposition.* Section(s) in which the playwright provides background information about his characters and their situations.
- *Initial moment.* That point at which the main character has become engaged in a major conflict.
- *Rising action.* Scenes in which the conflict is further complicated, leading to the main:
- *Crisis.* Beginning of the irreversible climactic action, culminating in:
- *Climax.* The final turning point in the hero(ine)'s fortunes, in which he or she has lost (tragedy) or won (comedy). The climax triggers the:
- *Falling action.* Scenes devoted to showing what the characters' lives are like after this major change in their situation; also called *denouement* (untying) or *resolution;* sometimes the falling action includes a:
- *Final reaction.* The outcome is put once more into doubt; with or without this reaction, the resolution moves to the end, known in tragedy as the:
- *Catastrophe.*

If you can establish these elements in roughly this order, you have both (1) explained how the playwright created a suspenseful, moving drama and (2) identified the plot structure as a *traditional plot:* You can be sure that if you analyze the structure of Sophocles' *Oedipus the King* or Shakespeare's *Hamlet* or *Othello,* or Noel Coward's *Blithe Spirit,* you will be able to report how they conform to the traditional structure. • ★

Like a diagram to illustrate the rising and falling action? You could put on the board, or on the screen via an opaque projector, this adaptation of Gustav Freytag's "Pyramid," derived from his book *The Technique of the Drama:*

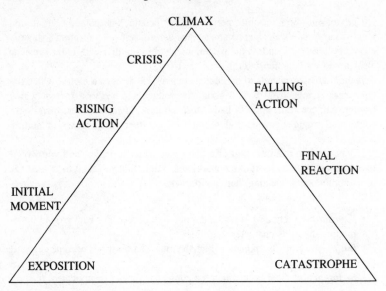

Nontraditional Plot in the Drama of _____

Even in the heyday of Greek drama—and that of Elizabethan drama—some playwrights did not produce plays tightly structured according to the scheme just described. In his *Poetics,* based on his analysis of classical Greek plays, Aristotle called dramas that consist of a series of disconnected incidents "episodic," and he rated them inferior. But dramatists have continued to enjoy the greater openness and freedom afforded them by the "episodic" plot. If you analyze a play by Chekhov, Beckett, Israel Horovitz, or some other "experimental" dramatist, you will find that in place of the traditional plot, the play uses a special structure designed to unfold its special message. For example, in Chekhov's *The Cherry Orchard,* no one really struggles against the tragic outcome, there is no major confrontation, no mounting tension. In Beckett's *Waiting for Godot* there seems to be no resolution at all. In neither play is there a major change of character. In reporting on each such play, it is your job to describe its unique structure and explain how the playwright has made it (or *not* made it) work toward his ends. • ★ ☐

   (**Wider scope:** Report on the critical reaction to the appearance of a play with an unorthodox structure. • ★ ☐)

Characterization in Drama by _____

In reporting on a playwright's success in characterization you should consider five questions:

1. Has the playwright created any personalities that I can identify—or at least sympathize—with? At first you may have only "gut" feelings to explain this sympathy, but as you consider our other questions you will discover a rational basis too.

2. Has the playwright made each such major character distinctly different, that is, human? Different in mannerisms, aspirations, philosophy, effect on others, speech rhythms, diction? How?

3. Has the playwright created problems that really test the characters, challenge them not only to change their life (outer) circumstances but also to cope with their own (inner) weaknesses?

4. Has the playwright provided credible *motivation* for each major step a major character takes?

5. Does the playwright assign each character a role in the development of other characters, of the action, of the theme? These are, after all, the ways in which a character impresses him/herself on the world!

By now you probably understand why you find, or cannot find, certain characters "sympathetic." And you are better prepared to evaluate the playwright's ability to create and develop characters. You can now even rate plays on the basis of their characterizations. Compare, e.g., Edmond Rostand's *The Romancers,* or Noel Coward's *Blithe Spirit,* with Paddy Chayevsky's *Marty* or *The Mother.*

In which do the characters change *only* their outer circumstances; in which do the characters *also* develop as people? Which, in other words, is a *situation drama,* with emphasis on plot, and which is a *character drama,* with emphasis on personality development? • ▲ ☐

The Famous "Three Unities" in the Drama of _____

In his *Poetics,* Aristotle said a drama should be an imitation of a single action, the scenes so integrated that if any of them were removed, the whole plot would collapse. He also reported that in the classic drama, the action had usually been limited to about one day. But Renaissance critics in Italy and France went much further. By 1570, they had adopted Aristotle's *unity of action,* made his *unity*

• average difficulty	○ previous knowledge	★ most libraries
▲ larger library	☐ visual component	♫ audio component

of time a strict requirement, and then added, on their own, *unity of place*—perhaps because action confined to one day could then not very well include extended travel.

On the English stage of the Elizabethan-Jacobean era, Christopher Marlowe and William Shakespeare (romanticists) ignored the "three unities" but Ben Jonson (a classicist) used them successfully in *The Alchemist*. After neoclassicist critics of the official French Academy rebuked Pierre Corneille for violating the unities in *Le Cid*, French playwrights observed them for nearly two centuries. Then Victor Hugo (romanticist) flouted them in *Hernani*. Since Hugo, dramatists feel free to use or to ignore the unities, depending on the effects they intend. Observing them makes credible character development—a gradual process—almost impossible, but it does help a playwright achieve fast action and dramatic intensity, as does Carl Foreman in his film *High Noon* and Tennessee Williams in *Cat on a Hot Tin Roof*.

To illustrate obedience to the three unities, you could analyze and report on Jean Racine's *Phèdre* (1677), and any or all of the Jonson, Williams, and Foreman works cited above; to exemplify violation of the unities, discuss any or all of these works: Christopher Marlowe's *Doctor Faustus*, Shakespeare's *Othello*, Corneille's *Le Cid*, Hugo's *Hernani*, Arthur Miller's *Death of a Salesman*, Peter Shaffer's *Amadeus*. In each case show how action, time, and place are treated in respect to the doctrine of the three unities, and how the playwright benefits from his observance or violation of the doctrine. Of course, you can take this topic in your study of *any* play: "Why＿＿＿＿Does (Not) Observe the Three Unities." • ▲ ☐

(**Wider scope:** Discuss the critical literature on the Unities, starting with Aristotle and the Renaissance critics and coming as far down to modern times as the scope of your assignment can include. • ▲ ☐)

Role of Language in Drama by ＿＿＿＿

True, for long sequences spectacle can dominate in drama (e.g., in the Buster Keaton film, *The General*). But with the exception of the pantomime, in which speech is ruled out by definition, drama usually relies on language for its clarifying, cumulative, and unifying effects. Even in silent films, dialogue as well as some narration were flashed on the screen as "subtitles." At the other extreme, when language predominated, as in Shakespearean drama, very often words would even set the scene. In general we can say that when language is one of the components of drama, it performs three functions:

1. It helps the actors establish the *pace* of the action. The dramatist can vary the length of their speeches. In *Antigone,* as tension mounts, Sophocles uses shorter and shorter speeches until the characters are engaged in swift give-and-take, rapid-fire, one-line speeches (*stichomythy*). As the immediate conflict subsides, or moves toward resolution, he gives the characters longer speeches again. In *Waiting for Godot,* Beckett uses stichomythic parallelism, sometimes to speed up the conflict, sometimes to orchestrate a harmonious feeling between Didi and Gogo. When Didi reflects or speculates, his speeches become longer, they slow down the action, force us all to wonder or even to think.

2. Language helps characterize each speaking person. There are four speaking characters in *The Triumph of the Egg,* a major short play by Sherwood Anderson and Raymond O'Neill. The language the playwrights assign them makes them distinctly different: Joe's speech is polite, fact-bound, critical, lacking in enthusiasm and color; Father may sound uneducated but his language is enthusiastic, rhythmical, figurative; Mother is more educated but dogged, lackluster in her speech; that Freddie is a mere child would be obvious to the audience if they had their eyes closed.

3. Language adds a verbal way—often the main way—for expressing the playwright's theme. Near the end of Michelle Cousin's *The French Way,* the main character sums up her relationship with her ex-lover: "He gave me myself." In Shakespeare's *Macbeth,* the main character sums up the way he feels about Life: "Life's but a walking shadow . . . a tale told by an idiot, full of sound and fury, signifying nothing."

Seeking ways of evaluating any drama you may be reporting on, you can always do a very revealing study by showing how the playwright's language performs (or fails to perform) one or more of these three functions. And you can always compare your own conclusions with those of the critics. ● ▲ ☐

Figures of Speech in the Drama of _____

Three types of figures of speech are especially important in drama.

1. *Verbal irony* excites dramatic interest in all its forms, as when: a character is saying one thing but meaning another; or revealing to us that he speaks out of ignorance; or asserting a belief that soon proves to be false. In Tad Mosel's TV play *My Lost Saints,* Mr. Hallet says at the end: "We all have to grow up some time." Irony: in the course of the action, all of the characters *have* grown *except* Mr. Hallet.

2. A *metaphor* is a verbal comparison between unlike things. Characters are

most apt to speak metaphorically when they express great emotion. In Anton Chekhov's *The Bear,* Popova says to Smirnov: "You're a muzhik! You're a crude bear!" But he's not literally a peasant but a gentleman farmer; not a bear but a man. She is speaking metaphorically to communicate her feelings about the way he *seems* to her.

3. A *symbol* is a thing, place, person, or situation that stands for something else, something larger than itself, often something material that represents something immaterial. In Reginald Rose's TV play *Thunder on Sycamore Street,* the slowness of Arthur's watch (which is mentioned five times) becomes symbolic of Arthur's reluctance to violate his neighbor's civil rights; Charlie's correcting Arthur's watch symbolizes Charlie's eagerness to involve Arthur in a lynching. In *The Bear,* Popova's repeated references to a bag of oats symbolize her changing attitudes toward her late husband (and toward Smirnov).

Your hook for a paper or an oral report: How successfully does the dramatist under discussion use figures of speech to increase dramatic tension? to reveal the emotional states of the characters? How sensitve to these questions have the critics been in reviewing this dramatist? (Are you the first one to study his figures?) • ▲ □

Themes in the Drama of _____

The theme(s) or message of a play are the sum total effect of its spectacle, characterization, and language. Thus a theme may be acted out, as when Didi and Gogo do the same irresolute, habitual things again and again, and/or it may be stated in dialogue:

DIDI: Habit is the great deadener.

A contrast between action and passivity may be made explicit in the behavior of Laertes and Hamlet and/or it may be summed up explicitly in a speech:

HAMLET: To be or not to be, that is the question . . .

In other words, when you report on the themes of a drama, do not content yourself with finding them only in the words. They may inhere in the *setting* (is it possible that Godot is there all the time, maybe as represented by the tree?) or even in the *properties* (notice that in Paddy Chayevsky's *The Mother,* two different styles of alarm clock announce the theme of conflict between older and younger people), or in the *sound effects* (as we saw in talking of *The Cherry*

Orchard), or in *nonverbal action* (as when Nora slams the door at the end of Henrik Ibsen's *A Doll's House*). Consider consulting the critics to spur yourself on to formulating your own conclusions. • ▲ ☐

SPECIFIC IDEAS ABOUT THE FULL-LENGTH PLAY

Religious Origin of Drama

What is it about theater that explains why—twice in the history of western civilization—drama grew out of religious ritual? Establish (1) the religious background of ancient Greek drama up to its life in the Athenian Theater of Dionysus, and (2) the religious origins of medieval European drama. Why did medieval drama move out of the church, away from direct church control, although ancient drama had been performed as a religious function throughout its history? What vestiges of the medieval religious stage remain in western theater today? • ▲

Theater of Dionysus Compared with Medieval Pageant Wagon

An excellent topic for an oral report because you'd want to put drawings on the board, and/or use slides or dioramas. Compare and contrast the two types of theater from the point of view of (a) *the actor:* what did he have to work with? (b) *the playwright:* what kinds of spectacle and sound effects were available to him? how were his performers trained? within what traditions was he expected to work? (c) *the producer:* who financed and managed the production? (d) *the playgoer:* what did he see? what conventions of place, direction, etc., were understood by the audience? who were allowed to attend? how were the playgoers accommodated? • ▲

(**Narrower scope:** Take just one or two of the four subtopics listed.)

• average difficulty	○ previous knowledge	★ most libraries
▲ larger library	☐ visual component	♫ audio component

Playgoer's Psychology Compared: Ancient and Medieval Theater

This requires either a good theatrical imagination or intensive research or a blend of both. What were the playgoer's expectations in each case? What was the ultimate religious meaning of the plays for the spectator in each time period?

Compare the Greek audience's *daylong* experience of, say, Aeschylus' *Oresteia* trilogy, and its concluding satyr play, with the medieval audience's *daylong* experience of a cycle of Biblical plays (Creation to Ascension!). Consider the religious context in both cases, e.g., the priest's part in the Greek performance, the religious conclusions in the Greek drama; the psychological significance of the Bible come to life, the mental tie-in with sermons and sacraments, the awe with which the audience must have gaped at who/what *went down* and *came up out of* that symbolic trap-door between earth and hell! Consider the probable state of mind in which the playgoer, in each culture, left the theater. • ▲

From Medieval Pageant Wagon to Elizabethan "Round O"

Compare the movable outdoor pageant wagon of the Middle Ages with the stationary indoor theater of Shakespeare's day. Contrast the two types of theater from the four points of view outlined above (a, b, c, d). Visual aids? • ▲ □

Playgoer's Psychology Compared: Medieval and Elizabethan

Compare the religious expectation and experience of the medieval audience with the secular expectation and experience of the Elizabethan audience. In what state of mind does the playgoer probably leave the theater, in each case? • ▲

Shakespeare's Stage and Arthur Miller's

From the four points of view detailed above (a, b, c, d), compare the "round O" with a typical (New York, Toronto, London) live-drama theater of today. Where is the poor person in each audience? the rich man? the woman? • ▲

Piñero's *Short Eyes:* **Stage Play and Movie**

From the four points of view detailed above (a, b, c, d), compare and contrast a production that appears on the stage with its film version. E.g., consider Miguel Piñero's classic of stage and screen: *Short Eyes*. What changes did Piñero make in the stage script to adapt it for the screen? • ▲ ☐

Piñero's *Short Eyes:* **Stage Critics, Film Critics**

Sum up three reviews of each version. Compare the critical reception that each version got. Did any critics compare or contrast the two versions? With what conclusions? • ▲

Joseph Heller's *Catch-22:* **Novel, Play, Movie**

Joseph Heller's *Catch-22* was published as a novel in 1961, Mike Nichols' production of the movie version (written by Buck Henry) was released in 1970, and Heller's own stage version premiered in 1971. Compare the three versions (the film is rerun on TV and in "art" theaters; the novel and Heller play are in paperback). Nichols tried to approximate the "spiral" structure of the novel's plot, circling back several times to Snowden's death. Why did critic Richard Schickel find that this approach betrayed Yossarian as a human being? What did Heller himself lose in reducing his encyclopedic novel to an evening's drama? • ▲ ☐

A Comparison: Film Play and Television Play

Compare these two types of theater from the four points of view detailed above (a, b, c, d). Stress advantages and disadvantages each has that the other lacks. • ▲ ☐

Paddy Chayevsky on Film and on TV

Paddy Chayevsky wrote a low-budget TV play called *Marty*. It was the first TV production to be rerun by popular demand. Then *Marty* was made into a low-budget movie. If you're lucky enough to be able to see both, make your own first-hand comparisons. How much expansion was Chayevsky allowed on film? How did he sustain the tension when he expanded the script (and the locations)?

If you have not been able to see both productions, read at least the TV script (available in Chayevsky collections and in anthologies of great TV plays); the movie producer might sell you a photo-offset copy of the film script. In any event, read the critical reviews of both versions and report on what the critics saw as the differences. If it's an oral report, get stills from the producer and blow them up on the classroom screen or wall with an opaque projector. • ▲ □

Novelists as Playwrights

What happens when successful fiction writers try their hand at writing for the stage? Does their ear for good dialogue, their sense of internal conflict, their wisdom about the essence of tragedy and comedy work well for them in this second medium? Consider the dramatic work of one or more of the following famous novelists: Ernest Hemingway, Joseph Heller, Kurt Vonnegut, Rosalyn Drexler, and Ursule Molinaro. In what ways are their plays equal, superior, or inferior to their novels? Compare your conclusions with those of the critics. • ▲

The Verne-D'Ennery Stage Successes

For fifty years, theaters in Paris alternated between *Around the World in Eighty Days* and *Michael Strogoff*, plays by Jules Verne and M. D'Ennery based on novels by Verne. Two possible Ideas here for papers/oral reports: (1) How did D'Ennery adapt each of Verne's novels? change the plot? exploit (the possibilities of) the spectacle? Have the changes added to or subtracted from the artistic value of the novels? (2) Since these two plays became "hits" for two generations, you are justified in asking and answering this question: What does the success of these two plays indicate about popular taste in drama? • ▲

The Verne-Todd Film Success

In 1956 Mike Todd produced a film version of Jules Verne's *Around the World in Eighty Days* which was an immense success. How did Todd change the story to make it more suitable for the cinematic medium? (N. B.: The balloon-flight episode was lifted out of Verne's *Five Weeks in a Balloon*.) How much of the film's success was due to Verne's reputation? to his basic story? to the film adaptation? to the international cast of stars (headed by David Niven, including the Mexican star Cantinflas)? to the fact that Todd used the (then) new wide screen? • ★ □

Around the World in Eighty Days: **Novel, Play, and Film**

Compare and contrast Verne's novel *Around the World in Eighty Days* with the D'Ennery stage version and the Mike Todd film version. (Include some ideas from the two topics above.) Given the limits of the two dramatic media, who made more sensational use of spectacle, Todd or D'Ennery? See any evidence that Todd was indebted to the French playwright? How was Verne's story changed for each medium, and what was the justification? Compare your conclusions with the critics'. • ▲ ☐

Stage History of *Michael Strogoff* and *Around the World in Eighty Days*

After running alternately for fifty years, Verne's two plays were "killed . . . dead," according to his grandson, Jean Jules-Verne. The simple but deadly reason he offers is just one of many "dramatic" events in the stage history of the Verne-D'Ennery plays. Start with the grandson's biography of his grandfather, *Jules Verne,* focusing on his accounts of the writing, production, promotion, and demise of the dramas. • ▲

Critical Reputation of *Waiting for Godot*

When Samuel Beckett's play premiered (in its French version: *En Attendant Godot*) in Paris in 1953, it was hailed by critics as a major breakthrough in the search for new dramatic techniques, and it ran for a French record of more than 300 performances. Yet at the play's American premiere, in Miami in 1956, half the audience left in disgust before the curtain rose for Act II. Today *Godot* is a classic in twenty languages, and any high school dramatic society enjoys putting it on. Research and report on the reasons for the ups and downs of the play's reputation. • ▲

Zola's Influence on Drama

Emile Zola's *The Experimental Novel* (1880) inspired changes not only in fiction but also in drama. Review the Ideas on Zolaism and naturalism (see INDEX) and/or check the two words in a handbook of literary terms. Explore

Zola's influence on drama by reading (in addition to Zola's essay) any or all of these naturalistic plays: Henrik Ibsen, *Ghosts; A Doll's House;* August Strindberg, *The Fathers; Miss Julie;* Gerhardt Hauptmann, *Before Dawn; The Weavers;* Maxim Gorky, *The Lower Depths;* Eugene O'Neill, *Anna Christie; Beyond the Horizon.* • ★

(**Wider scope:** Research of the critics' reactions to the premier productions. • ▲)

Zolaist Influence on David Rabe

David Rabe has written a trilogy of plays about the Vietnam War. *Streamers* was also made into a film by Robert Altman. The other two plays are *Sticks and Stones* and *The Basic Training of Pavlo Hummel* (which starred Al Pacino). To what extent do you see the century-old influence of Zolaism on Rabe's dramas? (See above.) In his case, to what extent has the determinism of Zolaism actually become outright fatalism? How do your conclusions compare with those of the drama critics? • ▲

Dramatic Technique of Amlin Gray

Describe the original dramatic techniques that Amlin Gray uses in his play *How I Got That Story.* What unusual dramatic effects does he achieve through these techniques? • ▲

(**Wider scope:** What was the reaction of the critics? With whom did they compare Gray as an innovative dramatist? • ▲)

Characterization by Amlin Gray

In *How I Got That Story,* playwright Amlin Gray depicts the character development of an Iowa-born reporter assigned to the Vietnam War. How would you describe this characterization? What techniques does Gray use to make the reporter's character changes clear to his audience? In Aristotle's terms (*Poetics*), what part does a character flaw play in the reporter's development? In Zola's terms (see above), how do heredity, environment, and social pressures influence the characterization? • ▲

(**Wider scope:** Compare your conclusions with the reactions of the drama critics who attended the premiere performances. • ▲)

Dramatizing the Vietnam War: Rabe and Gray Compared

Read one of David Rabe's three plays about the Vietnam War (see above) and compare it with Amlin Gray's *How I Got That Story*. How similar/different are the playwrights in: the dramatic techniques they use to represent their views of the war? in the emotions they arouse in us? in their relative success in reaching us emotionally, intellectually, ideologically? Compare your own reactions to those of the drama critics who reviewed the original performances. ● ▲

Drama of Two Wars: Shakespeare and Anderson/Stallings

Compare Shakespeare's *Henry V* with Maxwell Anderson and Lawrence Stallings' *What Price Glory*? (Both are often rerun on TV, but you may have to settle for your own silent reading of the original play scripts.) In each case, why do men fight? How do they prepare for combat? How do the Elizabethan playwright and the two modern American dramatists differ in their treatment of the horror of war? ● ★ ☐

(**Wider scope:** The screen versions of both these theater classics have been reviewed by major critics. How have they touched on the questions posed? ● ▲ ☐)

Drama of Two Wars: Shaw, Rabe, Gray

Compare Irwin Shaw's play about World War I, *Bury the Dead*, with any one of the Rabe plays or with the Gray play cited above. Consider how the two authors use the dramatic medium to get their message across; in each case, how convincing is that message? how original is the method? ● ▲

Critical Reputation of *Bury the Dead*

Irwin Shaw's play has had an almost unique career. Study its critical reception at the time it premiered, how the play figured in the news, Shaw's own changing ideas about the work. Start with *The New York Times Index*. ● ★

Political History of *Bury the Dead*

Why did Irwin Shaw change his mind about his play? To what extent was he influenced by the political climate? Which Shaw do you prefer, the one who wrote the play or the one who changed his mind? After reading the play itself, check *The New York Times Index* for its author's attitudes and the "political climate" in which his play figured. • ★

Two-Character Plays about War

War would seem to require large casts: think of Shakespeare's *Henry V* or of Maxwell Anderson and Lawrence Stallings' *What Price Glory*? Yet two recent war plays call for only two characters. Consider William Packard's *War Play* and Amlin Gray's *How I Got That Story*. In each case, explain how the playwright has succeeded in *representing the vast scope of war with the minimum cast needed for dialogue!* • ▲

Dialogue—with Just One Character!

The minimum cast needed for dialogue, we just noted, is two. But in *Krapp's Last Tape*, Samuel Beckett needs only one: Krapp, on his 69th birthday, engages in dialogue with tapes he recorded on earlier birthdays. What, as you interpret the play, is Beckett's message? about a man's identity? about his relation to himself? about man as a prisoner of time? about his own worst enemy? • ★

(**Wider scope:** How did the critics react to this first drama to make use of a man's voice today and yesterday? • ▲)

Ethics and Esthetics in Theater of the Absurd

Drama that finds humanity's existence to be ironic and aimless activity is called "Theater of the Absurd." However, the playwrights who so represent humanity's condition vary vastly in their techniques and emphases. Compare Beckett's *Waiting for Godot* with Harold Pinter's *Homecoming* and/or Luigi Pirandello's *Six Characters in Search of an Author* and/or Jean-Paul Sartre's *No Exit*. What conclusions can you infer about the necessity of morality and of art as propounded by the Theater of the Absurd? • ▲

(**Wider scope:** Consult histories of the drama for the critics' view on these questions. • ▲)

Play-within-a-Play: Shaw and Shakespeare

Compare and contrast Shakespeare's play-within-a-play in *Hamlet* with George Bernard Shaw's use of this device in *Fanny's First Play*. In each case consider the purpose and the results, with emphasis on the play-within-a-play as a form of acute dramatic irony. • ★

(**Wider scope:** Include Luigi Pirandello's use of this device in *Six Characters in Search of an Author* and Samuel Beckett's new twist in *Krapp's Last Tape*. What do the historians of drama, and the dramatic critics, see as the central idea that links all plays with plays-within-plays? • ▲)

Drama Criticism on Modern Pantomime

Beckett's *Film* and *Acts without Words* provided occasions for the critics to review the value of pantomime, its demands on writer, actors, audience, its history. Report on their various reactions to Beckett's work and to the revival of this genre. • ▲ □

Pantomime: Laurel and Hardy

How do Stan Laurel (born Arthur Stanley Jefferson) and Oliver Hardy use pantomime (dumb show) in their films to depict the condition of humanity? For what they want to express, why is pantomime often better than dialogue? • ▲ □

Concomitants of Pantomime

The Romans used music as a kind of "background" for their dumb shows. Check the details in the histories of drama. What other dramatic elements have modern pantomimists like Beckett used besides the silent acting? • ▲

Oppression and Moral Choice in Hansberry's Drama

In her three plays (*A Raisin in the Sun*, *The Sign in Sidney Brustein's Window*, and *Les Blancs*), Lorraine Hansberry deals with the severe effects of racial prejudice upon Black persons. Her dramas also deal with the necessity of moral choice and of people's ability to control their own destiny. Explain how she reconciles (or, in your opinion, does not reconcile) these seemingly contradictory themes. • ★

(**Wider scope:** What did the drama critics have to say about this question when her plays first appeared? • ▲)

Two Levels of Life in Hansberry's Drama

Several of Lorraine Hansberry's characters (see above) speak on two levels. They use the ordinary, colloquial English appropriate to their social class, the language of normal, factual, realistic discussion. Then suddenly they will break into highly poetic, subjective speech expressive of their fantasies or even of their unconscious knowledge. Report on the techniques she employs to represent these two levels of experience and on the unique dramatic effects the changeovers have on the audience. Compare your impressions with those of the critics and drama historians. • ▲

O'Neill and Hansberry: The Jungian Unconscious

Carl Jung, depth psychologist, postulated the existence, below each person's personal unconscious, of a collective ("racial") unconscious, a primeval "memory" which may sometimes emerge into the conscious life. Compare the techniques used to represent this emergence in Eugene O'Neill's *The Emperor Jones* and in Lorraine Hansberry's *A Raisin in the Sun*. • ★

(**Wider scope:** In a history of psychoanalysis, a handbook on Jung, or in Jung's writings proper, study the passages dealing with this secondary unconscious, *or:* Read the dramatic criticism of the premiere performances of the two plays. How did the critics appreciate these new Jungian probings in dramatic form? What connection did the critics see between O'Neill's and Hansberry's versions? • ▲)

Symbolism in Hansberry

A symbol, as we have seen, is something that stands for something else, usually larger than itself, often a material thing that represents something immaterial (like a psychological quality, a human ideal, or a national experience). A playwright's talent in using symbolism can be measured by the way his or her symbols grow naturally out of the characters' world—and the way they take root in the emotions of the audience. Discuss the validity and dramatic value, as symbols, of Mama Younger's potted plant (*A Raisin in the Sun*) and of Sidney's sign (*The Sign in Sidney Brustein's Window*). • ★

(**Wider scope:** What mark have Hansberry's symbols made in the history of the drama? in dramatic criticism? • ▲)

Lorraine Hansberry and Freytag's Pyramid

In what ways has Lorraine Hansberry, in her play *A Raisin in the Sun*, adhered to—and/or departed from—the traditional dramatic structure? Using Gustav Freytag's terminology (see INDEX), where do you find the bulk of her *exposition?* the *initial moment?* What constitutes the *conflict?* the *complication* or *rising action?* early *crises* and *climaxes?* *final crisis and climax?* *falling action?* *final reaction?* establishment of a new order of life (*resolution*)? What advantages has Hansberry gained by her design of the structure for this play? • ★

(**Wider scope:** Read Freytag's *The Technique of Drama* first-hand and/or check the reviews of Hansberry's play to see what the critics noticed about her plot. • ▲)

(**Still wider:** In Hansberry's *The Sign in Sidney Brustein's Window*, where would you locate the *major climax?* Describe the difficulty in deciding. What do your conclusions tell us about Freytag's Pyramid? about how modern dramatists use it? • ★)

1960s Children: Weller and Wilson Compared

Dramatic critic Walter Kerr said that Michael Weller's play *Moonchildren* might become "the definitive play about the young people of the 60s." Michael Phillips, on the other hand, has said, "My vote goes to Lanford Wilson's *Fifth of July*." Compare the two plays for their subject matter and dramatic treatment thereof. With which critic do you tend to agree? Why? Track down Kerr's and Phillips' remarks and see what else they've said that you can use. • ▲

Foil Characters in *King Lear*

Lear and Gloucester typify Shakespeare's frequent use of foils, that is, characters who serve as contrasts for each other. Explore the similarities and differences in their situations as parents, their personalities, their typical reactions to events, their speech patterns. In what ways do we know Lear better because of Gloucester's presence? • ★

Foils in *Hamlet*

See above on *Lear*. Study Laertes and Fortinbras as foils for Hamlet. • ★

(**Wider scope:** Check the origin of the use in drama of the word *foil*, and/or study the critical literature on Shakespeare's use of this device for aspects of it you yourself have missed. • ▲)

Foils in *Antigone*

Consider Ismene as a foil for her sister Antigone. How does Sophocles' characterization of Ismene enhance his characterization of Antigone? Find another pair of foils in this play. Discuss all four foil characters as separate people and as reflectors. • ★

Foil Characters in Drama by _____

As a routine search for Ideas, always consider whether the playwright you're reading uses foils. If he does, what effects does he achieve? • ★

Sophocles' Antigone: A Woman for All Times

Each generation has found new meanings in *Antigone* and has seen new aspects of Antigone's character. After you read the play for your own inferences of its value to us today, read the introduction to the Washington Square Press edition and (for as much as you can get out of it: this is advanced stuff) George Steiner's definitive work, *Antigones*. Show how audiences in three different periods in history (including our own) have seen Antigone as one of their own ideals. • ▲

Shakespeare's Cordelia And Sophocles' Antigone

Cordelia, Shakespeare's tragic heroine in *King Lear*, and Antigone, Sophocles' tragic heroine in *Antigone,* both face an impossible choice. Both are in a double bind, for they would be hurt by either of the only two decisions open to them. Explore the similarities and differences in the two women. To what extent is their suffering intensified because they are independent women in a man's world? • ★

(**Wider scope:** Have the critics and historians of drama already made extended comparisons of these two heroines, or is your study the first? • ▲)

Conflict Between Generations: Sophocles and Shakespeare

Compare the ancient drama *Antigone* and the Renaissance play *King Lear* as studies in the conflict between generations. This time include sons as well as daughters. • ★)

(**Wider scope:** In social histories of the two periods, find out what Sophocles' and Shakespeare's respective societies would have expected relations between the generations to be like. In each case, how does this add to the dramatic tension? • ▲)

Conflict Between Generations: Sophocles, Shakespeare, Miller, Beckett

Using notions from the Ideas above, add one more ancient play, Sophocles' *Oedipus Rex,* and one modern play, Arthur Miller's *All My Sons* or *Death of a Salesman,* or Beckett's *All That Fall.* Compare and contrast the intergenerational problems. How do they change from epoch to epoch? What do they signify? • ★

Conflict Between Generations: Oedipus and Kent State Killings

Notice that in Sophocles' classic play it's the father, Laius, who wants to kill his son, Oedipus, years before the son, fleeing the prophecy that he'd do it, unwittingly kills Laius. Notice too that when the older generation (a governor is a father figure) sent high school grads in the Ohio National Guard out against college students at Kent State University, dramatist Arthur Miller pointed out (in a *New York Times* piece) that we always emphasize the Oedipus Complex (father-hatred) and overlook "the Laial Complex" (hatred of the son). Read *Oedipus Rex* and at least *The New York Times* account of the KSU killings, as well as Miller's piece. Why has Miller's "Laial Complex" not caught on? • ★

(**Wider scope:** Read at least one of the several books about the Kent State killings. How do dramatists Sophocles and Miller prefigure in the investigations? • ▲)

Oedipus and Hamlet

Was Hamlet's inability to act a symptom of an Oedipus Complex? Sigmund Freud, discoverer of the "family complex" as he later preferred to call it, said yes. And his biographer, psychoanalyst Ernest Jones, said yes too. In his classic essay *Oedipus and Hamlet*, Jones explains the connections between Sophocles' play *Oedipus Rex*, Shakespeare's play *Hamlet*, and Freud's theory. He also refutes earlier explanations. Read all three works, checking Jones' quotations from the dramatists to get the full benefit of context, and report on the Jones-Freud interpretation of Shakespeare's masterpiece. • ★

(**Wider scope:** Include in your research some or all of the following: the critics that Jones quotes and refutes; Harry Slochower's essay on *Hamlet* in *Mythopoesis,* in which he extends the Freudian analysis to Shakespeare's imagery; post-Freudian explanations of the "family complex," especially Erich Fromm's and Harry Stack Sullivan's. • ▲)

Nature of the Tragedy of Marlowe's *Faustus*

Discuss Christopher Marlowe's hero in *Doctor Faustus* as caught between medieval and modern values and destroyed as a consequence. • ★

Is Goethe's *Faust* Autobiographical?

Several critics have drawn parallels between the intellectual progress of the hero in Goethe's *Faust* and that of the author himself. Goethe worked on this material for sixty years, producing the *Urfaust* in 1771, *Faust* Part One in 1808, Part Two in 1831. To what extent are you justified in considering *Faust* autobiographical? If you cannot do this in German (surely required for a master's or doctor's dissertation), you will still find enough papers in English on this subject (some of them quoting and translating crucial German studies). Make no compromise on English versions of *Faust* itself: read a recent, not a pompous (like the nineteenth-century translations) version. Try to add some discoveries of parallels that you yourself make. Would that make your paper publishable? • ▲

(**Narrower scope:** Trace the autobiographical parallels only from 1771 to 1808. • ▲)

Drama in the Bible: *The Book of Job*

Some modern Biblical scholars see *The Book of Job* as a philosophical drama, and some editors even print it in dramatic format. Consider the work in terms of: *dramatic conflicts; dramatic irony* (What does the audience know that Job and his friends do not? He acts in total ignorance of the *real* cause of his

suffering.); *dramatic climax* and *resolution;* poetic language; characterization.
• ★

(**Wider scope:** Comment also on a selected few scholarly papers, all so recent that you can be sure they summarize previous scholarship sufficiently for your purposes. • ▲)

MacLeish's *J. B.*: A Modern *Job*

Poet Archibald MacLeish has written a modern version of the drama of Job. *J. B.* combines MacLeish's own poetic passages with portions of the ancient Semitic (not just Hebrew: broader than that) masterpiece. *J. B.* enjoyed a good run on Broadway. What does MacLeish add to the ancient work? How is Job's problem brought up to date? How does the modern poet's interpretation of Job's suffering differ from the ancient poet's conception? • ★

(**Wider scope:** Research either or both: reviews by critics who saw the Broadway play; critical studies in surveys of modern drama. Discuss the overall critical reaction to MacLeish's themes and techniques. If you wish to concentrate on the theological reactions, limit yourself to reviews and studies in theological journals and treatises. • ▲)

The Book of Job: Hebraic and Arabic

The Book of Job, modern research indicates, was written by someone whose language included both Hebrew and Arabic expressions. What are the implications? Start with Marvin H. Pope's edition of *Job,* including his own translation, introduction, and notes (The Anchor Bible series). What did the reviewers of Pope's edition have to say on the subject of the book's vocabulary and its implications? Check reviews in theological journals especially.○ ▲

Robert Frost's Sequel to *The Book of Job*

Poet Robert Frost has given his interpretation of the Job story in his verse drama, *A Masque of Reason.* Compare Frost's work with the original Semitic drama for: characterization; themes; style and tone. • ★

(**Wider scope:** Compare the Biblical, MacLeish [above], and Frost versions. *Or:* What did the theological journals have to say about Frost's sequel? *Or:* Exactly what does Frost's title mean? • ▲)

Berkeley's Philosophy and Beckett's Drama

Two possibilities: (1) George Berkeley's idealist and monist philosophy can be summed up in his motto: *Esse est percipi* (To be is to be perceived). In his notes to his script for *Film*, Samuel Beckett expands this to: *To be is to be perceived by oneself*. To what extent is Beckett's note the theme of, and/or the key to, *Film*? (2) If you know Berkeley well, you could interpret Lucky's monologue in *Waiting for Godot*.○ ▲ □

(**Wider scope:** What have scholars, theologians, philosophers, and critics to say about Beckett's note? They would be commenting on *Film* in its book form, of course. What were their reactions to Lucky's speech? ○ ▲ □)

Samuel Beckett's Human Being: Chess Player, Chess Piece

In his plays and novels, Beckett sometimes represents human beings as chess players or chess pieces. If you limit your study to his drama, start with *Endgame*. Then get your critical bearings with Hugh Kenner's *Samuel Beckett: A Critical Study* and follow through with the other plays.○ ▲

(**Wider scope:** Include Beckett's fiction. ○ ▲)

The Goat-Girl In *Waiting for Godot*

When James Flannery, author of *William Butler Yeats and the Idea of Theatre*, produced Beckett's *Waiting for Godot* at the Beckett festival at the University of Rhode Island, *he cast the goat-boy as a goat-girl!* What could he have intended that to mean? Does it deepen or change Beckett's meaning? After you think this through far enough to deserve an interview with Flannery, write him at Emory University and request a telephone interview. ● ★

Why an All-Male Cast in *Waiting for Godot?*

Consider the meaning of the absence of women in Beckett's classic. Consult (1) the introduction that playwright-novelist William Saroyan wrote for the sleeve of the Columbia Masterworks recording of *Godot;* (2) the Monarch Note on *Samuel Beckett's "Waiting for Godot" and Other Works,* and (3) other critiques listed in the Monarch bibliography. ● ★

Drama in the Bible: *The Song of Songs*

Some Biblical scholars see *The Song of Songs* as the surviving fragment of an ancient wedding drama, and some editors print it in dramatic format. In works on the Bible as literature, study the genre of the ancient Near East wedding idyll. How does the *Song* fit into this genre? How and why, in spite of its erotic imagery, was the book included in the Hebrew Scriptures? How do theologians interpret the erotic imagery? How does their interpretation square with the theory of the wedding idyll? • ▲

Freudian Forces in *Waiting for Godot*

It seems easy to recognize Pozzo and Lucky as a familiar pair in history and psychology: master and slave, exploiter and victim, sadist and masochist. The pairing of Didi and Gogo is subtler. Suppose they represent two parts of the same personality, or of all personality? Consider the evidence that they represent what Freud calls Ego and Id, Jung the Persona and Shadow. Do they interact like Id and Ego? What does it signify that they can separate only at night, and reunite by day? • ▲

Meaning of Spectacle in Beckett's *Endgame*

What does the stage setting suggest? A corner of the chessboard, as the title also hints? Then what are the characters? Or does it suggest the inside of the skull, with the high windows as eyes? Then what are the characters? (See Idea above.) Or a disaster shelter? Then who is the boy outside? Or a cabin inside Noah's Ark? Then where is Noah, Ham's father? Better check the Bible story of Noah and Ham! Or does Beckett intend the setting to represent now some of these possibilities, now others? Check your speculations and conclusions with the most recent Beckett scholarship (see above). • ▲

Aristotle's *Poetics*, Then and Now

For centuries the *Poetics*—Aristotle's theory of drama, his definition of tragedy, comedy, tragic hero, catharsis, etc.—was regarded as the very touchstone of dramatic criticism. How does modern drama manage to be dramatic while ignoring many of his precepts? First study his little treatise (the fragment that remains to us). Then consider: Sophocles' *Oedipus Rex* (Aristotle's ideal);

Shakespeare's *Julius Caesar* or *Othello;* Arthur Miller's *Death of a Salesman, All My Sons,* or *The Crucible;* Samuel Beckett's *Waiting for Godot;* John Osborne's *Look Back in Anger;* Miguel Gomez Piñero's *Short Eyes.* Which of Aristotle's precepts are still valid? Which may or may not apply today? Which have definitely been shelved? Superseded by what? • ★ ☐

(**Wider scope:** Check your conclusions against those in recent publications on the relevance of Aristotle's *Poetics* now. • ▲ ☐)

Ten Great Heroines: A Comparison

How have male dramatists portrayed women who refused to accept the limited role that patriarchy offers them? Compare, for their ideas, talents in leadership, and other qualities, three or more of these heroines: Clytemnestra (Aeschylus' *Agamemnon*); Antigone (Sophocles' *Antigone*); Medea (Euripides' *Medea*; Portia (Shakespeare's *The Merchant of Venice*) or Lady Macbeth (his *Macbeth*); The Duchess of Malfi (John Webster's play of that name); Mrs. Millamant (William Congreve's *The Way of the World*); Nora (Henrik Ibsen's *A Doll's House*) or Hedda (his *Hedda Gabler*); Candida (Bernard Shaw's *Candida*). • ★

(**Wider scope:** Consult scholarly studies of the three characters you choose and/or feminist works by Simone De Beauvoir, Germaine Greer, Kate Millett, *et al.* • ▲)

Women as Playwrights

How many plays mentioned so far have been written by women? Note what the chorus in Euripides' *Medea* say would be the result *if* women had been allowed to write and publish. Consider the plays of Lillian Hellman, Eve Merriam, Lorraine Hansberry, Rosalyn Drexler, Claire Booth Luce, Ursule Molinaro. What do women write about now that they *are* allowed to write for the theater? What innovations have they made in this medium? • ▲ ☐

Tragedy and Comedy: The Classical Distinctions

In his *Poetics,* study Aristotle's definitions of tragedy and comedy. Illustrate the difference in Greek drama by comparing two works on the same (antiwar) theme: Euripides' tragedy *The Trojan Women* and Aristophanes' comedy *Lysistrata.* • ★

Effect of Commercials on Television Drama

Compare the emotional buildup possible in uninterrupted drama (e.g., a stage play like Arthur Miller's *The Crucible* or a movie-house presentation of Paddy Chayevsky's *Hospital*) with the emotional buildup possible in TV drama in which scenes are alternated with (louder) commercials. Check United States network practice in teleplay broadcasting with that of Britain's Third Program, Swedish television, Canadian television, Cable TV, or Public Television. *Perform this experiment:* Compare your own experience of a major film as you saw it in a movie theater with the version you see on television. How did the two experiences differ in emotional intensity? emotional aftermath? ● ★ ☐

Catharsis—Then and Now

In his *Poetics*, Aristotle says that a tragedy arouses "pity and terror" in the spectator and then effects a "catharsis" or purgation of these emotions. Note right off that virtually every writer on the subject has a different explanation of what Aristotle meant: *A comparative study of their views alone constitutes a major subject for oral reports/papers.* Presumably Aristotle meant that, on an intellectual level, the play convinces the spectator that, given the circumstances and the character of the hero, the tragedy is inevitable and hence, of necessity, acceptable. On an emotional level, Aristotle might have meant simply that, having experienced "pity and terror" vicariously, the spectator has got these specific reactions out of his system. But *perhaps Aristotle also meant* that the arousal of emotions has drained off repressed feelings *not* related to the play, feelings the spectator brought to the performance but (purged) now leaves behind in the theater. In this case, Aristotle would be regarding tragedy as a social "safety valve" to release feelings of dissatisfaction and discontent. The classical idea then would be that the audience goes home (or switches off the TV) chastened, readjusted to the *status quo,* accepting Fate, *purged of social discontent* as well as of personal frustration.

A modern answer, then, would be: Why *should* social grievance be drained off in the theater? Why shouldn't social problems be treated in the theater in such a way that the audience will want to do something about them *after* the play?

For example, Henrik Ibsen, in *A Doll's House*, offers *no* purgation in the theater. Rather he triggers resentments and shocks that conscientious playgoers might resolve only in political action outside the theater.

Compare serious plays typical of different periods: e.g., Sophocles' *Antigone,* Euripides' *The Trojan Women,* Shakespeare's *Othello,* Ibsen's *A Doll's House,* Arthur Miller's *The Crucible,* Lorraine Hansberry's *A Raisin in the Sun,* Lillian Hellman's *Watch on the Rhine,* the film version of John Steinbeck's *The Grapes of Wrath,* Samuel Beckett's *Waiting for Godot,* Miguel Piñero's *Short Eyes,* Meyer Levin's dramatization of *The Diary of Anne Frank.*

In each case, what emotions has the playwright aroused? Which are "purged" in the theater? (In this connection, note especially the function and effect of the final choruses or other concluding minutes.) Which plays leave you with emotions to take away, unpurged? What do you see as a possible *political function and intention* of Aristotle's theory of catharsis (and accordingly, of Greek drama itself? ● ▲ ☐

(**Wider scope:** Read recent, presumably cumulative studies of Aristotle's *Poetics,* to supplement your own reactions to the above plays and to the questions posed here. ● ▲ ☐)

Poetry in the Theater (1)

Sophocles, Shakespeare, Racine, Goethe, and many of their contemporaries composed their plays in verse. *Why is poetic drama a rarity in our time?* Consider two or more of the following full-length *modern* verse dramas: T. S. Eliot, *Murder in the Cathedral;* Maxwell Anderson, *Winterset;* Robinson Jeffers, *Medea;* W. H. Auden, *The Ascent of F6* or *The Dog Beneath the Skin;* Archibald MacLeish, *J. B.;* William Butler Yeats, *The Countess Cathleen.*

How has the poet, in each case, faced the question of the best verse form for the time of the action? (You might want to check the sections on verse form in Chapter 5. Who—Eliot, Auden, MacLeish, or Anderson—has worked out the best verse patterns for twentieth-century English speech? Who has been most successful in creating a unique poetic speech for each character? Which plays have succeeded on the stage? or "on the air"? Why? (For these last questions, check the reviews of the premiere performances.)

For Poetry in the Theater (2) see p. 120. ● ▲

What Today's Textbooks Teach About the Art of Writing Drama

Report on how today's writers are advised to write drama for stage and screen. Read at least three treatises, including the classics by Lajos Egri (*The Art of*

Dramat!c Wr!t!ng) and Michelle Cousin (*Writing a Television Play*), and at least one more recent work. On what do the authors agree? How do they differ in their approach? How does each author define ''drama''/''dramatic''? To what extent do they distinguish between commercial drama and artistic drama/literary drama? What in these books excited/shocked/disappointed you and why? How do the principles of drama they advance compare with the Ideas about drama you have been studying here? To what extent do these authors help you understand the techniques you see used on stage and screen? In your opinion, would these books help a talented writer to adapt to the dramatic media? How? • ▲ ☐

(**Wider scope:** What did the reviewers think of these books when they first appeared? • ▲ ☐)

What Anne Frank's *Diary* Gains/Loses on the Stage

See *The Diary of Anne Frank* in ''Ideas about Literary Nonfiction.''

Comparison: Two TV Plays about Nuclear War

Compare *The Day After* (ABC, 1983) with *Threads* (BBC, 1984). If you cannot get to view reruns, try to get scripts from the networks, or simply work from the critical reactions of leading TV reviewers. Start with *The New York Times Index*. How do the two telemovies compare for the techniques they use to get their messages across? The action of *The Day After,* as its title suggests, is confined to one day; that of *Threads* to thirteen years. What dramatic advantage does each play achieve because of its duration? How do their messages differ? Which work has the greater emotional impact? • ▲ ☐

(**Wider scope:** Compare either or both these plays with one or more of the nuclear-war novels of the Eighties. See INDEX, Nuclear War. • ▲ ☐)

GENERAL IDEAS APPLICABLE TO ANY SHORT PLAY

Our list of master themes (pp. 9–15) and our survey of dramatic techniques (pp. 83–93) will hold true for the short play too, but with this crucial distinction: Writers of short plays cannot design a plot, or develop characters, on anything like the scale enjoyed by writers of full-length plays.

First, what do we mean by ''short'' and ''full-length'' plays? The distinction varies somewhat with the medium. But generally, a short play is one designed to take up only part of an evening (or afternoon), while a "full-length" play takes up an entire evening (or most of the afternoon).

Stage Drama. The short stage play, called a "one-act play," consists sometimes of two or more scenes, but often of just one scene (e.g., J. P. Sartre's *No Exit*), the entire work played in about half an hour. By contrast, the full-length stage play runs from two acts, like Samuel Beckett's *Waiting for Godot*, to five acts, like Shakespeare's plays, running anywhere from two to five hours.

A good measure of the difference: When the manager of a "live stage" theater does not present a full-length play, he usually offers instead three or four one-act plays, like Beckett's *Ohio Impromptu, Catastrophe, What Where*. And he sometimes presents a single short play as a "curtain-raiser" before the full-length drama is performed.

Cinematic Drama. Originally all "movies" were short. The theater manager would usually make up a program of several brief works, say Charlie Chaplin or Laurel and Hardy comedies. By the time full-length "feature" films became available, they would run for at least 90 minutes (e.g., *High Noon*).

But even today a movie producer will occasionally offer us a program of several short screenplays, e.g., *Quartet*, dramatizations of four short stories by W. Somerset Maugham.

Radio and TV Drama. Short plays tailored especially for the broadcast media usually run from 30 to 60 minutes, comprising three or more short acts separated by bursts of commercials, like Reginald Rose's *Twelve Angry Men* (in its original TV version). By contrast, a "long" television drama may play for 90 minutes, two hours, or longer, like *The Day After*.

Any Short Drama. So, then, with 30 to 60 minutes in which to explore his or her themes, the writer of the short play usually focuses on one simple plot (e.g., Anton Chekhov, *The Bear*), in contrast to the complicated multiple plots allowed to the writer of long plays (e.g., Shakespeare, *A Midsummer Night's Dream*). With no time to spin out a long rising action, the short-play writer very often opens his or her work close to the climax (e.g., Rose's *Twelve*); or, if he or she does indulge in a leisurely complication, it will be compensated for with a swift, brief falling action (Edmond Rostand, *The Romancers*). Of course, the author can't often use a large *dramatis personae,* having rather to concentrate on a few characters. And with no time for long-range character development, the only kind likely to convince, he or she focuses on one or two facets of a character's makeup (e.g., the basic human decency in Captain Cassell that overcomes his Nazi training in Maxwell Anderson's *Miracle on the Danube*).

SPECIFIC IDEAS ABOUT THE SHORT PLAY

The "Tease" In Radio/TV Drama

To catch and hold the listener/viewer (before she tries other channels!), the radio/TV writer often uses a "tease," a few seconds of drama that typifies and introduces the play to come. For example, in a script the present author wrote for WNBC Radio, he called for the sound of a woman's high heels crossing a hollow sidewalk, followed by the high-low whistle of the typical sidewalk judge of female beauty, followed by a male voice saying, "Not bad." He felt that these three sounds would create such interest in the program to follow that the audience would hang on while the announcer formally identified the show. Lonne Elder III also opted for a simple tease in one of his TV scripts for the *NYPD* series: He called for an "establishing shot" of high ground above a boat marina on a river, then a quick zoom into some high bushes as a rifle is thrust out and fired. Every episode of *Dynasty* opens with the stock device (a kind of logo) of a quick series of action shots from the last episode.

A great deal of art, of knowledge of the audience, goes into the script-writer's composition of the few seconds of the "tease." Report on the results of *your survey of some twenty or more "teases" viewed all in the same week*. Which ones were genuine promises that would be fulfilled in the program proper? Were any tawdry or misleading, used simply to lure you away from the competition? Describe in detail a few that were outstanding examples of the TV writer's art and craft. Figure out an artistic way of organizing *your* material. Should you, for example, use a tease of your own or one of your examples, to gain *your* audience's attention? • ☐

The Problem of Exposition in Selected Short Plays

In the short play especially the dramatist can devote little time to exposition (background information about the characters, their general situation). He must so contrive his plot that all information we need about the *past* is unfolded while the conflict develops in the *present* and suspense is created about the *future*.

For their skill in handling exposition in the short play, compare three or more of the following: August Strindberg, *The Stronger;* Clifford Odets, *Waiting for Lefty;* Edward Albee, *The Sandbox,* or *The Zoo Story;* Edmond Rostand, *The Romancers;* Eugene O'Neill, *Bound East for Cardiff,* or *In the Zone;* the present author, *Joseph in the Pit* (in his *Making an Angel*); Michelle Cousin, *A Door You Can Close* (in her *Writing a Television Play*); Mario Fratti, *Our Family;* Samuel Beckett, *Ohio Impromptu,* or *All That Fall.*

Explain in detail how one playwright manages to incorporate exposition into ongoing action while another actually risks losing our interest while he halts the action so his characters can "fill us in" on past happenings, and still another seems to need *no* overt exposition at all, allowing us to infer the characters' previous experience from their present concerns. • ▲ ☐

Crisis-to-Climax in Selected Short Plays

The section where writers of the *well-plotted* short play must prove themselves as dramatists begins at the *main crisis* (the point at which the hero[ine] must launch an all-out effort or suffer defeat) and ends at the *climax* (when the crisis reaches its peak intensity, the turning point in the main character's fortunes). Analyze the structure of three or more of the following plays: August Strindberg, *Pariah,* or *Simoon;* Clifford Odets, *Waiting for Lefty;* Reginald Rose, *Thunder on Sycamore Street* (the original TV short version); Anton Chekhov, *The Bear;* John Synge, *Riders to the Sea;* Eugene O'Neill, *The Long Voyage Home,* or *The Moon of the Caribbees;* Edward Albee, *The Zoo Story,* or *The Sandbox;* Samuel Beckett, *Catastrophe.*

In each case, locate the beginning of the crisis and its end in the climactic moment, and evaluate the intensity of the action between these two crucial points. Is it brief or sustained, drawn out? Would you describe it as sensational, powerful, painful, explosive, almost unbearable? Or low-key, subtle, quietly building to quiet insight? Does the climactic moment lead to a psychological breakthrough? *Would the characters have been capable of it without this excruciating experience?* Does the climax lead us to an important psychological, social, or political realization? *In which plays can it be said there is no climax,* no plot, *in the usual sense, but rather just a cumulative effect?* • ▲

Edmond Rostand's Use of Setting in *The Romancers*

Report on Edmond Rostand's *The Romancers* as an example of how the playwright can use setting as the ultimate—realistic, symbolic, expressionistic—representation of both the conflict and the resolution. • ▲

The Romancers And *The Fantasticks*

Compare and contrast Edmond Rostand's straight comedy, *The Romancers*, with the musical comedy version by Tom Jones and Harvey Schmidt. As you and/or the critics see it, does the extended action in the second play add to or subtract from the charm of Rostand's situation? Why? • ▲

Critical Reputation of a Long-Running Hit

At this writing, *The Fantasticks* (see above) has been running in Greenwich Village for more than a quarter of a century. What did the critics say about its probable future when it premiered? What did they think of it in relation to Rostand's original comedy? How have the critics explained the long run— when substitution of new actors, or a tenth or twenty-fifth anniversary, or the return of a member of the original cast, justified a new review? • ▲

Who Killed Radio Drama in the United States?

Until World War II, radio was a major medium for dramatists. In U.S. dramatic history, consider such classic short plays as Maxwell Anderson's *Miracle on the Danube*, Archibald MacLeish's *Panic* and *Fall of the City*, Alfred Kreymborg's *The Planets*, Norman Corwin's *On a Note of Triumph*, Edgar Marvin's mystery dramas (one every two weeks for a major network!), and the award-winning plays of Nelson Bond.

In what ways is radio a natural medium for drama? Why was radio drama precipitately abandoned after World War II? Did you know that radio drama still thrives in many other countries, including Canada and Great Britain? That Samuel Beckett and other major playwrights still write plays for British radio? How do you account for these differences between U.S. and foreign practice? Start with histories of radio, broadcasting, modern drama; for exact dates, check *The New York Times Index.* • ▲

A Perfect Radio Play: Thomas' *Under Milk Wood*

Explain how Dylan Thomas was making maximum use of the unique characteristics of radio when he composed his play *Under Milk Wood*. Check its broadcast history, too, and the reactions of the critics (radio and book reviewers). • ▲

An "Ethnic Problem" in a Transferable Play

In his one-act play *Our Family,* Mario Fratti, author of forty plays (including *Nine!*), treats of the "double nature" of the Italian-American. But in his Preface he points out that directors, educators, etc., can adapt *Our Family* to apply to the "double-nature" problems of Hispanic-Americans, Greek-Americans, etc. Discuss the dramatic techniques that Fratti uses to get at problems so basic to all Americans who arrived after the "Indians" settled here.

To what extent are the separate personalities of the older generation, and of the younger, determined by their place of birth? By their family interaction? By their role as parents or children *regardless* of nationality? What might this family be talking about if they weren't at this moment self-conscious about their hyphenated nationality? • ▲

Classroom Production of *Our Family*?

Do you think *Our Family* (see above) is suitable for classroom production? If so, ask the publishers (check *Paperback Books in Print*) for permission to perform it. Then consider: set, props, casting, rehearsals. Assignment for those not engaged in the production: Write the drama review for tomorrow's (or the school?) paper, evaluating the play itself, its themes, its characterization, its success in getting its point across, the acting, the pacing of the action, the direction and staging, the total effect. • ★

Humor in Religious Medieval Drama

The classical Greek dramatists made a strict distinction between tragedy and comedy. But English drama, from its very inception in the religious plays of the Middle Ages, has intensified tragedy and comedy by contrasting them in the same play. Report on humor, buffoonery, caricature in the miracle plays *The Murder of Abel, Noah,* and *The Second Shepherd's Play,* in *Doomsday,* and in the morality play *Everyman.* • ★

Anonymity in Art and Drama of the Medieval Period

The author of *Everyman,* like the author of any medieval English play, is unknown. Like the stonecutters who produced thousands of individual gargoyles, he worked anonymously: *he* was *not* an individual. Why? The reasons will open to you an entirely different conception of the individual and his relation to the community. Start with histories of medieval culture, then of drama. If this is to be an oral report, you could use slides of some gargoyles, maybe even of a scene or two from modern productions of *Everyman*. • ★ □

Characterization of Bible Figures in Medieval Religious Drama

Demonstrate in detail how the (anonymous) writers of medieval religious drama deeply humanized such Hebrew Scriptures characters as Cain (*The Murder of Abel*), Isaac (*The Sacrifice of Isaac*), Noah's wife (*Noah's Flood*), and such New Testament characters as the shepherds (*The Second Shepherd's Play*). Compare the play texts with the Biblical passages they are based on; show how much detail of their own invention the playwrights added. • ★

The Character of God: Medieval and Modern

Compare God as he is represented in the medieval morality play *Everyman* and in Marc Connelly's *Green Pastures*. How has each playwright humanized the deity? In what ways does each version show that each culture (here, medieval English and modern American) conceives of God in its own image? • ▲

Christopher Marlowe and the Morality Play

Show how vestiges of the medieval morality play found their way into Elizabethan drama, e.g., setting, Good vs. Evil Angel, and Seven Deadly Sins in Marlowe's *Doctor Faustus*. • ▲

A Modern Miracle Play

The 1977 drama *Joseph in the Pit* by Walter James Miller (in his *Making an Angel*) is largely modeled on the typical miracle play. Approximately half an hour long, it's based on a classic Bible story. Like medieval drama, it's composed in verse. It offers a new interpretation of the character of Joseph and, like medieval drama, invents enough details to humanize the Biblical characters and to dramatize their domestic as well as religious relationships. It adds colorful details about the Holy Land that medieval dramatists were unaware of.

How does Miller explore internal (as well as external) conflict in the ten brothers? What does he see as the relation between mediocrities, like the brothers, and geniuses, like Jacob and Joseph? How does Joseph manipulate Reuben to manipulate the others? How well does the verse function to create the pastoral and Biblical mood? • ▲

(**Wider scope:** Compare *Joseph in the Pit* with a medieval miracle play of your choice, maybe one of those cited in Ideas above. • ▲)

Writers of Short Stories as Writers of Short Plays

How do writers already successful with short stories fare when they turn their talents to the short play? Compare one or more short stories by Kurt Vonnegut or Rosalyn Drexler or Ursule Molinaro with one or more of his/her short stage or TV plays. Does the author sound like the same person in both media? Or does the author reveal different sides of her/himself in each medium? Consider tone, dialogue, theme, ease inside the tight constraints of the short story/play. Check your reactions with those of the critics. • ▲

Poetry in the Theater (2)

Euripides, Marlowe, Molière, Grillparzer and their contemporaries composed many of their plays in verse. Why is poetic drama a rarity in our time—in the short play as well as in the full-length play? (See Poetry in the Theater (1) in the preceding section.)

Consider one or more of the following contemporary short verse dramas: Archibald MacLeish, *Panic,* or *The Fall of the City;* Alfred Kreymborg, *Planets;* Norman Corwin, *On a Note of Triumph;* Walter James Miller, *Joseph in the Pit* (in his *Making an Angel*); William Butler Yeats, *On Baile's Strand.* Which of these poets have found appropriate verse forms for the speech of the time period (present or historical) in which their plays are set? How has the poetic line affected characterization of the persons speaking it? Which of these plays have (or have not: check the critics) succeeded on the stage or on the air? • ▲

Jules Verne's Short Plays

Before he found his proper medium in science fiction, Verne labored for years for success as a playwright. His *Broken Straws (Les Pailles rompues)* was produced in Alexandre Dumas' Théâtre Historique in 1850 and privately printed soon after; another of his short plays, *Castles in California* (*Les Chateaux en Californie*), was published for home performance in *Musée des Familles* in 1852; still another, *Monna Lisa,* was published posthumously in *L'Herne* in 1974.

If you read French, you can explore at least two of these works in the original. In English you will find summaries and commentaries in several biographies of Verne. The first and third are especially clever (cynical?) about love and marriage.

Possible topics for papers/reports:

- Alexandre Dumas as Mentor of Jules Verne;
- Verne's Disappointments in Love as Reflected in his Short Plays;
- The Functions of the Curtain-Raiser: Verne's *Broken Straws;*
- The Concept of Drama for Home Performance Exemplified by a Verne Play Published in a Family Magazine;
- Dialogue (and/or Situation) in Verne's Short Plays: Foreshadowing His Techniques in Science Fiction. • ▲

Literary Explanations of Mona Lisa's Smile

"Why, among all the smiling faces ever painted," asks H. W. Janson in his *History of Art,* "has this particular one [Leonardo's *Mona Lisa*] been singled out as mysterious?" Jules Verne's short play *Monna Lisa* offers an original explanation (read it in French in *L'Herne* 1972, or read the full English summary of the play offered in *Jules Verne* by J. Jules-Verne, translated by Roger Greaves). Possible topics:

Verne's *Monna Lisa:* A Disappointed Lover's Explanation of da Vinci's Portrait (J. Jules-Verne chronicles the disappointments too);

Two Explanations of Mona Lisa's Smile: Verne's Play *Monna Lisa* Compared with Anthony Valerio's "Mona Lisa" (one of his fictions in *Valentino and the Great Italians*);

Three (or more) Interpretations (Add Janson's and as many other art historians' views as you wish). • ▲

The Curtain Raiser: Its Function and History

Anton Chekhov's *The Bear* and Jules Verne's *Broken Straws* are among thousands of plays written originally as "curtain raisers" (or lifters), i.e., short works to be performed before the main attraction of the night. Read at least two such plays, and consult histories of the theater for discussion of the functions of this dramatic form: its role as an "appetizer" before the main course, as an offering for the early birds while the late-comers straggle in for the main event, as a suitable form for developing and trying out new playwrights. Consider also highlights in the history of the curtain-raiser: e.g., curtain-lifters that became famous while the full-length plays they preceded are forgotten. • ▲

Characterization in *Under Milk Wood*

Discuss Dylan Thomas' play as an argument for radio drama as a vehicle for characterization. The narrator is a blind man: what he knows he knows largely from what he can hear. And he hears not only the sounds of events but sounds people make that reveal their character. How easy for the audience to identify with him! For we too are *blind* to what's happening in a radio play! We too have to assemble all our cues about a personality from what we *hear* her say, what we hear others say about *how* she acts. We concentrate on the inflections, the nuances of her speech. Most important, *we have to visualize the action*, construct the appearances of the characters, *entirely on the stage of our own minds*. We have to imagine, ponder, contemplate even more than we do at a visual performance. In any case, it's a different way of contemplating reality, and therefore a fresh approach.

Report on the peculiar suspense, and the means of characterization, that prevail in radio drama. • ▲

(**Wider scope:** Compare and contrast Thomas' *Under Milk Wood* with Samuel Beckett's radio play *All That Fall*. How many distinctive characters can you report on now? • ▲)

Beckett's Radio Play: *All That Fall*

This short, intense radio classic should interest you as the subject of a paper/oral report along any, several, or all of these lines:

1. Beckett's achieving all his desired effects through sound alone, a perfect example of how radio can stage a play entirely in the listener's ear;
2. The way Beckett uses blindness, sterility, physical infirmity as symbols of the condition of modern humanity;

3. How *All That Fall* possibly explains the symbolism (and maybe the fate) of the boy in Beckett's *Endgame,* and maybe also why Gogo is furiously angry at the boy in *Godot:* He represents new life, which people in *The Waste Land* (Eliot's) dread more than their own death;

4. The way Beckett represents, again, as in *Godot,* activity and passivity as equally destructive;

5. How *All That Fall* exemplifies the traditional dramatic device of revelation: Beckett resolves the play by withholding a piece of vital information until the end;

6. The fact that, since a radio play is easy to produce (speech and sound effects are directed into a microphone not visible to the audience), you could include in an oral report on *All That Fall* actual classroom production of a short passage. (Check and obey the permissions information given on the copyright page of *Krapp's Last Tape,* the Grove Press volume that includes *All That Fall.*) • ▲ ♒

The Boy in Beckett's Plays

Is the boy in *All That Fall* the key to the meaning of the boy in *Waiting for Godot?* and in *Endgame?* Try it out. See what ideas it opens up for you. Have any scholars/critics already considered the question? Or are you the first to write about it? • ▲

Critics and *Krapp*

Beckett's *Krapp's Last Tape* became the main "hit" of the off-Broadway season when it opened in Greenwich Village in 1960. How prepared were the critics for such a revolution in the technics of drama? What future did they see for it? Compare the early reviewers' reactions with those of the drama historians expressed in later treatises. • ▲

Three Moods in the Short Play

In any work of short fiction or short drama, the author usually attempts to create two or three moods in succession: an initial mood, ambience, atmosphere, the quality of the characters' lives *before* a big change occurs; then a different mood, one of transition, of uncertainty, confusion, as the big change is under way; finally, a totally new mood in the characters (and audience) produced by the outcome of the change.

A big problem with the short play is that the author actually has to create and accustom us to such different moods in maybe half an hour, at most one hour.

Try out this "three mood" approach when analyzing the structure of several short plays, including some of these: *The Second Shepherd's Play; Everyman;* Jules Verne, *Monna Lisa* (see above); Anton Chekhov, *The Bear;* August Strindberg, *Pariah;* Eugene O'Neill, *The Moon of the Caribbees;* Clifford Odets, *Waiting for Lefty;* Norman Corwin, *On a Note of Triumph;* Michelle Cousin, *A Door You Can Close* (see above); the present author, *Joseph in the Pit* (see above); Samuel Beckett, *Krapp's Last Tape, All That Fall;* Edward Albee, *The Zoo Story;* Israel Horovitz, *Rats, Line.*

Can you discover what the playwright specifically *did* to create each of these successive moods? Or is there, perhaps, no change of moods but rather a single, sustained, cumulative buildup of one mood? Does the secret of the moods lie in the setting, sound effects, how the characters respond to each other, the profundity or banality of their concerns? Pay particular attention to the *closing mood. Is the audience reconciled* to the ending? Has it experienced catharsis? Is it *gladdened* by the reassertion of human values? *Saddened* by the inexorability of circumstance? Or are they, as they leave the theater or turn off the radio/TV, *determined, like the players and the playwright, hereafter to find love, justice, happiness, more meaning in life?* • ▲ ⧂

Characterization—Action—Action—Characterization

Henry James pointed out that action and characterization are virtually the same phenomenon. For characters take action and action affects character. A "dramatic" example in a short play: In Anton Chekhov's *The Bear*, Smirnov is so provoked that he challenges his hostess, Popova, to a duel! But when he has his gun in hand, he finds he can't shoot her. His character precipitated the action of the duel, but that action forces him to change his view of himself . . . and of her . . . and of womanhood! And notice, it was *internal* conflict in one character that affected the *external* conflict in two characters. And it causes big changes in both of their makeups: the macho misogynist Smirnov now proposes to the woman who a few minutes before had hated him, and she accepts.

Complete a similar analysis of the rest of *The Bear*. Then subject Edmond Rostand's *The Romancers* to the same kind of scrutiny: Check the relationship between action and character, the evidence of productive internal as well as external conflict. In your paper/oral report, set forth your reasoning for your answer to this question: Which comedy has the greater psychological complexity? So, you see, Henry James to the contrary, it is still possible for a play to have an *imbalance* between characterization and action. If you're learning more about people, would you prefer more comedies like *The Bear* or more like *The Romancers?* • ▲

The Theme of Themes in Serious Drama

A common theme in serious drama is this: It's difficult to live a lie, to live in a way that violates one's own nature, or one's relations with others. The action of such a play then moves toward a character's (re)discovering this truth. In Maxwell Anderson's *Miracle on the Danube,* a Nazi captain could probably win acquittal if he could suppress his conscience for just the half-hour of his court-martial. But he yields to his conscience even though that means the firing-squad in the morning. In Paddy Chayevsky's *The Mother,* an aged widow discovers that, despite the wishes of her daughter, she cannot compromise her independence: She must support herself in a house of her own.

The movement of all literature, as we noted earlier, is from appearance to reality. In whatever short play you're going to report on, isn't this one of the needs of at least one of the characters? • ▲

• average difficulty	○ previous knowledge	★ most libraries
▲ larger library	□ visual component	♫ audio component

5

Ideas about Poetry

IDEAS APPLICABLE TO ANY POETRY

What do we expect from poetry that sets it apart from prose?

1. A much greater intensity, compactness, and suggestiveness of expression and experience;
2. A greater use of connotation, metaphor, and word music;
3. As a result of these, a greater appeal to mood and emotion as well as to intellect—that is, a greater appeal to the entire personality;
4. A special typographic arrangement that not only finalizes the music and the meaning but also declares that *this* composition must be judged by these *higher—that is, poetic—standards.*

With these essential qualitative differences, the poet works in all media and with all types of subject matter.

The poet writes fiction—we call it epic (e.g., Homer's *Iliad*), or verse narrative (e.g., Chaucer's "The Pardoner's Tale"), or ballad (John Keats' "La Belle Dame Sans Merci"), or even verse novel (Elizabeth Barrett Browning's *Aurora Leigh*).

He writes drama—indeed, the original playwrights wrote only in verse (Aeschylus, *Agamemnon*) and early modern dramatists worked mainly in poetic forms (Shakespeare, *Richard II*).

If we see philosophy, criticism, and social protest as nonfiction by nature, then *the poet writes nonfiction too* (Lucretius, *On the Nature of Things;*

Alexander Pope, *Essay on Criticism*; Erasmus Darwin, *Zoönomia;* Elizabeth Barrett Browning, "The Cry of the Children"). In addition to contributing to these genres in which prose writers now predominate, the poet enjoys a medium peculiar to poets alone. *He writes the lyric, the commemorative ode, the "occasional" poem, and other types of composition classified simply as poetry.*

Looking back, then, we can see that our master list of literary themes (pp. 9–15) provides a good starting place for thinking about the content of poetry too. And our lists of literary techniques (pp. 17–22, 83–92) hold true again if we just add those special emphases on music, metaphor, and typography mentioned above.

Later we develop some details of these special poetic techniques in terms of specific ideas you can use right off as the basis for papers/projects/oral reports. The study and use of such techniques is known as *versification* or *prosody.*

But first let's suggest an overall approach that might increase your understanding and appreciation of poetry.

Mood as an Aid to Understanding Poetry (1)

When you are assigned to read some poetry, or are working on a paper/oral report about poetry, try out the method of comprehension suggested here. As a matter of fact, you might find it worthwhile to report on the success you've had with this approach. You might well find that the method works for you; but you still have to study our Ideas about technique that follow this introductory Idea.

Absorb yourself in a poem long enough to feel that it has communicated a *mood*. Resist at first all *rational* efforts to clutch at the *overall meaning* of the poem at least until you've experienced its mood (or its series of changing moods). Describe the mood to yourself. What caused it? *The rhythms?* They speak first to the unconscious, and they can create feelings in us before we have been reached by the *import* of the words. Has the *music,* the *tones* of the language affected your mood? What did they connote? Has the *setting* of the poem affected you? Perhaps some haunting phrase? Perhaps one of the *metaphors* disturbed or at least surprised or impressed you? Metaphors can also affect the unconscious, striking rapport quickly between us and the poet, shocking us with their unexpected likening of unlike things. Which metaphor triggered the strongest emotional reaction in you?

Only when you've really *weighed the mood(s)* the poem has stirred in you should you yield to the urge to figure out its *consecutive, complete meanings,* including its logical and literal meanings. Your mood(s) will give you valuable clues to literal and total meaning; if you ignore them, and try to be too rational too fast, they'll persist and get in the way of your processes of understanding.

If you experiment with more than one poem, make them poems that really are contrasting in their emotional appeal. Good poems to try:

Gary Snyder: "August on Sourdough, A Visit from Dick Brewer"
Langston Hughes: "Ballad of the Landlord"
Amy Clampitt: "A Procession at Candlemas"
Walt Whitman: "When Lilacs Last in the Dooryard Bloom'd"
Allen Ginsberg: "Howl"; "Transcription of Organ Music"
Allen Tate: "Ode to the Confederate Dead"
Robert Frost: "After Apple Picking"; "Stopping by Woods on a Snowy Evening"
Adrienne Rich: "Rape"; "Diving into the Wreck"
Harvey Shapiro: "Battle Report"; "July"; "The Card"; "Winter Sun"
Michael Harper: "Tongue-Tied in Black and White"
Anne Sexton: "Ballad of the Lonely Masturbator"; "The Touch"; "The Kiss"; "For My Lover"
Sylvia Plath: "Daddy"; "Lady Lazarus"; "Suicide off Egg Rock"
Samuel Taylor Coleridge: "Kubla Khan"
T. S. Eliot: "The Love Song of J. Alfred Prufrock"
Percy Bysshe Shelley: "Ode to the West Wind"
Gregory Corso: "Marriage"; "Elegiac Feelings American"
Edmund Spenser: "Epithalamion"

If you decide to make your experience with this approach the subject of a paper/oral report, consider discussing just one poem. For if you really recount *all* the gradual ways in which you have assembled clues to meaning, one poem is about all you could do justice to. ● ▲

Mood as an Aid in Understanding (2)

If the method proposed above works for you in poetry, thus making you more sensitive to the undertones and connotations in literature, would it work too in

---

● average difficulty	○ previous knowledge	★ most libraries
▲ larger library	□ visual component	♫ audio component

the less concentrated forms—the short story, the novel, the personal essay? This could be the subject of a follow-up report, either written or oral. • ★

Music in Poetry: Three Components

Report on the *three basic patterns* that the poet writing in English uses to compose his *word-music: metric, rhythmic,* and *tonal*. At the start, use traditional poems for your examples: They are most likely to adhere to regular patterns, introducing us quickly to the basics. (We'll soon enough get to the nontraditional poets.) Thomas Gray's "Elegy Wrote in a Country Churchyard" (1751) might meet your needs perfectly.

1. First establish the *metric pattern* by using a stress mark that leans to the right (/) for each syllable that rises, or is accented; use a simple hyphen (-) for each syllable that falls or is not accented. When you find a syllable that rises but not so emphatically as other stresses in the line, use the half-stress mark which leans to the left (\ ). But whenever you are in doubt about full-stress or half-stress, simply use the full-stress mark. You are concerned here only with the *relative rise and fall* of the poet's language. Thus you might scan Gray's first stanza:

The curfew tolls the knell of parting day,

The lowing herd wind slowly o'er the lea,

The plowman homeward plods his weary way,

And leaves the world to darkness and to me.

You have discovered a definite pattern of *ten syllables* to the line, five stressed ones alternating with five unstressed. Since you will find that this pattern prevails throughout the poem, with few serious variations, you can now diagram the basic *meter* and describe it at this point in the nontechnical terms we have used so far.

2. Next note that the poet also uses three *rhythmic patterns* which he plays *with or against* the regularity of his metric pattern.

(a) The easiest to detect is the rhythm he creates by the way he arranges his words. In stanza 1 above, Gray so disposes his phrases that *pauses* occur only at the end of each line. He strengthens this pattern throughout stanza 2:

> Now fades the glimmering landscape on the sight,
>   And all the air a solemn stillness holds,
> Save where the beetle wheels his droning flight,
>   And drowsy tinklings lull the distant folds;

By now he has established a regular rhythm that fits into his metric unit—one pause after every 10 syllables. Now notice how he begins to vary this rhythmic pattern in stanza 3:

> Save that from yonder ivy-mantled tower
>   The moping owl does to the moon complain
> Of such, as wandering near her secret bower,
>   Molest her ancient solitary reign.

Here he so disposes his phrases that meaning now runs *without pause* past the ends of two lines, pauses twice within the third line, and then reasserts the regular pattern set up in stanzas 1–2; that is, a pause at—and only at—line's end. And now of course we have the additional subliminal excitement of expecting regular pauses after every 10 syllables but also, maybe, irregular pauses after—*any* syllable!

To achieve his variations in stanza 3, Gray uses two tricks of rhythm: *enjambement,* or the spilling over of meaning from one line into another (lines 1–2); and *caesura,* or an irregular pause within the line (as in line 3) as opposed to a regular pause at line's end (as in line 4).

Obviously, the rhythms established in stanzas 1–2 would become monotonous if they were not varied thereafter. By his unexpected, irregular use of *caesura* and *enjambement,* Gray achieves not only welcome variations in rhythm, but he tightens and loosens the tension, speeds up or slows down the movement, all as concomitants of meaning.

(b) Gray creates still other contrapuntal tensions by playing the meter against itself. Where we expect an unstressed syllable (-) in stanza 1, line 2, Gray uses a stronger one: *wind* rises at least to a half stress (\ ). And where we expect a stressed syllable (/) in line 4, he uses a weaker one: *and,* which here can rise only to a half stress (\ ). And so lines 2 and 4 differ subtly in their rhythms from lines 1 and 3.

(c) Gray also exploits even further the fact that stressed syllables don't all have the same *degree of stress* or even the same *duration of sound.* In stanza 2,

Now fades thē glimm'rĭng landscape on thē sight

doesn't *fades* seem to you to be a longer sound than *glim, on,* or *sight,* while *land* may receive a different stress from what *fades* gets? Poets will prefer one word over another simply because of the degree of stress they need for their rhythm at a certain point.

So far, then, you have seen how the traditional (formalist) poet achieves *musical tension:* First he establishes a definite *metric pattern.* Then he varies the *rhythmic patterns* made by pauses, by the meter itself, and by different degrees of stresses.

3. Finally, note how the poet uses several techniques to achieve his distinctive *tonal patterns.* Most important in Gray's case is his *end-rhyming* of first and third lines (*day / way*) and second and fourth lines (*lea / me*). Within the lines he uses *assonance,* or concentrations of certain vowel sounds. In stanza 1, it's the full "o": t*o*lls, l*o*wing, sl*o*wly, *o*'er, h*o*meward. And in line 3 he uses *alliteration,* or repetition of initial sounds:

. . . *p*lowman . . . *p*lods . . . *w*eary *w*ay . . .

Not the least of Gray's tonal effects is his *onomatopoeia,* or use of words that imitate the sounds they denote. The huge curfew bell makes a heavy, round sound: it *tolls;* little bells on the sheep collars, however, produce *tinklings;* the animals themselves are making low sounds, *lowing;* and the plowman, taking heavy steps, *plods.*

Find other examples of *end-rhyme, assonance, alliteration,* and *onomatopoeia* which, together with *meter* and *rhythm,* create the music of Gray's melancholy reflections.

To show how *the poet can vary his metric, rhythmic,* and *tonal patterns to suit his varying moods,* study at least two other traditional poems, say the opening passage of Alexander Pope's *Essay on Man* and either William Blake's *Songs of Innocence and of Experience,* or William Wordsworth's "Ode: Intimations of Immortality," or Samuel Taylor Coleridge's "Kubla Khan."

Scan the lines and diagram the basic meter; describe how the poet, by his phrasing, his use of line's-end pauses, caesuras, and enjambement, sets up a rhythmic pattern that works against, but within, the metric pattern; study his use of end-rhyme (and internal rhyme, if any), assonance, alliteration, and onomatopoeia to create his tonal patterns. Finally, report on how his *prosody*—the sum total of his technical devices—relates to his poetic effects and poetic message. ● ★

Five Fixed Metric Patterns

Report on the five stress patterns used most frequently in English poetry:

1. *Iambic.* Each stressed syllable is the nucleus of a *foot* of poetry. If the stress rises from one unstressed syllable, we call the foot an *iamb* (- /). The stress pattern Gray uses in his "Elegy" (above) is *iambic:* each typical line consists of five *iambic* feet.

2. *Trochaic.* If the stress is followed by one unstressed syllable, we call the foot a *trochee* (/ -). The first line of Gray's stanza 3 (above) opens with a *trochaic* foot, as does the opening line of stanza 7. The following line from Shakespeare's *Macbeth* consists of four *trochaic* feet:

$$\text{Double,} \mid \text{double,} \mid \text{toil and} \mid \text{trouble} \mid$$

3. *Anapestic.* If the stressed syllable rises from two unstressed ones, we call the foot an *anapest* (- - /). This line from William Cowper's "The Poplars Are Felled" contains four *anapestic* feet:

$$\text{And the whis} \mid \text{pering sound} \mid \text{of the cool} \mid \text{colonnade} \mid$$

4. *Dactylic.* If the accented syllable is followed by two unstressed ones, the foot is a *dactyl* (/ - -). This line from T. S. Eliot's *Murder in the Cathedral* contains four *dactyls* followed by one *trochee:*

$$\text{Golden Oc} \mid \text{tober de} \mid \text{clines into} \mid \text{sombre No} \mid \text{vember} \mid$$

5. *Spondaic.* A foot that consists of two stresses we call a *spondee* (/ /). Such a foot may be used in place of any of the above. Gray uses spondees in stanzas 3, 10, 11, 13, and so on. The present author's poem "Silent Spondee at the Morgue" (*New York Quarterly* 1986) ends with a *spondaic* line:

$$\text{That's that!}$$

And the following line from Henry Wadsworth Longfellow's *Evangeline* consists of five dactyls and a spondee:

This is the | forest pri | meval. The | murmuring |
pines and the | hemlocks |

We name a line of poetry according to the *number of times it uses the specified foot*. A line of one foot is *monometer*; two, *dimeter*; three, *trimeter*; four, *tetrameter*; five, *pentameter*; six, *hexameter*; seven, *heptameter*. Thus

That's that!

is a *spondaic monometer line;* the line above from Shakespeare is *trochaic tetrameter;* from Cowper, *anapestic tetrameter;* from Gray, *iambic pentameter* (the classic English line); the Longfellow line is *dactylic hexameter* (the spondee substitutes for one dactyl).

Use a series of lines from each of the poems cited so far (or their metric equivalents) to show how the poet first establishes his meter and his rhythm and then varies both. What effect is gained in each case by using a *rising meter* (- / or - - /) as opposed to a *falling meter* (/ - or / - -)? Which is the line used most frequently in traditional English prosody? Why? Why is it no longer the predominant line? ● ★

Four Looser Metric Patterns

Verse written in very strict metric patterns "will become same and tame," remarked the nineteenth-century English Jesuit poet, Father Gerard Manley Hopkins. Report on these four ways the poet can loosen metric verse to prevent such monotony:

1. S/he can use a regular meter but vary the number of feet in each line. In a chorus in *Samson Agonistes,* John Milton sets up a regular iambic pentameter line, then shortens and varies it:

But who | is this, | what thing | of Sea | or Land? |
Female | of sex | it seems |
That so | bedeckt, | ornate, | and gay |
Comes this way | sailing |
Like a | stately | ship . . .

For similar variations in iambic pentameter, you should analyze Matthew Arnold's "Dover Beach" and Robert Frost's "After Apple Picking."

2. Another way the poet can loosen regular verse is to follow medieval Anglo-Saxon prosody. The Old English poet used a line of four regular stresses but with any number of unstressed syllables. Notice the several variations accomplished in just two lines of "The Wanderer" (anonymous, translated by Charles W. Kennedy):

> Oft tō thē Wanderēr, weary ōf exile,
>
> Cometh God's pity, compassiōnate love

Hopkins used a version of Anglo-Saxon prosody which he called "sprung rhythm." In each line he used a fixed number of stresses but any suitable number of weak syllables. Thus each line could speed up or slow down, shrink or expand, as Hopkins needed.

3. Still another way the modern poet flexes a fixed meter is simply to add or subtract one syllable in each line. Thus in "For Once Then, Something" Robert Frost uses a trochaic pentameter line with an extra, unstressed syllable added. And here the present author shortens the standard ten-syllable line to nine syllables:

Cliff Dwellers at Mesa Verde

> Into the cracks in the tableland
> They tucked their pueblos, small adjustments
> In the cliffline, nests of clay and stick.
> Below the scorched mesa, embracing
> The sandstone damp with sea memory,
> They scooped out their cool cells for the drape
> Of loosened limb, for the shape of love
>
> They sketched their rooms in free hand: floors lift
> Like strata, walls surprise like outcrops,
> Bricks touch like spilled rocks that drifted
> Into status. Here they hardly dreamed
> Nightmares of the right angle, or schemed
> The tautest distance between two points,
> Or heard the pressures of perfect cubes

Notice the results: Some lines emerge with four accents; some can be read with five or even six; still, iambs predominate, and most lines end on a stress.

4. Probably the most common way today's poet relaxes metric verse, if he uses meters at all, is to substitute, whenever it's convenient, an anapest (- - /) for an iamb (- /), a dactyl (/ - -) for a trochee (/ -)

If you report on these ways the poet relaxes fixed meters—in order to make his music less monotonous, less the "same and tame," consider the overall effect he achieves in each case. • ▲

Just What Is Free Verse?

In the twentieth century many poets have abandoned strict metrics and followed the lead of Walt Whitman, who established free verse as a more suitable medium for expressing the temper of modern life. Like the architect Louis Sullivan, Whitman sensed that form should follow function—that form should be designed anew and special for each new work.

As we have shown, the traditional poem establishes its form rather quickly. Actually it *imposes* a prefabricated order on new subject matter. The free verse poem rather finds, sometimes struggles to find, the unique order *implicit* in this new subject. Contrary to the layperson's belief, free verse poetry *does* rely on rhythmic and musical devices, but it uses them in a different way in each poem. Hence it seems more authentic psychologically, truer to the life of discovery, openness, change.

In free verse, the poet works not with meters and feet but with word clusters; he balances words against words, phrases with phrases, clauses with clauses, line against line, pauses with pauses. He repeats key words and phrases to link one line to another. Three of his basic formal devices, then, are *parallel structure, recurrence,* and *caesura.*

Report on this approach to poetic form by selecting passages from Whitman's *Song of Myself,* especially sections 1, 11, 32, 51, and any others you need to make your points. • ★

• average difficulty   ○ previous knowledge   ★ most libraries
▲ larger library   □ visual component   ♫ audio component

Six Types of Tonal Patterns

Report on the six types of tonal patterns that poets use—that is, the varieties of sound-repetition and sound-play they employ in their effort to create moods through word-music.

Full rhyme. Poets are using full rhyme when they match the concluding sounds of two different words or phrases. Thomas Gray, in his "Elegy," rhymed 128 lines all with one-syllable rhymes, e.g.:

> The boast of heraldry, the pomp of *power,*
>> And all that beauty, all that wealth e'er *gave,*
> Await alike the inevitable *hour.*
>> The paths of glory lead but to the *grave.*

But often poets will rhyme more than just the final syllable. In "Kubla Khan," Samuel Taylor Coleridge opens his second section with seven lines that rhyme their *last two syllables,* in this case all in falling feet (/ -):

> But O, that deep romantic chasm which *slanted*
> Down the green hill athwart a cedar *cover!*
> A savage place! as holy and en*chanted*
> As e'er beneath a waning moon was *haunted*
> By woman wailing for her demon *lover!*
> And from this chasm, with ceaseless turmoil *seething,*
> As if this earth in fast thick pants were *breathing,*
> A mighty fountain momently was forced . . .

Full rhyme is usually *end rhyme;* however, it can appear in mid-line as well, as in Walter James Miller's *Making an Angel:*

> You could not *stare* into my comet *glare*

Half Rhyme. Notice that in the above examples, *full rhyme* means correspondence of both final consonants and final vowels. But the poet can use just one or the other to achieve *half rhyme.* Thus Coleridge matches only the concluding consonant sound in the line that follows the quote above:

> A mighty fountain momently was *forced:*
> Amid whose swift intermitted *burst*
> Huge fragments vaulted . . .

This rhyme of the concluding consonant sound only is called *dissonant rhyme*. This is a favorite sound effect with Emily Dickinson, who begins her poem 432:

> Do People moulder equally,
> They bury, in the *Grave?*
> I do believe a species
> As positively live
>
> As I . . .

Notice that in both *forced/burst* and *Grave/live,* only the *concluding* consonants correspond. The World War I poet Wilfred Owen was adept at rhyming the *last two* consonant sounds in his end words. Thus in "Futility" he rhymes *seeds/sides* and *star/stir:*

> Think how it [the sun] wakes the *seeds,*
> Woke, once, the clays of a cold *star.*
> Are limbs so dear-achieved, are *sides*
> Full-nerved—still warm—too hard to *stir?*

In his preface to the 1931 edition of Owen's works, fellow-poet Edmund Blunden invented the term *pararhyme* (for such matching of words with identical consonant sounds and different vowels. Famous examples of Owen's end-pararhyme are *escaped/scooped* and *grained/ground* used in Owen's "Strange Meeting." Notice how in the following lines from "Exposure" Owen uses two pararhymes (*flake/flock, wand-/wind*) as internal rhymes:

> Sudden successive flights of bullets streak the silence.
> Less deathly than the air that shudders black with snow,
> With sidelong flowing *flakes* that *flock,* pause, and renew;
> We watch them *wand*ering up and down the *wind*'s nonchalance.

The matching of s*ilence* and noncha*lance* is, of course, one more instance of dissonant rhyme used as end rhyme.

Occasionally a poet will use pararhyme in two consecutive concluding words, as Miller does in "Old Surfcaster Blues" (*Artemis X,* 1987):

> the *mass hug*
> of a *moss hag*

The other half of half-rhyming is, of course, the matching of only *vowel* sounds, which we call *assonance*. It is sometimes used as end rhyme, as in *Making an Angel:*

> Always there were two Julys
> Yours and m*i*ne

but it occurs frequently as internal half-rhyming, as when the "Surfcaster" says:

> I w*a*de b*a*ck
> through sl*a*ckening w*a*ve
> and bl*a*ckening d*a*ymare

where one set of assonant rhymes—w*a*de, w*a*ve, d*a*y—alternates with a set of half and full rhymes—b*a*ck, sl*a*ckening, bl*a*ckening.

The oldest rhyming device in English poetry is *alliteration*, as we can see in our quote from the medieval poem "The Wanderer." *W*anderer and *w*eary alliterate. Initial rhyme, as we also call it, occurs too in the Owen line:

> With sidelong *fl*owing *fl*akes that *fl*ock . . .

Notice that Owen also combines alliteration with assonance in the opening words of that poem:

> *Su*dden *su*ccessive flights . . .

Not often a rhyming device but definitely contributing to *tonal patterns* is *onomatopoeia*, or the use of words that actually imitate the sounds they describe. Consider the opening section of Miller's "Z: In Memory of Louis Zukofsky" (*Literary Review*, 1982):

> Baking a grateful face in a blue and gold day in the Appalachians,
> I'm lazing on a lawn listening like a well-fed cat ears back to the
>   suasions of cicadas.
> At peace even with cyclists snarling up the hill with jets lumbering
>   toward a landing,
> I'm lazing like him who when he loafed invited his soul and by God
>   got RSVPs.

Here the poet establishes onomatopoeia not only for its own sake as music, but because it plays an important part in the narrative experience. For

> *suasions of cicadas*
> cyclists *snarling* up the hill
> jets *lumbering* toward a landing

all prepare us for a climactic moment related to

> *a cricket scraping its limited instrument.*

Notice again that tonal devices are rarely used alone but rather in concert. In "Z" there is internal assonant rhyme (B*a*king, gr*a*teful, f*a*ce, d*a*y, Appal*a*chian, l*a*zing, su*a*sion, cic*a*das) and there is simple alliteration:

> . . . *l*azing on a *l*awn *l*istening . . .

as well as interlocking alliteration:

> *B*aking . . . *g*rateful . . . *b*lue . . . *g*old . . .

Emphasize in your report that the newer rhyming devices—dissonance and pararhyme especially—give the twentieth-century poet much richer resources for his music and the moods it creates. • ▲

Line Arrangements in Poetry: Strophes and Stanzas

Report on the variety of line-arrangements the poet may use. Your aim is to show the distinctly different effects each form can have on the music and on development of theme.

Strophes and Stanzas. The all-inclusive term we use for any unit of line arrangement in verse is the *strophe*. But if all the strophes in a poem have the same regular structure, we call them *stanzas*. The word *strophe* then tends to designate units of line arrangements in a poem that has different, irregular structures. Check back and note that Gray's "Elegy" is organized in stanzas, Whitman's "Song of Myself" in strophes. Coleridge's "Kubla Khan" is also *strophic*.

Stanzas. There are many well-established stanzaic forms, and of course any poet may invent new ones. (See Eileen Simpson's description, in her memoir *Poets in Their Youth,* of John Berryman's search for a new stanza form.) But don't worry too much about the nomenclature. You need only describe a stanza, and its characteristic effects, accurately. If you know that Gray's stanza is a *quatrain,* great; if you don't, describe it as a four-line stanza.

Quatrain. When she uses quatrains, Dickinson (see above) casts them as alternating tetrameter and trimeter lines, rhyming usually on the shorter lines: a *b c b.* This particular quatrain form is known as the *ballad stanza.* But the quatrain can contain lines of any length and different rhyme schemes. The quatrain Gray used in his "Elegy" is cast in pentameter lines rhymed *a b a b.* Quatrains may be unrhymed.

Couplet. We call two successive lines of verse linked by rhyme a *couplet.* The lines may be unequal in length, but usually they are of identical metric pattern. For an iambic tetrameter couplet, see Milton's "L'Allegro." For iambic pentameter couplets, study Pope's *Essay on Man* or Phillis Wheatley's *To the Right Honorable William, Earl of Dartmouth.* By Pope's time the iambic pentameter line had been established as the *heroic* meter for English, the best line for epic, narrative, dramatic, and philosophical poetry. So the rhymed iambic pentameter couplet is also called the *heroic couplet.*

In the Neoclassical Age, the *closed couplet* was almost mandatory: that is, each couplet had to contain a unit of thought concluded by the rhyme. *Enjambement was taboo.* But by the Romantic Age, the *open couplet* flourished: meaning could flow over from couplet to couplet, as in Keats' *Endymion.* (See below, "Revolution in a Couplet.")

Couplets are usually run in succession, without breaks, in larger units of irregular length, called *verse paragraphs,* which may run up to fifty or more lines.

Blank Verse. Shakespeare uses the heroic couplet extensively, especially in his earlier plays. But for most of his career he used *unrhymed iambic pentameter,* usually called *blank verse,* and sometimes *heroic blank verse.* (Don't call it free verse! Or vice versa! Blank verse has that definite metric pattern; free verse doesn't.) Blank verse has been used by major poets from Christopher Marlowe to Robert Frost. Blank verse may be arranged in stanzas, as in Wallace Stevens' "Sunday Morning," but it usually appears in blocks of irregular length—that is, in verse paragraphs.

Terza Rima. Like the couplet, *terza rima* is not so much a stanza as a link, a unit, in continuing verse. Lines are arranged in *tercets,* rhyming *aba, bcb, cdc, ded,* and so on, until the poet closes the series by *moving from a tercet to a rhymed quatrain: xyx, yzyz,* or just *to a couplet: xyx, yy.* Invented by Dante for his *Commedia,* terza rima was introduced into England by Chaucer and used by Percy Bysshe Shelley, Robert Browning, and William Morris. Never a dominant form in English rhymed poetry, it may interest you as the forerunner of the *unrhymed tercet* so popular in today's poetry, probably because of its advantage as a continuing cycle of beginning, middle, end, beginning, etc.

Rime Royal. Chaucer favored this stanza (see *Troilus and Criseyde*), formed of seven iambic pentameter lines rhymed *ababbcc.*

Ottava Rima. Sir Thomas Wyatt introduced this stanza into England; it was the medium of the Italian epic poets Ariosto and Tasso. It has eight iambic pentameter lines rhymed *abababcc.* Study Lord Byron's brilliant use of it in *Don Juan.*

Spenserian Stanza. For his *Faerie Queene,* Edmund Spenser invented a stanza that comprises two iambic pentameter quatrains and a concluding iambic hexameter, interlinked by a rhyme scheme of *abab, bcbc, c.* Byron, Shelley, and Keats liked it too.

Sonnet. Strictly speaking, the sonnet is not a stanza form, since a complete sonnet consists of just one strophe. But often poets write *sonnet sequences,* in which case each sonnet becomes, in effect, one stanza. In both its Italian and English forms, the sonnet consists of 14 iambic pentameter lines, rhymed. The *Italian sonnet* is composed of an *octave* (eight lines), usually rhymed *abbaabba,* and a *sestet* (six lines), often rhymed *cdcdcd* or *cdecde.* You will find the Italian form among sonnets by Thomas Wyatt, John Milton, William Wordsworth, and John Keats.

The *English sonnet* is composed of three quatrains followed by a couplet, usually rhyming *abab, cdcd, efef, gg.* Invented by Henry Surrey, the English sonnet is best typified in Shakespeare's sequence, after whom it is often called the *Shakespearean sonnet.*

The sonnet is almost always rhymed, but Keats and others have used its basic form without rhyme. The sonnet offers you a prime example of how format and subject matter must interrelate. Where does the meaning—and so the mood—undergo change? With what effect? • ★

The Magic of Metaphor

You might find this an exciting topic: "The Function of Metaphor in the Poetry of _____."

Poetry operates on both our verbal and nonverbal sensibilities. Perhaps it reaches us first with its *rhythm,* which stirs the unconscious mind, wakes up the imagination. We start translating the poem's verbal *imagery* into pictures in the "mind's eye," scenes soon filled with noises, smells, tastes, contact as well as sights. In just two lines of "The Haunted Palace," Poe appeals to two of our senses:

> Along the ramparts plumed and pallid,
> A winged odour went away.

Soon, if not at once, the poet hits us with the magic of a *metaphor,* a lightning-like experience in which we thrill to his insight into the similarity between dissimilars:

> John Henry—he curses in giraffe-tall words . . .

Melvin B. Tolson tells us. And Frank Bidart describes a woman whose voice

> death and memory have made
> into a razor blade without a handle . . .

Such comparisons excite us emotionally as well as intellectually. Note that all three of these appeals—*rhythm, image, metaphor*—are at work at once as Miller describes:

> Elpenor's "dramatic moment"—
> When he rises like a dead minnow
> In the bucket of my memory—

It's no exaggeration, then, to say that the comparisons invoked *shock* us into accepting a hitherto unlikely relationship. So you must consider too how your poet's use of metaphor contributes to the *suspense.* This is a factor hardly ever mentioned in discussion of metaphor. (Be the first on your block, etc.) For having assimilated a shocking analogy like Bidart's or Tolson's, we are now wide awake and hopeful—no, demanding!—in a special dimension of ourselves. Romantics like Shakespeare arouse and satisfy us frequently—he aims a metaphor at our emotional and rational apprehension at least once every ten or fifteen lines. But William Butler Yeats, a romanticist who turned classicist, used metaphor sparingly, perhaps thereby increasing the suspense.

In "Easter 1916" his low-key music reaches us with its short lines, its enjambement, its dissonant rhyme (*faces, houses*) alternating ominously with full rhymes, all setting up a plain scene in plain diction:

> I have met them at close of day
> Coming with vivid faces
> From counter or desk among grey
> Eighteenth-century houses.

The poet tells us how he has never taken "them" seriously, assuming that like himself, they were cast in roles of clown or jester. Of course, they and he were not literally so, so this is metaphoric:

> Being certain that they and I
> But lived where motley is worn

And Yeats keeps us in suspense about that image for twenty lines or so before he caps it with another metaphor. He is talking of one of the Easter 1916 martyrs to the cause of Irish freedom:

> He, too, has resigned his part
> In the casual comedy

Thus the revolutionaries have separated themselves from the clowns; they

> Are changed, changed utterly;
> A terrible beauty is born.

The author of the poem "Z" (see above), before he launches his metaphors, pre-sensitizes us not only with long rhythmic lines of free verse, assonance, and onomatopoeia, but with the figure of speech known as *apostrophe:* He addresses the poet Zukofsky, newly dead, as though he were still alive and present. The living poet reminds his dead colleague of their problems when teaching poetry in a technical institute:

You and I Lou Lou and I . . .
Taught [Whitman] to engineering majors who suspected all of us

> Of some hoax some humbug passed on from Homer to Horace to Herrick to
> him and you and me
> But horrors not to them: The class it seemed sat damlike against any chance
> of seepage

And there it is, the poet's main, most effective technique: to make the reader see
the unknown (e.g., how a certain class looked) in terms of the known (how a
dam looks, works). And so the reader hopes that more points will be made in
terms of metaphor. The poem ends:

> Always—as in your poetry played on a violin fitted with secret organ stops—
> You sounded only the radius. Meaning the total terrorful circumference.

The musical and mathematical analogies both say, in different ways, that
Zukofsky always said more than he seemed to be saying. To paraphrase Robert
Frost, poetry is the medium in which you say one thing and mean another.

Terminology. Whenever the poet likens two unlike things, we call it *metaphor* (we all wear motley because life is a "casual comedy"; "You sounded
only the radius"). But if he or she uses the equal sign of *like* or *as* ("rises like
a dead minnow"; "the class . . . sat damlike"), we might identify it as a
special kind of metaphor by calling it a *simile.* In either case, the poet's use of
metaphor (the generic term) should signal, as well as achieve, both an emotional and intellectual highpoint in the poem.

Research. If your interest in metaphor takes you into poetry of the past, you'll
have no trouble finding poems by Poe or Yeats. But if you want to study
contemporary metaphor, you might have to seek out recent anthologies or even
the "literary magazines." For example, if you can't locate their books, look for
Melvin B. Tolson's "The Birth of John Henry" in Dudley Randall's anthology,
The Black Poets; Frank Bidart's "Elegy, Part V: *Lineage*" in Helen Vendler's
magnificent *Harvard Book of Contemporary Poetry;* and the present author's
"Z" in *The Literary Review,* 26 (Fall 1982). • ▲

• average difficulty	○ previous knowledge	★ most libraries
▲ larger library	☐ visual component	ଌ audio component

SPECIFIC IDEAS ABOUT POETRY

Major Documents in Twentieth-Century Prosody

Interested in reporting on modern prosody in greater detail? Start with four major documents: The 1931 edition of Wilfred Owen's *Poems,* edited by Edmund Blunden, who discusses and names Owen's pararhyme and other techniques; *A Hope for Poetry* by Cecil Day Lewis, a study of the influence of Hopkins and Owen on the W. H. Auden generation of poets; the fourth edition of *The Poems of Gerard Manley Hopkins* (1967), edited by W. H. Gardner and N. H. MacKenzie, which contains Hopkins' own full explanations of his prosody; and Robert Hass' essay "Listening and Making" which appeared in *Antaeus* in 1982 and was reprinted in *Random Review 1,* edited by Jonathan Galassi, a brilliant study of prosody from Walt Whitman to Louis Zukofsky and Gary Snyder. Consult too rhyming dictionaries, poets' handbooks, and studies of contemporary poets in *The American Poetry Review, Poetry: A Magazine of Verse,* and *The New York Quarterly* (the craft interviews, the first series of which has been reprinted in *The Craft of Poetry,* edited by William Packard; the second, expanded edition is titled *The Poet's Craft*). • ▲

Rationale Behind the New Prosody

The two greatest American poets, as we've noted, introduced major innovations in prosody in the nineteenth century: Walt Whitman's free verse and Emily Dickinson's extensive use of dissonance and assonance as end rhyme. In the twentieth century, the great Anglo-Irish poet William Butler Yeats then used a combination of dissonant end rhyme and full end rhyme in such major poems as "Easter 1916." The World War I English army officer Wilfred Owen, before his death at the Battle of the Somme, invented pararhyme as end rhyme and accentuated assonance, alliteration, and alliterative assonance in a small body of poetry of large impact on contemporary poets. Meanwhile, the English priest, Gerard Manley Hopkins, dead for several decades before the bulk of his work was published in 1918, had reintroduced accentual verse as "sprung rhythm," and he too had a major impact on later poetry.

Why, at this point in the history of Anglo-American poetry, did poets *need* to make such departures from traditional prosody? What is the rationale, the motivation, for innovations like free verse, sprung rhythm, half rhyme?

Start with histories of literature and poetry to get the overview; read the four major documents described in the Idea above; study the key poets; check the journals for up-to-date discussions of all the principal figures mentioned above.
● ▲

Free Verse and the Psalms

Our description of Whitman's form as based on special patterns of parallelism, recurrences, and caesuras could just as easily be applied to *The Book of Psalms* in the Bible. Whitman was quite conversant with the Scriptures. Read several psalms and compare them with several sections of *Song of Myself* and report on: The Influence of the Hebrew Psalmist on Whitman's Free Verse. ● ★

(**Wider scope:** Check both the Whitman scholars and the scholars of the Bible as literature for their discussions of prosody; consider also the effect of the operatic *recitativo* on Whitman; the biographies should provide context for Whitman's sudden departure from traditional prosody. ● ▲)

The Hass Theory of Free Verse

Free-verse rhythm, says Robert Hass in his "Listening and Making" (*Random Review 1*), "is not a movement between pattern and absence of pattern, but between phrases based on odd and even numbers of stresses." To Hass, three and five are open numbers, two and four closed numbers, with corresponding psychological effects. Study especially Hass' discussion of Whitman's "A Farm Picture" and then apply it to "When Lilacs Last in the Dooryard Bloom'd" and "Passage to India." ● ▲

(**Wider scope:** Try out Hass' theory on such free-verse poets as Harvey Shapiro, Adrienne Rich, and Galway Kinnell. What has the critical reaction been to Hass' study? ● ▲)

Two Free-Verse Poems Compared

Compare Allen Ginsberg's "Howl" with Karl Shapiro's "I Am an Atheist Who Says His Prayers," two long contemporary poems, different in mood and in purpose, but both poems of analysis and belief. What are the technical means by which each poet achieves his effects? Under what circumstances do you see free verse as an effective medium? ● ▲

(**Wider scope:** Add to the discussion a Whitman poem of analysis and belief, and of comparable length, e.g., "Passage to India." Do the critics agree with your answers to the questions posed above? • ▲)

Two Stanzas: "Binary Terms"

A poem of two stanzas, says Helen Vendler (editor of the *Harvard Book of Contemporary Poetry*), "is almost always occupied with binary terms—choice, contrast, comparison." Check this in: William Blake, "O Rose Thou Art Sick"; Wallace Stevens, "The Emperor of Ice Cream" (*The Collected Poems*); Walter James Miller, "Cliff Dwellers" (quoted in full above); John Ashbery, "Street Musicians" (*Houseboat Days*), and any other two-stanza poem you would like to include—perhaps one from Emily Dickinson. • ▲

(**Wider scope:** Does Vendler's hypothesis still work when you extend your examination to any poem of *two strophes?* For example, such poems by Robert Bly, Harvey Shapiro, Adrienne Rich, Sylvia Plath, Samuel Exler; poems you discover in *The Beloit Poetry Journal, The New York Quarterly, American Poetry Review, Pulpsmith, Croton Review, Chelsea Review?* • ▲)

Polyphonic Prose and Its Impact

A nineteenth-century poet, Paul Fort, wrote verse which was printed in prose format. Amy Lowell developed this form sometimes with meter and full rhyme, sometimes with free verse and assonance, always with poetic motifs. A third poet, John Gould Fletcher, gave this genre the name of "polyphonic [all-sounding] prose." Read at least two examples from each poet and report on the history, characteristics, and advantages of this blend of poetry and prose. • ▲

(**Wider scope:** After you've sketched out your own reactions, check those of the critics and include them in your discussion. • ▲)

Scansion of Whitman

If you scan Whitman's lines as we did some of Gray's, you will discover that although his free verse is *not conceived* in feet and meters, it very often *moves freely in and out of metric patterns*. You can demonstrate this by reporting on your scansion of passages like this one, from the beginning of *Song of Myself*:

I celebrate myself, and sing myself,
And what I assume you shall assume,
For every atom belonging to me as good belongs to you.

I loafe and invite my soul,
I lean and loafe at my ease observing a spear of summer
        grass.

My tongue, every atom of my blood, form'd from this soil,
        this air,
Born here of parents born here from parents the same, and
        their parents the same,
I, now thirty-seven years old in perfect health begin,
Hoping to cease not till death.

Creeds and schools in abeyance,
Retiring back a while sufficed at what they are, but never
        forgotten,
I harbor for good or bad, I permit to speak at every hazard,
Nature without check with original energy.

Note that Whitman's free verse is really a combination of several modes of formal prosody. His basic pattern is *free iambs:*

$$\bar{\text{I}} \; \text{cel}\acute{\text{e}}\text{br}\bar{\text{a}}\text{te} \; \text{m}\acute{\text{y}}\text{self} \; \bar{\text{a}}\text{nd} \; \text{s}\acute{\text{i}}\text{ng} \; \text{m}\bar{\text{y}}\text{self}$$

or

$$\bar{\text{Ret}}\acute{\text{i}}\text{r}\bar{\text{i}}\text{ng} \; \text{b}\acute{\text{a}}\text{ck} \; \bar{\text{a}} \; \text{wh}\acute{\text{i}}\text{le} \; \text{s}\bar{\text{u}}\text{ff}\acute{\text{i}}\text{ced} \; \bar{\text{a}}\text{t} \; \text{wh}\acute{\text{a}}\text{t} \; \text{th}\bar{\text{e}}\text{y} \; \acute{\text{a}}\text{re}$$

His pattern alternately tenses to spondees and relaxes to either anapests:

$$\acute{\text{Born}} \; \acute{\text{here}} \; \bar{\text{of}} \; \acute{\text{par}}\bar{\text{ents}} \; \acute{\text{born}} \; \acute{\text{here}} \; \text{fr}\bar{\text{om}} \; \acute{\text{par}}\bar{\text{ents}}$$
$$\text{th}\bar{\text{e}} \; \acute{\text{same}}, \; \bar{\text{and}} \; \text{their} \; \acute{\text{par}}\bar{\text{ents}} \; \text{th}\bar{\text{e}} \; \acute{\text{same}}$$

or to dactyls:

Natūre wíthoút chéck wíth ōrigínaī énergȳ

With Whitman it is important to show caesuras in your scansion, since his balancing of word clusters is also a *rhythm of intervals*:

I celebrate myself │ and sing myself
 And what I assume │ you shall assume • ★

Ezra Pound's Prosody

Read T. S. Eliot's *Ezra Pound: His Metric and Prosody*. Select several of Pound's poems that Eliot considers crucial to a study of Pound's prosody. Report on how one poet views the prosody of another. What did this early book of Eliot's (1917) on the early poetry of Pound add to your knowledge of prosody? about how to discuss it? • ▲

(**Wider scope:** Any or all of the following corollaries: How Eliot's analysis applies to some subsequent period of Pound's poetry. How Eliot's own poetry reflects his study of Pound. How the critics and/or literary historians view this youthful study of a poet Eliot later allowed to edit his own work (*The Waste Land*—three words, please!) • ▲)

Melville, Whitman, and the Civil War

Compare and contrast the small body of Civil War poetry left us by two of our major writers, poet Walt Whitman and novelist-poet Herman Melville. On what do the free-verse writer, with his expansive strophes, and the severely formal poet, with his tight stanzas, agree? How would you compare/contrast their themes, observations, metaphor, music? • ★

(**Wider scope:** After you have formulated your own answers to the above questions, compare them with those of the critics/literary historians. Look especially for comparisons of the two poets; and/or check the poets' observations on the war with their personal involvement in it. How close did each poet get to combat? to the forces in the field? • ▲)

Whitman, Hopkins, and Sprung Rhythm

In his constant search for the best form for an idea or an image, Walt Whitman sometimes actually fell into the kind of accentual verse that Father Gerard

Manley Hopkins called "sprung rhythm." Its characteristics: it uses the same number of accents per line but a varying number of unstressed syllables. Hopkins could not have influenced Whitman—publication of the English priest's poetry was almost all posthumous. It's simply that in the search for music with flexibility and freedom, both poets hit upon similar patterns. (Compare Whitman's "A Farm Picture" with Hopkins' "Spring and Fall" (or any sprung-rhythm poem). Scan Whitman's piece as six accents to the line, Hopkins' as four. Note the importance of the caesura, especially to Whitman, but its special effects too in Hopkins. (For other aspects of "A Farm Picture" look ahead for "The Music of 'A Farm Picture'.") • ▲

Shakespeare's Three Stages in His Use of Blank Verse

Shakespeare's plays reveal his continuing search for new freedoms in his blank verse (unrhymed iambic pentameter). He used regular, end-stopped blank verse in, e.g., *Love's Labour's Lost;* then he tried looser rhythms by varying the meter and using more enjambement, as in *As You Like It*; near the end of his career, he used not only the run-over line but often blurred the end of the line either by ending it with a weak syllable or adding a weak eleventh syllable, as in *Cymbeline*. What effects did these changes in his prosody have on the sound of the dialogue? on the dialogue as poetry? as drama? • ★

(**Wider scope:** Compare your own observations with those of scholars and historians who study Shakespeare's prosody in detail. • ▲)

Computer Research in Blank Verse Style

As you read the blank verse of Marlowe, Shakespeare, Wordsworth, Browning, Tennyson, et al., you are aware that although they are all presumably using the same metric form, they each produce a qualitatively different iambic pentameter line. Now, the computer helped scholars establish the *Iliad* as the work of one man. (For a lead to the technical details, check *The New York Times Index* for 1961 for the story "Iliad One-Man Job, Computer Indicates.") So why can't the computer establish the essential stylistic differences (phrasing, patterns of half-stresses, assonance, alliteration, etc.) in the blank verse of several major poets like those we've listed? Design your project, program the computer, to suit the scope of your assignment. Are these results publishable? Check whether anybody has already done similar research; if so, do different poets or check for finer points. • ▲

Non-Computer Research on Blank-Verse Styles

Without the computer, you would not be able to conduct such an ambitious study as is suggested above. But you could still conduct research on blank-verse styles by doing thorough scansion of meter, rhythm, patterns of pauses and caesuras, enjambement, patterns of assonance, etc. on at least 200 lines of each poet's work, as many poets as the scope of your assignment suggests. You could get the feel of the terrain by consulting such a work as T. S. Eliot's remarks on the blank verse of Christopher Marlowe in *The Sacred Wood*. • ▲

Prosody in Other Languages

We have spoken so far of the patterns that the poet writing in English uses to compose his word music. If you have studied Greek, Latin, or any modern foreign languages, make a report on the prosodic techniques the poet uses in that language and in that period. How are they similar or dissimilar to English prosody? Relate the differences in prosody to differences in the nature of the language. • ▲

John Milton's Prosody in English and Latin

Take at least ten of Milton's poems in each language. How do they compare in their use of: variations in meter; end-stopped lines; enjambement; caesuras; frequency of spondees, or any other feature you detect? Is Milton Milton in both languages? • ▲

(**Wider scope:** Have the Milton scholars done any such comparative study? If so, you might examine different works in order to supplement their studies. If not, is yours publishable? • ▲)

Revolution in a Couplet!

In the Neoclassical Age, critics and poets preferred the *rhymed closed couplet*. This usually has a pause at the end of the first line and the completion of a thought at the end of the second, where the rhyme locks in a unit of meaning. Thus Pope:

> A little learning is a dangerous thing;
> Drink deep or taste not the Pierian spring.

In the Romantic Age, however, poets rebelled against the closed couplet in favor of the open couplet, in which meaning can spill over from line to line (*enjambement,* as above). Thus Lord Byron flouts convention:

> I say no more than hath been said by Dante's
> Verse, and by Solomon and Cervantes.

And John Keats revels in the runover line:

> A thing of beauty is a joy forever:
> Its loveliness increases, it will never
> Pass into nothingness; but will keep
> A bower quiet for us, and a sleep
> Full of sweet dreams, and health, and quiet breathing

Report on this revolution in poetic form, sampling not only the prosody of Pope, Byron, Keats, but the critics who supported each faction (including those who attacked Keats). • ▲

(**Wider scope:** Link this rebellion in a couplet to the larger issues, literary, cultural, political, of the periods involved. • ▲)

The Imagist Beginnings of Modern Poetry

Trace the beginnings of twentieth-century Anglo-American poetry in the short experimental poems of the Imagist movement. It flourished in England and the United States about 1910–1920. Focus on T. E. Hulme, F. S. Flint, Richard Aldington, Amy Lowell, and the imagist works of Ezra Pound, William Carlos Williams, D. H. Lawrence, and Wallace Stevens. Glenn Hughes' study of Imagism provides a good start for the history of the movement and its influence. Include other histories as the scope of your assignment suggests. • ▲

Nuyorican Life in Its Poetry

Poet and dramatist Miguel Algarín says in his afterword to his anthology *Nuyorican Poetry,* "A poem describes the neighborhood of the writer for the reader." What description of Puerto Rican life in New York can you assemble

from this book? On what do most of the poets agree about New York? disagree?
• ▲

   (**Wider scope:** How much critical attention did the anthology get? • ▲)

Nine-Year-Old Poet: Jorge Lopez

Born in 1966, Jorge Lopez was a published poet by 1975. Start your research
with his poems in *Nyorican Poetry: An Anthology of Puerto Rican Words and
Feelings.* Notice that having an adult coaching you helps you to become a child
prodigy: six-year-old Wolfgang Amadeus Mozart had his father Leopold,
"Georgie" Lopez has had poets Miguel Algarín and Miguel Piñero as his
mentors. (They are also the editors of the anthology.) • ▲

Adrienne Rich: Sociological Poet

One of the strongest themes in *The Fact of a Doorframe: Poems Selected and
New, 1950–1984,* is the evil of patriarchal society. As you and/or the critics see
it, with what techniques, what success, has Adrienne Rich made this material
poetic? • ▲

Gary Snyder's Leave-Taking and Japanese Tradition

Report on Gary Snyder's "August on Sourdough, A Visit from Dick Brewer,"
putting it in the tradition of the leave-taking poetry of Japan. Compare Snyder's
work with poems on the same theme by Buson and Basho. Robert Aitken's
book about Basho, *The Zen Wave,* will supply background. Robert Hass' essay
"Listening and Making" (see above) will be helpful as a start. • ▲
   (**Wider scope:** Note Hass' remarks on what earlier critics would have thought
about [and missed in] Snyder's poem. What critical reception did Snyder's
poem get originally? • ▲)

Pound and Lowell: Attitudes toward History

In her *Harvard Book of Contemporary Poetry* (p. 4), Helen Vendler thinks that
in their attitudes toward history, Ezra Pound acted like an archaeologist col-
lecting miscellaneous "shards of culture," but Robert Lowell like a chronicler
who knows "we cannot avoid, even against our will, forming a gestalt of what
we inherit." Test this hypothesis. As the scope of your project dictates, assem-

ble a number of works of the two poets that are generally conceded to be "historical" in their concerns. Does Pound assume less responsibility, and Lowell more, to find patterns of meaning in history? Is it possible Pound counted on the unconscious processes to form the gestalt, in both himself and his readers, while Lowell derived the gestalt more deliberately, more rationally?

What do you *and/or the critics* conclude about the authenticity of Vendler's comparison? • ▲

Piñero and Crane: Attitudes toward History

Compare Miguel Piñero's poem "The Book of Genesis According to Saint Miguelito" with Stephen Crane's "God Fashioned the Ship of the World Carefully." Compare them both with chapters 1–4 of *The Book of Genesis* in the Bible. In what ways are the two poems similar in their characterization of God? In what ways do they depend on the Bible story for their effects? Why do certain American institutions and customs figure here? Note that "Let me make one thing perfectly clear" was a characteristic expression of President Richard Nixon, a documented big-time prevaricator. In what ways does Crane's poem illustrate the advantages of a compact, single image? How does Piñero's show the advantages of expansiveness? How do they compare in their prosody? (For Piñero, see *Nuyorican Poetry,* cited above.) • ▲

François Villon and Saint Miguelito

In an introductory note to his third book of poems, *Mongo Affair,* Miguel Algarín compares the title character of his long "El Capitan San Miguelito" with the fifteenth-century poet François Villon. Why is the comparison apt? What clues do you see in the poem to the identity of El Capitan (and see above)? In case your own sources miss the point, remember that medieval Villon's "intensely personal message. . . . ranks him with the moderns," according to *The Concise Columbia Encyclopedia.* Villon's *Little Testament* and *Testament* are available in recent translations by poet Galway Kinnell, and Algarín's book from Nuyorican Press, 703 East 6 Street, New York, NY 10009. • ▲

(**Wider scope:** Have the poets, including Algarín himself, published anything more extensive about his comparison? If not, should you, using his remarks as the launching pad of your study, try to make it publishable? • ▲)

Philosophy in Poetry: Beckett and Descartes

Beckett's long poem *Whoroscope* purports to be some philosophical musing by René Descartes, founder of the Cartesian system of philosophy. If you know your Descartes, review, explain, criticize the poem. ○ ▲

Darwinism in the Poetry of Thomas Hardy

Establish a good summary of Darwin's theory of relations among living things. Show how Darwin's concepts influenced Hardy's perception in such poems as "The Ivy-Wife," "The Subalterns," "The Convergence of the Twain" (lines on the loss of the *Titanic*), and five or six others. ● ▲

(**Wider scope:** Work directly from Darwin's own text. ○ ▲)

Crane and Hardy: Views of Divinity

Compare Thomas Hardy's poem "Hap" with Stephen Crane's "God Fashioned the Ship of the World Carefully." How does "Crass Casualty" figure in both poems? (Hardy means "Casualty" and "Hap" in their old sense of *chance, luck, fortune;* why not compare the definitions of all these words in the sections on their synonyms in a good dictionary?) Compare the two poets' views of the controlling forces in the Universe. How would you know, without checking their exact dates, that both poems were written after Darwin's emphasis on the role of Chance in evolution? Show how each poet's techniques (music, metaphor, etc.) relate to his message. ● ▲

Elizabeth Bishop and Lord Byron
Compared for Their Use of Travel

With the nineteenth-century English poet Lord Byron, travel was an exciting subject for narrative poetry, e.g., *Childe Harold's Pilgrimage*. With twentieth-century American poet Elizabeth Bishop, travel—in all its aspects of pilgrimage, culture-shock, exile, a goad to reminiscence, a new perspective, etc.—is her main subject for lyric poetry. Compare some twenty or so of her travel lyrics (*Complete Poems*) with comparable passages of Byron's *Harold* for their tone, music, strophic form, metaphor, content, themes. ● ▲

(**Wider scope:** Has any critic, including Helen Vendler, already written extensively on this comparison? If so, incorporate relevant portions of their criticism but try to use poems they have not yet focused on; if not, is your essay even more suitable for publication? • ▲)

Anne Bradstreet's Influence on Dickinson and Berryman

English-speaking America's first poet of merit was Anne Bradstreet (1612–1672). Her *The Tenth Muse Lately Sprung Up in America* appeared in London in 1650; a second, enlarged edition was published in Boston in 1678; and her complete works in 1867. What influence has our first poet had on later American poets? With the guidance of the critics/scholars, check her influence on any or all of these: Edward Taylor; Emily Dickinson (especially her domestic metaphor); John Berryman (especially his book-length poem, *Homage to Mistress Bradstreet*). • ▲

Blake Anticipated Freud, Scholar George Claims

In her *Blake and Freud*, Diana Hume George declares that poet-artist William Blake anticipated the major tenets of psychoanalysis a hundred years before Freud. If the scope of your assignment suggests it, limit yourself to just one or two of George's topics—like "Innocence and Experience" or "Freud and Feminine Psychology"—and do a thorough reading of the Blake poetry discussed under that heading. Report then on her "Introduction" and that one aspect of her work. Before doing your final draft, check on the special conventions for quoting a long prose passage and several lines of poetry. • ▲

(**Wider scope:** Check on the critical reaction to George's study, especially in literary and psychological journals. • ▲)

Algarín, Ginsberg, Hughes and Ethnic Poetry

The Jewish "scene" had already been well established in fiction, but Allen Ginsberg was the first to explore it on a big scale in poetry. Langston Hughes had already acquainted us with the Afro-American milieu and, most recently, Miguel Algarín, with three volumes of his own poetry and an anthology to his credit, has introduced us to Puerto Rican life in New York. Report on these poets (five or more poems by each?) and how they explain their minority culture to the dominant culture. Consider metaphor, diction, message, initial and lasting appeal. • ▲

(**Wider scope:** Increase either the number of poets considered or the number of their poems. Has such a comparison been published? If not, is yours publishable? • ▲)

American Poetry and the Presidency

President Theodore Roosevelt assisted the poet Edward Arlington Robinson with a federal job. Check on his specific advice to the poet. The Kennedy family had Robert Frost recite his poem "The Gift Outright" at John F. Kennedy's Inauguration as President. President Jimmy Carter, a great admirer of the Welsh poet Dylan Thomas, invited forty American poets to a White House reception in 1980. How did the press react to these events? How did the poets benefit by this sort of recognition? Discuss the Presidency as a Supporter of Poetry. • ★

Meaning and Symbolism in Jean Toomer

Study not only his poetry but also his sketches and stories (collected in *Cane*). What do you and/or the critics see as the central symbols in his work? • ★

Influence of Folk Poetry on Black Literary Poetry

Start with anthologies that include black folk poetry (like Dudley Randall, ed., *The Black Poets*) and then focus on books by some or all of the following poets: Robert Hayden, Melvin B. Tolson, Etheridge Knight, Larry Neal, Sterling A. Brown, Margaret Walker. What do you and/or the critics see as the influences? • ▲

The John Henry Legend in Black-American Poetry

Discuss the legend of that "steel-drivin' man," John Henry, as it begins in anonymous black balladry and recurs in contemporary poetry, e.g., "The Birth of John Henry" by Melvin B. Tolson. For a start, consult anthologies like Randall's (cited above). What do you and/or the critics see as the influences? the innovations and elaborations? • ▲

Langston Hughes' Poetry and the Blues Form

First study the verse patterns used by blues composers. What effects do you see (and/or the critics document) of the blues on Langston Hughes? For an oral report especially, play poems from one of the numerous records of Hughes poetry, some of himself as the reader. • ▲ ♎

Claude McKay's Poetry of Religious Conversion

Claude McKay is best known for his early poems on racial themes. Study his later works which, more personal, chronicle his development from atheism to Catholicism. What do you and/or the critics see as the technical concomitants of his philosophical reorientation? • ▲

Influence of Pope on Phillis Wheatley

Study the debt of this early black poet (1753–94) to the Neoclassical poet Alexander Pope. Compare her verse forms with his for rhyme scheme, end-stopped rhyme, closed couplet, enjambement, caesura. How do they compare in philosophy? • ▲

The Harlem Renaissance

Study the poetry produced during the flowering of Afro-American literature in Harlem during the 1920s. What part did W. E. B. DuBois' magazine *Crisis* play in this movement? Narrow or widen the scope of your report by including consideration of some or all of these poets: Langston Hughes, Claude McKay, Countee Cullen, and Jean Toomer. What killed the Renaissance? • ▲

Black Poets, White Poetry (I)

Harlem Renaissance poets Countee Cullen and Claude McKay have been criticized for writing under the influence of the English Romantic poets John Keats and William Wordsworth and even of the seventeenth-century poet John Milton. Follow one or both paths of study: Compare Cullen's and McKay's style with that of the English classic poets mentioned; compare Cullen's and McKay's style with that of Langston Hughes and Jean Toomer, poets considered as being closer to their own time and place. What do you and/or the critics see as the significant differences and similarities? • ▲

Hayden, Brooks, Danner: Eliot, Crane, Pound

Study the influence of T. S. Eliot, Hart Crane, and Ezra Pound on the *techniques* of Robert Hayden, Gwendolyn Brooks, and Margaret Danner. What do you and/or the critics see as the connections? How do the black critics regard the influence? • ▲

Black Poets, White Poetry (II)

Black poets of the Sixties and Seventies turned away from the values and the poetry of white society, and started to create a new black poetry of their own. Study especially the poetry of Amiri Baraka (the former LeRoi Jones) and Don Lee. What do you and/or the critics see as the difference between the new and old black poetry? For an oral report especially, play selections from LeRoi Jones' Library of Congress tape, or his Jihad Productions record, and/or Lee's Broadside Voices tape, or his Jihad tape. • ▲ ♋

Stoker "Shine" Legend in Neal and Knight

A legend is a popular story of heroic deeds that may change in its details as it is passed on from one storyteller to another. Some changes are imaginative additions to fill in gaps in the narrative or to accommodate the storyteller's own point of view or interpretation. Compare the legend of "Shine," a black stoker on the ill-fated ship *Titanic,* as it is treated in the poetry of Etheridge Knight and Larry Neal. In addition to comparing their content, consider the technical means they use to get their effects. If you're unable to locate books by these poets, try these two anthologies: Dudley Randall, ed., *The Black Poets;* LeRoi Jones (now Amiri Baraka) and Larry Neal, ed., *Black Fire.* • ▲

(**Wider scope:** 1. Locate other versions in Afro-American poetry and fiction; compare them with the Neal and Knight versions. 2. Check discussions of the legend in scholarly journals, including black periodicals. 3. Compare Knight's and Neal's stories of the *Titanic* disaster with that of Thomas Hardy cited above. 4. Consult *The New York Times Index* for 1912, histories of the period, encyclopedias, *The New York Times Index* for 1986 for salvage operations and light they throw on the disaster, all for more background on any of the above. Did the salvage operations prompt any reprints of Neal and Knight? • ▲)

Black Poets' Influence on American Language

Did you know that we owe the expression "up against the wall" to Amiri Baraka? The phrases "integration of negroes with black people" and "talking black and sleeping white" to the poet Don Lee? If you'd like to report on the black poets' influence on American speech, first check library card-catalogues, etc., check the Index to *American Speech,* read the introductions to several anthologies, write to the editors of *Black Scholar, Black World,* etc., for leads. ○ ▲

John Berryman's Id Externalized

In his *Dream Songs,* John Berryman externalizes his own id in a "character" named Henry. For the real-life model for Henry, see the memoir *Poets in Their Youth* by Berryman's first wife, Eileen Simpson. Report on Henry and the id as necessary subjects for Berryman, on the stanza form he invented for these *Songs* (Simpson here too), the tone of the work, its aims, conclusions, and influence. Simpson will lead you to other sources, as will reviews of her book. ● ▲

(**Narrower scope:** Limit the number of sections of this long poetry series that you can handle given the scope of your project: term paper? master's essay? No limit for the Ph.D. candidate! ● ▲)

The Eclogue—Then and Now

Several modern poets have used the eclogue as a vehicle for their sociopolitical ideas. See for example Robert Frost's "Build Soil," Louis MacNeice's "Eclogue from Iceland," W. H. Auden's "The Age of Anxiety," and Allen Ginsberg's "Ecologues of These States 1969–1971" (yes, *his* title puns on *ecology*). Why have they chosen this ancient and "pastoral" form? In a history of literature trace the evolution of the eclogue from Vergil's *Bucolics* to Edmund Spenser's *Shepherd's Calendar* to the eighteenth-century "town eclogues." What characteristics of the eclogue remain constant from Vergil to Ginsberg? ● ▲

(**Wider scope:** Check with the critics at every stage. ● ▲)

The Wordsworth Collaboration

Just how much did Dorothy Wordsworth contribute to her brother William's poetry? How much of her help was acknowledged? How much of her anonymity was a matter of personal choice, how much of the sexist attitudes of the day? The most recent biographies of sister and brother, or reviews thereof, might be the best starting place, with reading of the crucial poems mandatory. • ▲

Ginsberg, Merrill, Kaminsky, and Nuclear Disaster

Compare Allen Ginsberg's, James Merrill's, and Marc Kaminsky's poems on nuclear disaster. How do they make poetry out of the subject? Discuss the way their music, imagery, diction, metaphor all function to make their point. Why do Kaminsky and Ginsberg require notes? Check *Rolling Stone* for the original layout of Ginsberg's work. • ▲

   (**Wider scope:** How do the critics answer these questions? • ▲)

How Does a Poem Work? See "A Farm Picture"

Report on this little gem of a poem by Walt Whitman as a perfect answer to the question "How does a poem work?" Scan it with special attention to line's-end pauses and caesuras:

> Through the ample open door │ of the peaceful country barn,
>
> A sunlit pasture field │ with cattle and horses feeding,
>
> And haze and vista, │ and the far horizon fading away.

The poem is in sprung rhythm (see above). Each line has the same number of accents but a varying number of unstressed syllables, and a caesura. But notice how the place of the caesura shifts in the last line. The phrases now are not three accents long but two and four, not an odd number but an even number. What are the effects of this change, musical and thematic? Of the alliterative series of three *p*'s in line 1, of four *f* sounds in lines 2 and 3, of the two *z* sounds in line 3; of the assonant rhyme of three *a*'s in line 3; of the pararhyme of *feeding* and *fading?* of the absence of any verb (and therefore of a sentence)? How does the music contribute to the themes and the overall meaning? What does it say about poetry that a three-line work can elicit so much consideration? Check INDEX for definitions of technical terms used here. • ★

Two Views of Painters: Vasari's, Browning's

Giorgio Vasari's sixteenth-century *Lives of the Most Eminent Painters, Sculptors, and Architects* is our chief source of information about Renaissance artists. Robert Browning based two of his dramatic monologues—*Fra Lippo Lippi* and *Andrea del Sarto*—on Vasari's accounts. Compare and contrast Vasari's and Browning's treatments of one or both painters. Who gives us the more dramatic, more realistic, more poetic portrait? On what bases did Browning select and reject material Vasari offered, and invent additional material of his own? How can the liberties Browning has taken be justified? • ▲

(**Wider scope:** Do later biographical accounts of the painters throw any new light on their lives and circumstances? How do these compare with Browning's interpretations? • ▲)

Dramatic Monologue, Then and Now

Robert Browning brought to perfection what he called the "dramatic lyric" but what critics prevail in calling the "dramatic monologue." This is a poem written in the first person, from the point of view of one character, whose speech not only gives us the setting but the identities of other people present and even implies, through his reactions, what they are doing/saying. Uttered at a crucial point in the speaker's life, such a monologue can reach peaks of dramatic irony (see INDEX) as he unwittingly reveals more of his own nature than he intends to, or even more of the nature of his listeners than he himself presumably is aware of. Browning begins *in medias res,* as in *Andrea del Sarto:*

> But do not let us quarrel any more,
> No, my Lucrezia; bear with me for once;
> Sit down and all shall happen as you wish.

Other poems of his that will help you establish the characteristics of the genre are: *My Last Duchess, The Bishop Orders His Tomb, Fra Lippo Lippi, Soliloquy of the Spanish Cloister.*

Compare Browning's achievements in this form with Alfred Lord Tennyson's in *Ulysses,* T. S. Eliot's in *The Love Song of J. Alfred Prufrock,* and *Portrait of a Lady,* William Butler Yeats' in his "Crazy Jane" poems, and Frank Bidart's in *The War of Vaslav Nijinsky* (this last, like Browning's, based on a historical person). • ▲

(**Narrower scope:** Compare two of Browning's dramatic monologues with Bidart's. • ★)

Dramatic Soliloquy, Dramatic Monologue

In his development of the dramatic monologue, Browning was guided by Shakespeare's soliloquies. He even titled one of his monologues *Soliloquy of the Spanish Cloister*. But there are vital differences: The speaker of the dramatic soliloquy is alone in a setting already familiar to the audience, while the speaker of the dramatic monologue himself establishes setting and the presence of other characters. What Browning studied in Shakespeare, then, must have been his characters' psychological acumen, including self-analysis, at moments of high-pitched emotion.

Illustrate in detail the differences and similarities between such dramatic soliloquies as:

* Ransom's opening soliloquy in W. H. Auden, *The Ascent of F6;*
* Richard III's soliloquy "Now is the winter of our discontent" in Shakespeare's *Richard III;*
* Hamlet's "To be or not to be," "How all occasions do inform against me," and Claudius' "O my offense is rank," in Shakespeare's *Hamlet;*

and such dramatic monologues as those by Browning, Tennyson, Eliot, Yeats, and Bidart cited above. • ▲

Poet and Biographer on Dancer Nijinsky

Compare Frank Bidart's dramatic monologue *The War of Vaslav Nijinsky* with related materials in biographical works about the celebrated dancer. What liberties has Bidart taken? How may they be justified? • ▲

(**Wider scope:** What are the critics' reactions, especially in the dance magazines and journals? • ▲)

Rudyard Kipling's Changing Reputation

By 1900 Rudyard Kipling was the most popular poet in the English-speaking world. By the outbreak of World War I he was considered passé. But in the mid-1980s there started a revival of interest in his work. Consider the reasons for the rapid rise, rapid fall, and slow recovery of his reputation. Include: (1) the exotic setting of many of his poems ("Mandalay"); (2) his singing the praises of the common soldier ("Danny Deever"; "Tommy"); (3) his championing of chest-thumping masculinity; (4) his firm belief in the rectitude of British imperialism (his series about the Boer War) and in the superiority of the white race ("The White Man's Burden," written to encourage the Americans in their suppression of Filipino nationalism); (5) the rare poem in which he seems to have realized the value of national humility ("Recessional"). Consider the widespread belief among critics by 1940 that Kipling's verse was verbose, monotonous in its music, reactionary in its orientation. What are the reasons given now, by today's critics and reviewers, for the resurgence of interest? Which is the poem most likely to enjoy a steady popularity? • ★

Kipling and Gilbert: Four-Syllable Meters

As we have seen, two-syllable meters (rising: *iambic;* falling: *trochaic*) and three-syllable meters (rising: *anapestic;* falling: *dactylic*) are the most common in English. In the late nineteenth century, however, four-syllable verse enjoyed a vogue in the hands of W. S. Gilbert and Rudyard Kipling. Four-syllable rising is called *double iambic* (- / - \ , or - \ - /), as in Gilbert's *The Played-Out Humorist:*

Quixotic is his enterprise, and hopeless his adventure is

Four-syllable falling meter is called *double trochaic* (\ - / -, or / - \ -), as in Kipling's "Mandalay":

"Come you back, you British soldier, come you back to Mandalay!"

Notice that in the four-syllable foot, the stresses alternate between full (/) and half stress (\ ), or vice versa, leaving only one full stress in every four syllables. Do a full scansion of "Mandalay" (or of Kipling's "In the Neolithic Age") and of a passage from the Gilbert operetta libretto. What is the effect of such a large proportion of half stresses? In two- and three-syllable meters they are reserved for special effects. What do you and/or the critics see as the strengths and weaknesses of the four-syllable foot? • ▲

(**Wider scope:** Check books on prosody, rhyming dictionaries, handbooks of literary terms, etc., for more examples, more commentary. • ▲)

The Real Hero of Homer's *Iliad*

Some modern readers and critics see Hector, not Achilles, as the hero of Homer's war epic. What evidence do you see that Homer himself favored

Hector? In that case, what would the "message" of the epic be? Or is Hector a foil for Achilles? Is it possible for there to be two leading characters? If Achilles remains the undisputed hero, even after Homer has presented Hector in a sympathetic light, then what do you see as the poet's conclusions? After you formulate your own observations, check them out with Homeric critics who treat characterization in depth. Good start: the "Supplementary Materials" in the Pocket Books edition of Homer. • ★

The Common Man in *The Iliad*

What does Odysseus' treatment of Thersites tell us about Homer's society? If Agamemnon was conducting an assembly, what were Thersites' rights? (Compare the assembly that Telemachus conducts in *The Odyssey*.) What evidence do you see that Thersites' complaints are justified? How similar are they to Achilles' complaints? What do you see as the real grounds for Odysseus' punishment of Thersites? Why does Homer give Thersites the fullest description accorded anyone? Why did Thersites' ideas have to be put in the mouth of an ugly man? Check the word *thersitical* in an unabridged dictionary; again note the association of dissent with ugliness. How credible do you find the army's reaction to Thersites' speech? From Homer's treatment of the common man, which class in his society, do you imagine, was paying for his services? • ★

(**Wider scope:** Compare your answers to the above questions with typical critical discussions of Homer's characterization, starting perhaps with the Pocket Books edition and its "Supplementary Materials" cited above. • ▲)

Homeric Simile

Homer is famous for his *extended similes,* analogies in which one or both of the things compared are described elaborately, even including a long digression. Start with the similes used in *The Iliad,* Book IV, to describe how Menelaus' thighs are stained with blood; in Book XII, how the stones fall thickly in combat; in *The Odyssey,* Book V, how Odysseus rejoices on the third day of his ordeal at sea; in Book VIII, how Odysseus weeps after the bard has told the story of the Wooden Horse at Troy. Since the function of the simile is to explain the remote and the fictitious in terms of the immediate and the real, what do these similes tell us about the real life of Homer's audience? What do these long digressions tell us about the concentration of Homer's listeners? their imaginative powers? What would be a modern equivalent—free association? or what? • ★

(**Wider scope:** Compare your own observations with those of several modern critics of Homer. • ▲)

Longfellow's Similes in *Evangeline*

Henry Wadsworth Longfellow uses more than 80 similes in *Evangeline*. Some are comparisons in just a few words (e.g., lines 64, 138, 270); others are comparisons extended over several lines (e.g., 630–633, 1270–1275). Many similes are allusions to the Bible (e.g., lines 152–153, 485–486, 596–597). What is the overall effect of such frequent use of simile? What do you and/or the critics see as Longfellow's success with simile? • ★

(**Wider scope:** How many of Longfellow's similes qualify as Homeric simile [see Idea above]? Compare the Homeric similes cited above with the extended similes you find in Longfellow. • ★)

(**Wider still:** If you take a liking to Longfellow's long narrative style, extend the above studies to his *Hiawatha*. • ★)

Fact and Fiction: Longfellow's *Evangeline*

How much of Henry Wadsworth Longfellow's long narrative poem *Evangeline* is historically accurate? Note that historians disagree as to the motives the English had in sending the Acadians into exile; what are the latest views? To what extent does Longfellow make Acadian society a socialistic one, with ethical emphasis on cooperation rather than competition? Which specific characters are based on actual historical figures? Which historical facts did the poet change for the sake of poetry, story, plot, characterization? Start with histories of the colonial period, of the Acadians, and with biographies and literary studies of Longfellow; check *PMLA* and other MLA publication indexes. • ▲

Foil Characters in *Evangeline*

What effects does the poet achieve in making the fathers of Evangeline and Gabriel so different? and Evangeline so different from her father? See INDEX for "Foil." • ★

Absence of Evil People in Longfellow's *Evangeline*

What do you and/or the critics see as the overall effect of the absence of evil people among the main characters of *Evangeline?* of the idealization of the heroine? • ★

A Realistic Character Study of Evangeline and Gabriel

We know so little about the object of Evangeline's quest—Gabriel—that we begin to think of him mainly as a reflection of her feelings for him. Could he any longer be a real person for her, so that we could say she *knows* whom she seeks? Can you find any evidence that he seeks her? or avoids her? What would modern psychology say about Evangeline's search for him? Has he become a disembodied symbol for her? if so, what does her Quest symbolize? Check the most recent critical histories of nineteenth-century American literature, the latest scholarly studies of the poem, the psychological journals (e.g., *American Imago, Journal of Mental Imagery*). • ▲

Detective Work: The Homeric Questions

Three of the great scholarly questions have been: When did Homer compose his epics? Were they, indeed, composed by one man? Who was he? The first epic simile mentioned above (Book IV, *The Iliad*) proved to be an important clue to the date of composition. It indicated that *The Iliad* was composed in its final form after the technique of dyeing ivory had been introduced into Asia Minor from the East! T. L. Webster even studied the way Homer's patterns and themes correlate with eighth-century B.C. trends in Greek pottery! Even the computer has been brought into the Homeric questions. Check the 1961 *New York Times Index* for the front-page story headlined "Iliad One-Man Job, Computer Indicates."

The subject for papers/oral reports is as long or as limited as you want to make it. Start with the latest books on Homer. The Pocket Books editions (with "Supplementary Materials") might get you started; generally speaking, such supplementary materials in any editions will give you good leads to the never-ending detective work on Western civilization's oldest known author. • ▲

Detective Work: How Did Marlowe Die?

For centuries, the poet Christopher Marlowe's death was believed to be the result of a spontaneous tavern brawl. Thanks to modern detective work by J. L. Hotson (*The Death of Christopher Marlowe*) and M. Eccles (*Christopher Marlowe in London*), we now know that his death was elaborately planned and staged to appear as a spontaneous event. Report on the discovery of Marlowe's murder as exemplary of the scientific methods of modern literary scholarship. Of course, both Hotson and Eccles evoked full evaluations from their critics when their treatises appeared: Check especially those in scholarly journals and subsequent books and papers. • ▲

Detective Work: How Coleridge Composed

S. T. Coleridge published his "Kubla Khan: Or, a Vision in a Dream" as a psychological curiosity: He had composed it immediately after (opium-) dreaming its contents. Modern critics have probed for more details of the creative process involved. The seminal work is John Livingston Lowes' *The Road to Xanadu: A Study in the Ways of the Imagination*. In your search for other critics' reactions be sure to include Kenneth Burke's essay "Kubla Khan." • ▲

American Science and English Poetry

The American botanist William Bartram published in 1791 his *Travels through North and South Carolina, Georgia, East and West Florida, the Cherokee Country, the Extensive Territories of the Muscogees, or Creek Confederacy, and the Country of the Choctaws*. This work had an extraordinary three-fold effect on European cultural life: (1) It reported Bartram's discovery of hundreds of species of flora and fauna hitherto unknown to European science; (2) it offered spectacular evidence that Rousseau's theory of the "Noble Savage" might be true; (3) it had a remarkable effect on the poetry of the English Romantics, e.g., Samuel Taylor Coleridge's "Kubla Khan" and William Wordsworth's "Ruth" and "She Was a Phantom of Delight."

Two trains of Ideas here for papers and reports:

1. "The Interaction of Science and Poetry: Bartram's Effect on the Romantics." (You could extend this to include the influence of other scientists on the poets, who kept well abreast of new developments.) • ▲

2. "Why is Bartram So Well-Known in Europe and Hardly Known in His Own Land?" (For one thing, his ideas about the Noble Savage, a blend of scientific objectivity and Quaker openmindedness, did not fit well with state and federal policies toward the Native American, etc.) • ▲

Faust—His Doings at Los Alamos (1945)

Compare the use of the Faust legend by two English-speaking poets working nearly four centuries apart: the Elizabethan playwright Christopher Marlowe's *Tragical History of Doctor Faustus* and the World War II American GI Karl Shapiro's "The Progress of Faust." Who is the "fair Phrygian"? Is she "the face that launched a thousand ships"? Note that the Faust legend had a life of its own outside sophisticated literature, as Shapiro's allusion to the peasants' puppet plays indicates. Note too that Marlowe's source was doubtless Johann Spies' *Volksbuch* (chapbook), translated into English before Marlowe worked on his dramatic version.

What does Shapiro's account imply about the nature of nuclear war? militarism? about Baconian science, the Age of Reason, the French Revolution? (Quite a controversial poem!) How does each poet put chronology to good use for his purposes? Compare Marlowe's "mighty line" (as Ben Jonson called his blank verse) to Shapiro's low-key, often eleven-syllable line, rhyming version. How well does each poet's meter suit his subject matter, interpretation, intentions? • ▲

(**Much wider scope:** If you become fascinated by the Faust theme, read a good recent translation of J. W. von Goethe's *Faust.* How does Goethe's interpretation, in his Part Two especially, compare with Shapiro's? • ▲)

Rimbaud, "The Beats," The Myth of Revolt

The French poet Arthur Rimbaud ran away from home at age 15, wrote "The Drunken Boat," his most famous poem, by the age of 17, published his classic *A Season in Hell* at 19, gave up literature before he was 20, and, always in flight from the ordinary and the bourgeois, settled in Abyssinia. His Hell is not the conventional place for the guilty dead, like Dante's, but rather a life on earth of repression by family, church, government. In his *Hell,* he wrote "I accustomed myself to create visionary literature with extraordinary images and symbols." See also *The Illuminations*, published in 1886, fifteen years after it was written.

Report on Rimbaud's influence on one or all of the American "Beat Generation" writers, Allen Ginsberg, Gregory Corso, Gary Snyder, Jack Kerouac. • ▲

Influence of Poet X on Poet Y

All creative artists develop their own style by combining (a) techniques they select from forebears they admire with (b) their own original ideas and talents. Report on the literary influence of an older poet on a younger, an influence generally conceded by most critics. Compare them in terms of characteristic music, diction, phrasing, metaphor, tone, meaning. How much does the younger poet owe to the older? What is it in the younger poet's style that is uniquely his/hers?

Here are some typical lines of influence in twentieth-century Anglo-American poetry as observed by critics and scholars:

William Butler Yeats ⟶ Theodore Roethke

William Butler Yeats ⟶ ⎫
W. H. Auden ⟶ ⎬ John Berryman

William Carlos Williams ⟶ ⎫
Marianne Moore ⟶ ⎬ A. R. Ammons

Wallace Stevens ⟶ ⎫
W. H. Auden ⟶ ⎬ James Merrill

Robert Frost ⟶ ⎫
William Carlos Williams ⟶ ⎬ Adrienne Rich

Wallace Stevens ⟶ ⎫
T. S. Eliot ⟶ ⎬ John Ashbery

Ezra Pound ⟶ ⎫
T. S. Eliot ⟶ ⎬ Robert Lowell

Robert Hayden ⟶ Michael Harper

Robert Lowell ⟶ Frank Bidart

In a study of this nature, it's taken for granted that you would consult the critics and historians of poetry. ○ ▲

• average difficulty	○ previous knowledge	★ most libraries
▲ larger library	☐ visual component	♬ audio component

Auden and Shapiro on the Average Man

Both W. H. Auden's poem "The Unknown Citizen" and Karl Shapiro's "Elegy for a Dead Soldier" give a detailed picture of "the average man." Compare the two poems on several or all of these grounds: (1) their overall judgment of the ordinary person, (2) what the poets see as the cause of this person's condition, (3) what they see as the relation between the citizen and the modern state, (4) the details each poet uses to characterize his subject, (5) their relative sympathy for the average person, (6) their use of irony, (7) their tone, (8) the different prosodic techniques, especially their metric patterns, rhyme schemes, use of enjambement. What do these poems, separately or together, make you want to *do?* ● ▲

(**Wider scope:** Include Auden's "Sonnet on a Dead Chinese Soldier," who "added meaning like a comma." ● ▲)

Return of the Long Poem in American Publishing

In the 1980s, the book-length narrative poem made a comeback in commercial publishing in America. Start with Marc Kaminsky's *The Road from Hiroshima* and Leo Connellan's *The Clear Blue Lobster-Water Country*. What do these works establish as the scope of today's narrative poetry? How do they compare in techniques and themes? Based on such works, what do you and/or the critics see as the future of the long narrative poem in American commercial publishing? ● ▲

Publication of Poetry and the Small-Press World

The key word in the previous idea is "commercial." For half a century, American commercial publishers have issued very little of the good poetry being written. The bulk of that responsibility has been borne by the "noncommercial" or "small" presses. For example, it was City Lights Press of San Francisco that launched Allen Ginsberg on his career with *Howl*. To get the full picture about the long narrative poem, then, we have to ask: How many such works have *the small presses* published? And how much attention have the commercial reviewers paid to *them?* The research paths you'll have to follow will be the same as for the next Idea. ● ▲

The Small Press World: Its Place in American Literature

Since most small presses publish mainly poetry, this is the genre through which to explore this world initially. Keep in mind, though, their role in developing new fiction. Your best guides: a local librarian sympathetic to the "small press" and the "little mag" who (1) subscribes to the *Directory of American Poets and Fiction Writers* and *Poets and Writers,* their trade journal, to such other directories as *The Poet's Market,* and to such other periodicals as *Small Press* and *Small Press Review;* and (2) can lead you to recent issues of librarians' journals that publish occasional columns/articles about small press offerings. From the *Directory of American Poets and Fiction Writers* you can get addresses of enough key people in this "alternative world" to get you started: poet-publishers Suzanne Zavrian, Bill Zavatsky, Len Fulton, Robert Hershon, others they will refer you to, who can give you leads to your questions about the history, aims, functions, state of the small press world. You are now investigating the biggest "unknown" phenomenon in the history of literature! • ▲

Longfellow's and Kaminsky's Long Narrative Poems Compared

No two long narrative poems could be more different than Henry Wadsworth Longfellow's *Evangeline* and Marc Kaminsky's *The Road from Hiroshima.* Your comparison should reveal vast changes, in the past century, in the perception of the function of the genre, the development of techniques suitable to that function and to the modern psyche and its tastes in poetry. Check carefully into differences in plotting, characterization, setting, tone, style, use of figures of speech, connotation, overall message. • ★

• average difficulty	○ previous knowledge
▲ larger library	□ visual component

★ most libraries
♫ audio component

6

Ideas about Literary Nonfiction

GENERAL IDEAS APPLICABLE
TO ALL NONFICTION

As its name makes clear by negation, *non*fiction is *not* about imaginary situations. It is rather that vast body of writing about *real* persons, events, places, things, ideas, and issues in which the author is under obligation to distinguish between the known facts, on the one hand, and interpretation, conjecture, and preferences, on the other. One glance over our checklist of master themes of world literature (pp. 9–15) and you realize that nonfiction is the genre that gives us the most consistent reminders, the steadiest feedback on the big questions. Our continuous concern with closing the gap between illusion and reality, with the relation between ourselves and the rest of the world, with defining patriotism, love, justice in day-to-day life, makes us a nation of readers of history, philosophy, (auto)biography, memoirs, travel accounts, scholarship and criticism, scientific reports and speculation, textbooks, "how-to" writing and other instructional prose, news stories, "feature articles," and magazine pieces on any conceivable topic.

Most nonfiction is strictly practical and utilitarian in nature, designed and rendered for one-time use. But some of it—from Montaigne's essays to Alex Haley's *Roots*—can be enjoyed, reread, and discussed for its style, tone, and structure as well as for its content. Such literary nonfiction is our concern in this section.

Themes in Nonfiction: Explicit or Implicit?

By their very nature—as works in which suspense is highly valued—*plays and stories tend not to declare their themes explicitly*. It was because the most important themes in drama/fiction might be implicit, to be inferred by you, that we gave you a checklist of "master themes," just to nudge your perceptions along. However, also by its very nature—as the genre that tries to enlighten and counsel as directly as possible—*nonfiction tends to declare its themes explicitly and early*.

Very often nonfiction will state its subject, even its conclusions, in its title and/or in its opening sentences. True, sometimes the author of a highly impressionistic nonfiction piece—e.g., Tom Wolfe—might be just as coy about making his "point" as James Joyce is in fiction. But that's rare.

Depending on the scope of your assignment, compare three or more essays/articles by as many different authors for the way they state their theme: At which point in the development? Is it posed early as a question, answered at the end? Or are the questions and answers given together, with the rest of the piece devoted to proof, discussion, implication?

Since an author's placing of the fullest statement of his meaning is likely to determine all the rest of his structure, you might prefer to discuss theme and structure together (see next Idea). Your crucial concern, as in all literary criticism, is the effectiveness of the author's tactics. • ★

Structures of Ideas in Short Nonfiction

Form in literature has two purposes. It must create curiosity about the subject and it must satisfy that curiosity. Depending on the scope of your assignment, compare three or more nonfiction pieces by as many authors for the way they excite and feed curiosity. Most likely their forms will resemble some general pattern known to all practitioners of the prose art. Here are several of the standard patterns:

Classical (logical) structure. The author states his thesis, his controlling idea, in his introduction; devotes the body to arguments or evidence for his thesis; concludes with a summary of the main points he has established.

Report Form (single). The writer devotes her introduction to a history of the problem, her aim, scope, and method of attack; the body to a description of the work done and a discussion thereof; the final section to conclusions.

Double-Report Form. The writer devotes her introduction to an overall summary of both the problem/question, the work done, and the conclusions/ answers; the second part to a detailed restatement of both the problem and the solution.

Inverted Pyramid. So it's called in the newspaper world. The "lead" contains general-summary answers to the questions Who? When? Where? Why? What? and How? (known as "the five W's"); the lead usually plays up one of the W's; the second part of the article gives detailed answers to the curiosity aroused by the lead; the third part, either near the end or interwoven with part two, gives background information. The name of this pattern is based on the fact that the broadest statements are made at the top, and the story then narrows down to finer and finer details.

Inductive Approach. The classical (logical) structure, the double-report form, and the inverted pyramid are all *deductive:* that is, they go from the general to the specific. The single-report form is *inductive:* it goes from the specific to the general, working step-by-step from questions through to answers. When the essayist or magazine-article writer is confident he can attract and hold his reader's attention that way, he too might use an inductive approach. He could begin with specific examples, anecdotes, illustrations that foreshadow his declaration of the broad problem, which he can then proceed to discuss on an argumentational level, working toward conclusions and/or recommendations. Short essays—like newspaper editorials—are often written with the inductive approach.

Narrative Structure. The author recounts the *story* of his/her discovery, treating, in chronological order, the way a problem/question arose, how he or she went about finding the answers, with maybe some reflections on the significance of the journey at the end. *New Yorker* profiles are usually narrative and inductive in form. A classic example is William Whitworth's "On the Tide of the Times" in the September 24, 1966 issue.

Impressionistic Structure. While the narrative structure results, in some sense, in a personal story, admittedly somewhat subjective, it still keeps its focus on the aim and the sequence of the quest. The impressionistic article is so highly personal, so largely devoted to the author's impressions, that it abandons the chronological and the logical for the psychological form: it is structured mainly by free association. A classic example (taken from the same period as Whitworth's so as to make comparison easier within the history of the genre) is Tom Wolfe's "Ramito! Jibaro Hero!," a Sunday piece reprinted in Gerald Walker's *Best Magazine Articles of 1966*.

Fiction Structure. Starting in that same period, the Sixties, when nonfiction writers deliberately went about raising the artistic level of their work, they began structuring their articles as much as possible like short stories. For a classic example see Gay Talese's piece on Joe Louis in *Esquire* (1962).

Combination Structures. The experienced writer combines these forms in any way that arouses his or her audience's attention and satisfies their curiosity. He or she might use an inverted pyramid for the first section, an inductive approach for the second, and so on. Nothing will teach you so much about how to improve your own writing as a careful analysis of the patterns designed by the pros.

To analyse the pattern used in any single piece of nonfiction, compare it with the types described here. For a complete report on these patterns, find one example for each of the nine structures discussed above. • ▲

Structures of Ideas in Nonfiction Books

Structuring a nonfiction book, the author might (1) simply use an expanded version of one of the forms described above, or (2) use a combination of these forms, a different one perhaps in each chapter, or (3), as a result of the 1960s revolution in nonfiction, structure his/her book like a novel. For example, the opening chapter might be a complete statement of the questions to be taken up, with an analysis into subtopics; most of the succeeding chapters then would each take up one of the subtopics, each organized internally according to one of the forms for a short piece; the final chapter(s) would be a thorough statement of the conclusions justified by the previous discussion. *Or* the opening chapter might give a complete summary of both the questions/ problems and the answers/conclusions, the following chapters being devoted to working out the details. *Or* the book might open, like a well-crafted novel, *in medias res,* and develop through flashbacks and postponed revelations, like the classic "nonfiction novel" *In Cold Blood* by Truman Capote.

Ideas here: (1) Select at least two nonfiction books on the same subject (the space effort? environmental problems? the Vietnam War?) that use quite different structures. Show why each structure is (or is not) suitable for the subject and the author's approach and aims. (2) Keep reading reviews in *The New York Times Book Review, The New York Review of Books,* or in one of the professional journals in your own major field, until you have two or more critiques of the structures the authors use, at least one of them saying that the arrangement of materials does not work well. Read the books yourself. Are the critics right? Report on this alert as one of the services we expect the critic to render. • ▲

Point of View in Nonfiction

As our discussion of structure suggests, authors of nonfiction may use either the third-person, objective-observer point of view, or the first-person, subjective approach. In formal reports, especially, the third-person approach is usually required as being "more objective." Actually, it's just as easy to distort the facts in the third person; and sometimes use of the first person helps the reader to concentrate on the subject matter. Certainly the famous profiles developed by *The New Yorker* seem to lose nothing in objective content just because the author also adds some subjective information.

According to the scope of your assignment, select at least two first-person articles and at least two third-person pieces, all from magazines of established literary reputation, and compare the psychological effects of the two approaches on the reader. • ▲

Use of Metaphor in Nonfiction Writing

Even in the most practical writing, authors find it advisable to use metaphors to help their readers at least to visualize the subject, at best to thrill to it. (Check INDEX for definition.) Thus in an article on wines in *Gourmet* magazine, Frederick S. Wildman, Jr., describes how he went "wandering through what is now known as one of the world's great vineyard regions—the necklace of counties that surrounds San Francisco Bay." And in his classic report on *The Water Supply of the City of Rome*, Sextus Julius Frontinus describes water rushing in from the aqueducts and slowing down in the catch-basins as "taking fresh breath . . . after the run." Read several articles in magazines of literary merit and report on "How Metaphors Help the Nonfiction Writer to Communicate the Excitement of His Subject." • ★

Characterization Techniques in Today's Nonfiction

Since the 1960s, nonfiction writers have used fiction techniques to recreate actual persons who appear in their writing. *Ideas here:* Check INDEX and review characterization techniques used in drama and fiction. Then, adjusting to the scope of your assignment, report on two or more recent nonfiction classics: How do their authors build characters? Select nonfiction works like Tom Wolfe's *The Kandy-Kolored Tangerine-Flake Streamline Baby, The Right Stuff;* Norman Mailer's *Armies of the Night, Miami and the Siege of Chicago;* William

O'Rourke's *The Harrisburg Seven and the New Catholic Left;* Truman Capote's *In Cold Blood.*

Or apply the same question to recent biographies, e.g., Bruce Cook's *Dalton Trumbo;* Peter Brent's *Charles Darwin;* Hilary Mills' *Mailer;* W. Jackson Bate's *Samuel Johnson.* You might find it easier to discover your authors' methods by concentrating on the way they bring to life the *minor* characters in the action. • ★

SPECIFIC IDEAS ABOUT LITERARY NONFICTION

Setting Recreated in Travel Literature

Just as characterization is the great test of biographers, so is setting to travel writers. What techniques do they use to put their readers down in a strange valley among strange people? Which travel writers make every place sound like Paradise, which make each place unique? Depending on the scope of your assignment, either (1) compare five travel pieces that appear in publications like *National Geographic, Travel and Leisure,* or the Travel Section of the Sunday *New York Times;* or (2) analyze the techniques the authors use in classic travel books like William Bartram, *Travels through North and South Carolina, Georgia, East and West Florida, The Cherokee Country, etc.;* Charles Dickens, *American Notes;* Sidney Lanier, *Florida;* D. H. Lawrence, *Mornings in Mexico, Sea and Sardinia;* Ken Gangemi, *The Volcanoes from Puebla.* • ★

The "New" ("Gut") Journalism: History and Philosophy

In fall 1962 Gay Talese published an article in *Esquire* called "Joe Louis: The King as a Middle-Aged Man." In tone and approach, most of the piece read like quality fiction. Soon after, Truman Capote published *In Cold Blood,* his account of the life and hanging of two young murderers. True, this was nonfiction, but it was organized and treated like drama. Capote called it his "nonfiction novel" and it was very readily adapted to film.

What prompted this revolution in nonfiction writing—"dethroning the novel as the number one literary genre," as Tom Wolfe boasted: "starting the first new direction in American literature in half a century"? Why is it called "gut" journalism? For the history of the new journalism movement, see Dan

Wakefield's "The Personal Voice and the Impersonal Eye" in June 1966 *Atlantic;* Wolfe's three articles in *New York* magazine (starting February 14, 1972), or his expanded treatment in *The New Journalism: With an Anthology Edited by Tom Wolfe and E. W. Johnson*; and Michael L. Johnson, *The New Journalism*. For the philosophy of the movement, by one of its greatest practitioners, read Seymour Krim's *Views of a Nearsighted Cannoneer* and *Shake It for the World, Smartass.* • ▲ ☐

The "New" Journalism: How Different from the "Old"?

In "The Birth of 'The New Journalism'; Eyewitness Report by Tom Wolfe" (*New York*, February 14, 1972), note the periodicals which pioneered in the new nonfiction techniques (*Esquire, The New York Herald Tribune, New York*, etc.). Study several issues of these periodicals from the Fifties, i.e., in the heyday of the "old" journalism; then read Sixties issues containing typical "new" journalism pieces cited by Wolfe. What is the literary difference between the old and the new, especially in tone, subject matter, structure, style? • ▲

"Gut" Journalism: Its Classic Books

Study and report on the literary maneuvers used in several of the classic books of the "gut" journalism movement, e.g., Truman Capote's *In Cold Blood;* Norman Mailer's *Advertisements for Myself, Armies of the Night, Of a Fire on the Moon, The Prisoner of Sex, The Executioner's Song;* Tom Wolfe's *The Right Stuff, The Kandy-Kolored Tangerine-Flake Streamline Baby;* William O'Rourke's *The Harrisburg Seven and the New Catholic Left.* • ▲

Thoreau's *Civil Disobedience:* Its World-Wide Influence

One of the most influential nonfiction works of all time is Henry David Thoreau's *Civil Disobedience*. This essay directly taught Mahatma Gandhi how to free 400,000,000 Indians through bloodless revolution. It has been the bible for nonviolent dissenters in Thoreau's home country, especially during and since the 1960s. In the 1980s Justice Myron Bright, senior judge of the U.S. Eighth Circuit Court of Appeals in St. Louis, rendered this opinion: "We must recognize that civil disobedience . . . is ingrained in our society and the moral correctness of political protestors' views has on occasion served to change and better our society." He cited as major steps in the history of civil disobedience the Boston Tea Party, the signing of the Declaration of Independence, the freeing of the slaves by operation of the underground railroad, and current protests against nuclear annihilation. *Ideas here:* Report on the 1985 trial of five Catholic peace activists as reviewed by Justice Bright; on Thoreau's essay as the basis for Bright's decision; how Bright updated Thoreau; why dissenters have to be carefully trained in the exercise of civil disobedience; Gandhi's practice of Thoreau's theory; Thoreau's practice of his own theory—why he refused to pay his taxes and went to jail; what is it about Thoreau's writing techniques that help make the essay so cogent and influential? • ★

The Sixties as Seen by Didion, Cleaver, Bernard, Mailer

The 1960s was a period of social turbulence in which students, blacks, women, civil rights workers, citizens opposed to war, all struggled for a greater voice in the nation's—and in their own—affairs. For four different but overlapping views by four vigorous and perceptive writers, compare and contrast Eldridge Cleaver's *Soul on Ice,* Sidney Bernard's *This Way to the Apocalypse,* Norman Mailer's *Miami and the Siege of Chicago* and *Armies of the Night,* and Joan Didion's *The White Album.* What do you and/or the critics see as the merits/demerits of these movements? of these books as literature? • ▲

(**Wider scope:** Follow through on some of the writers that these four authors refer to: Whom did they see as their main influences? • ▲)

Essays: "Attempts," Formal and Informal

An essay is a short prose composition on some limited topic. It gets its name from the inventor of the genre, Michel Eyquem de Montaigne (1533–1592), who called his short prose pieces "essais," French for "attempts." The essay attempts to explore a subject and reach some better understanding of it—sometimes an understanding as distinct from a conclusion: as a skeptic, Montaigne hesitated to settle on any final conclusions on anything. His style is definitely personal, familiar, conversational, subjective, even when his content is more informative, insightful, and profound.

Sir Francis Bacon (1561–1626) adopted Montaigne's name *essays,* for his own short compositions. But Bacon's style is compact, impersonal, authoritative. And so, in retrospect today, we divide essays into two broad types: the *informal* (or familiar or personal) essay, like Montaigne's, and the *formal* essay, like Bacon's.

Scan the table of contents of Montaigne's 94 and Bacon's 58 essays. Select one or two by each on similar or related topics. Compare them (with specific quotes) for their style, tone, themes. Who is more interested in advancing a method, a process, of thinking? Who is more concerned with presenting polished conclusions? Who is more readable? Who is more quotable? • ★

(**Wider scope:** Include in your study the nineteenth-century American writers Ralph Waldo Emerson and Oliver Wendell Holmes. How does the distinction between formal and informal essays serve you now? Apply the same questions. • ★)

The Essay: Four Stages in Its Development

Interested in a more thorough study of types and stages of the essay? By the eighteenth century, when the distinction between the Montaignean "informal" and the Baconian "formal" essay was firmly established, leading writers began to seek a middle ground. Joseph Addison (1672–1719), Richard Steele (1672–1729), Samuel Johnson (1709–1784), and Oliver Goldsmith (1730–1774) produced essays for periodical publication that were neither so personal, so subjective, as Montaigne's, nor so severely formal as Bacon's. This great diversification in tone and approach led naturally to the fourth stage of essay development in the twentieth century. Now the formal essay has branched out into many types, many of them better known by such names as the magazine article, "the lead editorial," the "op/ed" piece, the master's essay, the essay-review, the position paper, the "Introduction" or "Foreword" or "Afterword," the engineering report, etc. And the informal essay also enjoys perennial popularity. On September 15, 1986, for example, we read over morning coffee a *New York Times* review of *We Irish: Essays on Irish Literature and Society* by Dennis Donoghue and then, in the October *Esquire,* an article by Gay Talese called "White Widows," which the editors had tagged, at the top of the page, "ESSAY."

To discuss the history of the essay, then, you might have to read more than four to represent its four stages of growth. Try to assemble essays on one or two related themes with a roster of authors somewhat like the following to represent the main stages: (1) Montaigne; (2) Bacon; (3) Addison or Steele, Johnson, Goldsmith, Charles Lamb, William Hazlitt, Ralph Waldo Emerson, Oliver Wendell Holmes, Henry David Thoreau, Oscar Wilde; (4) E. B. White, Joseph Wood Krutch, and at least three others representing the spread of types today: e.g., Susan Sontag, Gay Talese, O. H. Ammann (his 1926 report on the George

Washington Bridge), William Packard, Ralph Nader. Compare their essays for tone, organization, treatment of theme. Which ones are formal, casual, loose in structure? which formal, strictly businesslike, logical? which aim for timelessness, which for immediate and admittedly ephemeral attention?

In conclusion: What do you and/or the critics see as the changing function of the essay in the last four centuries of western culture? • ▲

Montaigne's Tolerance and Modern Philosophy

Voltaire, the Encyclopedists (especially Denis Diderot), and many nineteenth-century philosophers looked upon Montaigne as their teacher. His tolerance for diversity of opinion, his skepticism about absolutes, helped undermine dogmatism and thus prepared the way for pioneering modern thought. Consult biographies, histories of literature and of philosophy, and report on "Montaigne: A Catalyst of Modern Philosophy." • ▲

Your Teacher's Head: What Montaigne Advises

". . . one should choose a teacher who has a well-made head rather than a well-filled head." Thus Montaigne stressed the importance of acquiring judgment rather than mere information. *Some ideas here:* (1) In histories and encyclopedias of education, research "Montaigne's Influence on Education." (2) Read several of Montaigne's essays that bear directly or indirectly on education. In what ways does he portray the good and the bad teachers that you have known? Write on "Montaigne in Today's Classroom." • ★

Montaigne's Broadmindedness: Result of Mixed Ancestry?

To what extent are Montaigne's celebrated tolerance, open-mindedness, and skepticism a result of his mixed ancestry and unfortunate experiences with French religious politics? He was himself a French Catholic; his mother was descended from Spanish Jews; three of his brothers and sisters were French Protestants. He was thus personally affected by the St. Bartholomew's Day massacre (of Protestants by the Catholic monarchy); and he was imprisoned during the civil strife of 1588. He said of his own politicoreligious neutrality that he passed for a Papist among Protestants, and a heretic among Catholic zealots. What do you and/or the biographers, critics, and literary historians see as the connections between his family ties and experience, on the one hand, and his ideas on the other? • ▲

Montaigne's Main Doctrines: Ataraxia, Acatalepsia

Find and report on several passages in Montaigne that illustrate two of his main doctrines:

- *Ataraxia:* the necessity of suspending intellectual judgment indefinitely, because the truth consists of the sum total of all points of view; and
- *Acatalepsia:* the belief that against every true statement that is made, an opposite statement can be made that is also true. • ★

Montaigne's Love of Beasts: One of His Main Arguments

Montaigne's theriophily, or love of beasts, provides him with some of his main arguments. Report on his essays "Of Cannibalism" and "Apology for Raymond Sebond" to show how he makes use of comparisons between humans and beasts. • ★

Montaigne's Conception of Human Character

Is an act of heroism a matter of character or of circumstances? Report on Montaigne's concept of the self (is it many selves?) in his essay "The Inconsistency of Our Actions." • ★

Montaigne and Freud: Role of the Irrational

What does Montaigne see as the value of the irrational and the nonverbal in a world dedicated to reason? To what extent does he foreshadow Freud in this area? Start with his "Apology for Raymond Sebond" and "The Inconsistency of Our Actions." • ★

Joseph Addison's Attack on "Rules" in Literature

In collaboration with Richard Steele, Joseph Addison published *The Tatler* (1709–1711), a triweekly periodical of news and opinion. In his lead essay in *Tatler* #163, "Ned Softly the Poet," Addison ridicules the kind of writer who *composes* by the rules; and in *Tatler* #165, "Character of Sir Timothy Tittle," he satirizes the kind of critic who *judges* literary works by the rules. (For background on these rules, see INDEX for Three Unities and Prosody; check especially on Rhythm as opposed to Meter.) Report on "Addison's Essays on the Rules versus the Imagination." • ★

Joseph Addison's Treatment of Women

After two years of publishing the *Tatler* (see Idea above), Addison and Steele collaborated on *The Spectator,* a daily sheet. How did Addison treat women in these two periodicals? Start with the young lady who routs the critic in "Character of Sir Timothy Tittle (*Tatler* #165); include among the essays you study "The Uses of *The Spectator*" (the famous #10), "Dissection of a Coquette's Heart" (*Spectator* #281), and "The Fine Lady's Journal" (*Spectator* #323). • ★

Spectator and *Catch-22* on Roger de Coverley

Perhaps the most famous of the characters to appear in the *Spectator* was Sir Roger de Coverley, a typical country squire. The series of essays devoted to Sir Roger's circle is usually called—and often published separately as—"The Roger de Coverley Papers." Joseph Heller resurrected Sir Roger in his World War II novel *Catch-22* where he reappears as Major —— de Coverley. Compare the two characterizations of de Coverley. What is Heller saying about Addison's conception? Why is de Coverley suitable for Heller's purposes? Why is Heller's de Coverley without a first name? And what does *roger* mean in the Air Force? For de Coverley's significance for Addison's eighteenth-century audience, consult a standard history of literature; for his place in Heller's world, see "Mythic Imagery in Catch-22" in *Journal of Mental Imagery,* 1982, 6, pp. 145–156, and/or the Monarch Note *Joseph Heller's "Catch-22."* • ▲

Why Give "Days and Nights" to Addison's Volumes?

Dr. Samuel Johnson said: "Whoever wishes to attain an English style familiar but not coarse, and elegant but not ostentatious, must give his days and nights to the volumes of Addison." And this famous prose style is best studied in Addison's essays. One of his most successful disciples was Benjamin Franklin. *Ideas here:* (1) Answer the questions posed in the headline above. Analyze some of the essays and arrive at your own description of Addison's style. (See Style in INDEX.) Test out Johnson's description; give examples of his points. What other characteristics of Addison's style would you like to acquire for your own? (2) Read Ben Franklin's *Autobiography* and *Poor Richard's Almanac*. What evidence do you see that Franklin had studied Addison's style? What do Franklin's and Addison's styles have in common? In what ways does Franklin fall below Addison's standard, and in what ways does he surpass him? Report on "A Study of Style in Addison and Franklin." • ★

Old-Style Biography, New-Style Biography

Biography is one of the oldest literary forms. Probably it started as oral literature, tales of heroic ancestors passed on by word of mouth from one generation to the next. And probably that's how the oldest conception of biography developed: namely, that it should set up ideals of behavior based on the exploits of successful leaders. In any event, the oldest written biographies all seem conceived as proving or illustrating a thesis or a moral. The stories of the patriarchs in the Hebrew Bible aim to establish their prestige as God's handpicked agents; the four Gospels in the New Testament argue that Jesus was the Messiah and the Son of God; Plutarch's *Parallel Lives* show that the Greeks had fared well in the world of action; and the medieval hagiographies exemplify the traits that lead one to become a saint and to justify the adoration of saints.

This conception of biography as providing models of how to live can be seen at its moralizing worst in Parson Mason Locke Weems' life of Washington. Weems not only put impossibly priggish lines into the boy's mouth ("Father, I cannot tell a lie, I did it with my little hatchet"); he invented whatever material he needed to serve his purpose, like the entire scene of the to-do over a cherry tree.

The tendency to idealize and whitewash the subject persisted into the early twentieth century. Lytton Strachey had to write his collection of four short biographies of *Eminent Victorians* in order to correct the hagiographies then in print about them. And of course, most "campaign biographies"—life stories of candidates for public office—either glorify or vilify the person under "study," depending on which party the author supports. Good examples: biographies of Herbert Hoover published during the Presidential campaign of 1931.

Today's concept of the function of biography is that it should provide as complete and objective an account of a real life as possible. What were the saint's vices, failures? What did the youthful George really do in his spare time?

What did Jacob and Joseph do for fun? What were their relations with their sisters and mothers (female relatives of heroes are rarely mentioned in the Bible)? Old-style biography omitted whatever did not suit the writer's predetermined purpose; it was deductive in its approach. New-style biography accumulates the full truth from every available source—interviews, correspondence, family papers, previous accounts. Inductive in its approach, it reconstructs the character from the evidence, unflattering mixture of strengths and weaknesses though it may be.

The first such definitive biography was James Boswell's *Life of Samuel Johnson*. Good current examples are James Thomas Flexner's four-volume life of Washington, Nigel Hamilton's three-volume work on Field Marshal Viscount Montgomery of El Alamein, and Ernest Jones' three-volume life of Freud.

The psychological approach to biography—fostered first by the Romanticist interest in subjectivity and later by the Freudian movement—attempts to recreate the inner experience of the subject. Freud's *Leonardo da Vinci* is an early example. Already acknowledged as a classic in psychobiography is Bernard Solomon's *Beethoven*.

Now, along these lines you have *numerous Ideas for papers:*

- Compare Nathaniel Hawthorne's campaign biography of his college friend, Franklin Pierce, with that of President Pierce written more than a century later (revised edition, 1958) by R. F. Nichols. How are the two biographers' respective relations to their subjects reflected in their books? What does Nichols include about Pierce's pre–White House life that Hawthorne did not?
- Compare all of the campaign biographies of Herbert Hoover. Why did some of them doubt that Hoover had worked on the translation of Georgius Agricola's Latin treatise that bears Hoover's name?
- Compare Weems' life of Washington with Flexner's; what did their critics say at the time of publication? Discuss one as deductive (in the sense mentioned above), one as inductive, and explain the ways in which the difference in approach is obvious.
- Compare the life of Jesus of Nazareth as officially portrayed in the New Testament with those written by secular authors, Ernest Renan, Ian Wilson, *et al.*
- Compare a medieval biography of a saint with a modern secular account.
- Consider one or more of Lytton Strachey's subjects in *Eminent Victorians:* in each case, read at least one pre-Strachey biography. How do the two

authors' accounts differ? How do you and/or the critics regard the differences?

- Compare Izaak Walton's *Life of Dr. John Donne* (1640) with R. C. Bald's *John Donne: A Life* (1970); and/or Walton's *Life of George Herbert* (1670) with Margaret Bottrall's *George Herbert* (1954) or with Amy M. Charles' *The Life of George Herbert* (1977). What is the difference in the "admirer's approach" and the biographer's method?
- Consider one or more of Plutarch's *Lives;* compare it or them to a later author's account.
- Compare Freud's study of da Vinci with any standard pre-Freudian account. How do you and/or the critics regard the differences?
- Report on the three stages in biographical treatment of Beethoven: one published soon after his death; another in the twentieth century before Solomon's; and Solomon's. What do the differences reveal about changing concepts of the responsibility of the biographer? • ▲

Advantages/Disadvantages of the Brief Biography

Many a classic work in biography is actually a series of brief accounts of several, even many subjects. What are the advantages of such a treatment? Notice that usually there is some declared link among the subjects, evident in the very titles: Giorgio Vasari's *Lives of the Most Eminent Painters, Sculptors, and Architects;* Samuel Smiles' *Lives of the Engineers;* Lytton Strachey's *Eminent Victorians;* Paul de Kruif's *Microbe Hunters;* Ulick O'Connor's *All the Olympians: A Biographical Portrait of the Irish Literary Renaissance;* Russell F. Weigley's *Eisenhower's Lieutenants.* Sometimes the linkage is more subtle, as in Plutarch's *Parallel Lives* or John Aubrey's *Brief Lives.* Possibilities:

- Read one or more of such "group portraits" and consider the advantages the author reaps by treating several people together. Does it better enable him to make generalizations about a period? about a profession? to establish causes for behavior? to catch his subjects in apposite interactions? Consult the critics' as well as your own reactions.
- Read just one of the "brief" lives and compare it with a longer study of the same subject. What advantages does each study enjoy because of its duration? How well did the author of the "brief" study condense his materials, or select and reject materials from what was available to him? • ▲

Samuel Johnson as Portrayed by Different Biographers

James Boswell's *Life of Johnson* is "the most famous single work of biographical art in the whole of literature," writes W. Jackson Bate. Yet Bate himself saw the need for, and wrote, another *Samuel Johnson,* which was such a masterful feat that *The New York Times Book Review* called Bate "Man of the Year." Why was another biography necessary? Boswell knew Johnson well; in a sense, Johnson posed for a portrait by Boswell. But Bate had the advantage of two centuries' perspective on both Johnson and Boswell. Where is Bate able to correct Boswell or put Johnson in better perspective? Compare the man Johnson and his influence as seen by Boswell and Bate. • ▲

Delmore Schwartz as Portrayed by Different Memoirists

Both Eileen Simpson, in her *Poets in Their Youth,* and William Phillips, in his *A Partisan View,* depict the poet Delmore Schwartz. How do their impressions compare? How do they supplement/complement each other? What do the outright differences suggest about observation of human character? Why do we need *both* memoirs? • ▲

(**Wider scope:** Extend your comparison to other figures that both authors comment on, e.g., Philip Rahv, Robert Lowell. • ▲)

Alienation of the Hero/ine: A Theme in Recent Biography

The theme of alienation, isolation of the individual hero/ine, seems to characterize many recent biographies and autobiographies. Check it out in at least two or three of the following:

- *Chaplin: His Life and Art* by David Robinson. A genius is driven into exile because of his political views and personal life style.
- *The True Confessions of an Albino Terrorist* by Breyten Breytenbach. A South African poet winds up in solitary confinement.
- *Once upon a Time* by Gloria Vanderbilt. Born rich, you can still starve—emotionally.
- *Henry VIII: The Politics of Tyranny* by Jasper Ridley. He cut himself off from the international Church of the Apostolic Succession, made himself pope of a new national church—and survived.

- *Ease My Sorrows* by Lev Kopelev. An officer in the Soviet Army in World War II, he boldly stood up for the human rights of German civilians; as a result he served a long prison term; he is now an expatriate writer in the West.

What generalizations seem in order about the relationship between genius, heroism, and loneliness? • ▲

President Nixon's Resignation: Value of Psychohistory

In 1972 Bruce Mazlish published his *In Search of Nixon: A Psychohistorical Inquiry.* He applied psychoanalytic techniques to the character of the President, focusing on Nixon's preoccupation with crises and hard work, his paranoia, his body tensions and stiff self-control, his role-playing, self-image, outstanding personality traits. Mazlish concluded that "Time and events alone will tell us whether Nixon has correctly 'analyzed' his American dream, or whether a deeper interpretation would be better for the health and well-being of America and the world."

In 1974, at the height of the Watergate investigation, President Nixon resigned under the threat of impeachment. He accepted a pardon from his successor, President Gerald Ford. (Accepting a pardon is by definition an acknowledgment of guilt; that was the reason Dante refused one.)

To what extent has Mazlish's psychohistorical approach been justified and corroborated by "Time and events," by the revelations that forced Nixon's resignation? What do you and/or the critics see as the predictive value of psychohistory? What did the critics who disagreed with Mazlish in 1972 have to say in 1974? • ▲

President Nixon's *Six Crises* and Mazlish's Interpretation

Read President Nixon's autobiography, *Six Crises,* and consider whether Bruce Mazlish's interpretation, offered in his 1972 book *In Search of Nixon: A Psychohistorical Inquiry,* was borne out by events of 1974. When you check *The New York Times Index* for articles about the crucial events, go back to 1969 for Richard Rovere's *New York Times Magazine* piece about the perversity in Nixon's career which "seems to make everything go wrong." If perfected, what salutary effect could Mazlish's "deeper interpretation" of public figures have on politics and democratic rule? • ▲

Family and Non-Family Biographies of Verne

Since the appearance of Lytton Strachey's *Eminent Victorians,* we have been acutely aware of the difference between the whitewashed, "authorized biography" and the independent, more objective life study. Biographers of Jules Verne provide you with unusual (i.e., not-so-studied-already) examples. Jules Verne's family kept his surviving papers to themselves; and the early studies of him were either written by the family or based on what they would allow access to. The early family (i.e., "coverup") biographies were by Marguerite Allotte de la Fuÿe and Kenneth Allot. Many French psychoanalytic studies appeared before Jean Jules-Verne, the author's grandson, finally acknowledged the family secrets about (1) Jules Verne's family life, about his strained relations with his conservative, uncultured wife, his liberal son, and his religious relatives, and (2) his secret extramarital life. The first full-length nonfamily biography is by Peter Costello. The titles of all these works begin with the name *Jules Verne.* The only psychobiographical studies in English appear in Walter James Miller's *Annotated Jules Verne* (two volumes, 1976–1978). Report on "Family Influence on Studies of Jules Verne: What They Were Hiding and Why." • ▲

Frederick Douglass' Literary Restraint

Ex-slave Frederick Douglass had every reason to describe his physical and mental suffering in fiery, emotional fashion. Instead he narrated his *Life and Times* with objective realism, irony, and understatement. His goal was to convince his white readers that the slave possessed intelligence and sensitivity. How then does his literary control work to his advantage? Work from the final (1893) version of his *Life.* • ★

(**Wider scope:** Compare Douglass' style in his autobiography with his style in his published lectures and with his manner of public speaking, as described by others. • ▲)

Afro-Americans Picture Themselves

Survey the social and/or psychological situation of the American Black as depicted in the autobiographical writings of Frederick Douglass, Booker T. Washington, W. E. B. DuBois, Richard Wright (don't neglect his essay in *The God That Failed*), James Baldwin, Malcolm X, *et al.* • ★

Critical Reactions to Black Autobiography

What do you and/or the critics see as the literary value of the autobiographies of Black leaders listed in the Idea above? Note that Wright and Baldwin also distinguished themselves as writers of fiction, while Douglass, Washington, DuBois, and Malcolm X wrote only nonfiction. That may suggest your selection of works to compare: "Black Novelists as Autobiographers" or "Black Autobiographers as Writers." Review our sections on literary techniques (INDEX) before you set up your categories. • ★

DuBois, Wright, and Race Prejudice

Compare and contrast the ways Richard Wright and W. E. B. DuBois (see above Ideas) contended with race prejudice in the U.S.A. Early in life Richard Wright sought relief by joining the Communist Party but left it thoroughly disillusioned (*The God That Failed*) and joined the expatriate colony of American Black artists living in France. DuBois, a Harvard Ph.D. and cofounder of the National Association for the Advancement of Colored People, started as a civil rights leader demanding equality in America; discouraged here, he turned to world-wide Black liberation, became a communist, and moved to Ghana. • ★

St. Theresa of Avila's *Life* and Modern Biographies

St. Theresa is regarded as one of the most remarkable women of all time. She was a leading figure in the Catholic Counter-Reformation; her writings are celebrated as both literary masterpieces and major works in the cause of mysticism. Read her *Life,* written as a spiritual autobiography for her confessors, and note the effectiveness of her imagery, humor, and candor. For a closer-to-definitive view of her accomplishments read at least two recent biographies (e.g., H. A. Hatzfield, E. A. Peers) and a commentary by either E. W. T. Dickens or R. T. Petersson. What interpretation of her experience with the angel and his arrow do some modern authors offer? See INDEX for Bernini's sculpture of that event. • ▲

Influence of Milton's Poetry on De Quincy's Prose Style

In his *Confessions of an English Opium-Eater* and his *Suspira de Profundis,* a collection of essays, Thomas De Quincy developed an intricate, sonorous, and poetic prose style. Critics are fond of saying that he was influenced by John Milton. Pick out two sections of De Quincy's work that appeal to you as especially sonorous and poetic. Analyze them for their sentence structure, their rhythms, and their sound patterns (INDEX: Prosody). Select two passages from Milton—say one from "Lycidas," one from *Paradise Lost*—for a similar analysis. Why is a Miltonic style so suitable for De Quincy's subject matter? Report on "Specific Ways in Which Milton Influenced De Quincy." • ▲

The Diary of Anne Frank: Nonfiction and Drama

The Diary of Anne Frank, a classic document of the Holocaust in Nazi-occupied Europe, has twice been dramatized, first by the American-Israeli novelist Meyer Levin, then by Frances Goodrich and Albert Hackett. Although the Goodrich-Hackett version became a Broadway success, the Levin version is preferred in many quarters. (See Idea below: "Personal Crises.") *Possibilities:* "Nonfiction as a Source of Drama"; "How a Diary Lends Itself to Dramatization"; "How a Diary Lends Itself to Different Dramatic Treatments"; "What Anne Frank's Diary Gains and Loses on the Stage"; "A Comparison of the Frank Diary as a Reading Experience and as a Theater Experience"; "Whose Drama Is More Faithful to Anne Frank—Levin's or Goodrich-Hackett's?" • ▲

No Laughing Matter: Heller's and Halsey's Versions

Two distinguished American authors, both satirists, have used the same title, *No Laughing Matter,* for their accounts of harrowing personal experiences: Margaret Halsey, nonfiction writer, describing a marital crisis, and Joseph Heller, novelist and dramatist, detailing (with coauthor Speed Vogel) a near-fatal illness. As you and/or the critics see them, compare and contrast their techniques, themes, overall conclusions about life in these times. • ▲

Personal Crises: Heller, Halsey, Levin

Compare and contrast the techniques and themes of Heller's and Halsey's books (above) and novelist Meyer Levin's *Obsession* (an account of his psychological ordeal when powerful people in the theater succeeded in having his dramatic version of *The Diary of Anne Frank* withdrawn in order to give the assignment to other dramatists). Compare the critical reactions (including criticism of Levin's worth, especially, in the psychological journals). • ▲

Eldridge Cleaver's Use of Platonic Dialogue

Read—as Cleaver did while in prison—Plato, at least his dialogues *Symposium* and *Phaedo*. Then read Cleaver's "The Allegory of the Black Eunuchs" in his *Soul on Ice*. What use has Cleaver made of the Platonic/Socratic approach to ideas? How has Cleaver varied and adapted Plato's techniques? For example, how does the narrator relate to the main character in both cases? What is the advantage of the dialogue for the development of ideas? Note the relation between *dialogue* and *dialectic*. • ★

Eldridge Cleaver and St. Paul's *Epistles*

How are Eldridge Cleaver's "letters" in *Soul on Ice* influenced, in style, tone, tactics, and theme, by the Epistles of St. Paul (in the Christian *New Testament*)? • ★

Scientists and Writers: Symposium in Washington

The full transcript of the proceedings of the Conference on Science and Literature held at the Library of Congress in 1981 should provide you with a choice of one or several Ideas for papers/oral reports. The conference brought together some forty scientists (George Wald, Sir Fred Hoyle), science-fiction writers (Gene Roddenberry, Jerry Pournelle), and poets (Diane Ackerman, William Meredith). What do the scientists and writers see as their common problems? Their problems with each other? What works do they allude to that seem important for the public-at-large to read? What were the reactions of the critics on the two occasions of the conference as immediate news (1981) and as the basis of a book (1985)? The book is probably available in your library but surely from Central Services Division, Library of Congress, Washington, DC 20540. • ★

William James' *Psychology*: Its Value a Century Later

William James, founder of psychology in America, published his *Principles of Psychology* in 1889. How is the book regarded in the profession today? Which of his concepts have been superseded, which are still valid, which have been most influential? To what extent is the work valuable as a document of the history of ideas? • ★

James' *Religious Experience* and Studies in Identity

In what ways is William James' *Varieties of Religious Experience* (1902) a precursor of modern studies of the "identity crisis"? • ★

William James: Psychologist, Philosopher, Literary Stylist

William James, medical doctor and philosopher who set up the first psychological lab in America, is regarded as one of the greatest scientific writers of all time. From the following works select the one(s) closest to your own interests: *The Will to Believe, Principles of Psychology, Varieties of Religious Experience, Pragmatism, A Pluralistic Universe.* What do you and/or the critics see as the basis for his reputation as a literary stylist? • ★

Japanese-Americans and Pearl Harbor (I)

After Japan attacked the U.S. bases in Pearl Harbor, the American government decided to incarcerate all Japanese-Americans living on the west coast in War Relocation Camps further inland. Do a critical study (themes, techniques) of the Japanese-American nonfiction produced by Pearl Harbor and its aftermath. Start with Bill Hosokawa's *Nisei: The Quiet American,* Mine Okubo's autobiography, *Citizen 13660,* Senator Daniel Inouye's "One Sunday in December" in his autobiography, *Journey to Washington.* (See Idea II on page 253.) • ▲

Autobiographies Reveal Similarities in Experience of Minorities

Each minority group in America has a different history. Some are descended from immigrants who came here voluntarily; others from people brought here as slaves, in chains; others from Indian, Hispanic, Polynesian or Japanese settlers of territory conquered by the Anglos. Yet, as minority groups, they also have much in common. Explore these similarities and dissimilarities as they are revealed in several of these and other autobiographies:

- American Indian: *Black Elk Speaks,* as told to John Neihardt; *Sun Chief, Autobiography of a Hopi* by Don C. Talavesca.
- Japanese-American: *Journey to Washington* by Senator Daniel Inouye; *Citizen 13660* by Mine Okubo.

- Filipino-American: *America Is in the Heart* by Carlos Bulosan.
- Afro-American: See Idea above, "Afro-Americans Picture Themselves."
● ▲

Marcuse Gainsays Freud on Eros and Civilization

In his *Civilization and Its Discontents,* Sigmund Freud concludes that civilization, based on repression of instincts, makes mass neurosis inevitable. But in his *Eros and Civilization: A Philosophical Inquiry into Freud,* Herbert Marcuse disagrees and postulates instead a nonrepressive society that would draw more on libidinal energy and so return humankind to physical and mental health. Report on this major debate in modern philosophy. If this is your first venture into the field, you should use such guidebooks as Robert W. Marks' *The Meaning of Marcuse* and Arthur Mitchell's Monarch Note on *The Major Works of Herbert Marcuse: A Critical Commentary.* ○ ▲

(**Wider scope:** Include "Brown Refutes Freud," below.) ○ ▲

Brown Refutes Freud on Eros and Thanatos

In *Beyond the Pleasure Principle,* Sigmund Freud proposes that there are two major types of instinct: Eros, or love and life, and Thanatos, or death, and that they are in conflict in the psyche. But in *Life against Death,* Norman O. Brown proposes that the conflict is caused by repression and so it can be ended when repressions are abolished. He sees then a reunification not only of Eros and Thanatos, but also of Id and Ego, male and female. Report on this chapter in a major debate in modern philosophy.○ ▲

(**Wider scope:** For a broader study of rejection of Freud's death instinct, start with Reuben Fine's *A History of Psychoanalysis.* ○ ▲)

Tolerance, Objectivity: Real or Just a Tactic?

These concepts are basic to our belief in American democracy. But some philosophers say that ideas of tolerance and objectivity are mere disguises for repression. Report on this major debate of modern times by reading the essays by Robert Paul Wolff, Barrington Moore, Jr., and Herbert Marcuse in *A Critique of Pure Tolerance.* The two guidebooks mentioned above ("Marcuse Gainsays Freud") will work here too.○ ▲

(**Wider scope:** Include reaction by the critics to this collection of essays when it appeared in 1965, and again in 1969, when it was published with a postscript by Marcuse. Of special interest will be Eliseo Viva's *Contra Marcuse* and Mitchell's comments on it in the Monarch Note cited above. ○ ▲)

Post-Freudian Concepts of the Oedipus Complex

How have later psychoanalysts modified Freud's theory of the Oedipus (family) complex? Consider Carl Jung, Karen Horney, Erich Fromm, Harry Stack Sullivan, Erik Erikson, R. D. Laing. For guidance while reading the primary sources, check recent encyclopedia articles, histories of psychoanalysis, books on the Oedipus complex—e.g., Patrick Mullahy's—and biographies of the principal thinkers. ● ▲

The Feminist Movement: Classics Pro and Con

Read at least three of these modern classics of the feminist movement: Virginia Woolf, *A Room of One's Own;* Simone de Beauvoir, *The Second Sex;* Betty Friedan, *The Feminine Mystique;* Germaine Greer, *The Female Eunuch;* Kate Millett, *Sexual Politics;* Joan Goulianos, . . . *by a Woman Writt.* Report on "The Feminist Case as Made by——" ● ▲

(**Wider scope:** "The Case for and against the Feminist Movement." For the *pro* views, study at least three of the above; for the *con* views read (1) Norman Mailer's *The Prisoner of Sex*; (2) two or more reviews of the feminist books that appeared in religious journals published by fundamentalist sects; (3) writings on the subject by George Gilder and Lionel Tiger. ● ▲)

Simone De Beauvoir Refutes Psychoanalysis

Report on the great French feminist philosopher's argument against psycho-analysis in the Introduction and Chapters I and II of her classic *The Second Sex.* What have the critics—including critics for psychological journals—had to say about her views? ● ▲

De Beauvoir's Ambivalence to Historical Determinism

Report on De Beauvoir's mixed reactions to the philosophy of Marx and Engels as presented in Chapter III of *The Second Sex.* What have the critics—including critics for Marxist organs like *Science and Society,* and for "capitalist" organs like *The New York Times Book Review* and *The New York Review of Books*—had to say about her views? • ▲

De Beauvoir's Study of Myths of the Woman in Literature

Simone De Beauvoir, in her classic feminist work *The Second Sex,* sums up the role of women as it is viewed in the works of five authors (D. H. Lawrence, Stendhal, *et al.*). Read at least three of the writings she evaluates. In what ways do you find her approach validated? subjective? opening new vistas of literary criticism? • ▲

Koch, Charles, and Adams: Three Views of Jefferson

Demonstrate how Adrienne Koch (*Jefferson and Madison: The Great Collaboration*) and Joseph Charles (*The Origins of the American Party System*) differ from Henry Adams (*History of the United States during the Administrations of Jefferson and Madison*) in their studies of the Jeffersonian period. Contrast them first in their (a) approach and then in several of their (b) specific interpretations. Include their different interpretations of Jefferson's alleged conflicts, contradictions, and self-reversals; of the fate of the embargo; of the organization of an anti-Federalist movement. • ★

Two "Educations" Of Henry Adams

Henry Adams wrote an autobiography—*The Education of Henry Adams*—remarkable in several ways. He spoke of himself in the third person, presumably to gain greater perspective on himself; he was motivated to write about his education in order to discover the reasons for his own failures to do anything memorable or important (compared to his distinguished ancestors, e.g., John Quincy Adams); he was troubled by the role of accident rather than purpose in his own life, by the fact that humanity generally seems driven by blind forces.

Several decades later the scholar Max Baym wrote *The French Education of Henry Adams.* What had Adams omitted, or not perceived about himself, that justified another study of that portion of his life? To what extent is Baym influenced by Adams' style? • ▲

(**Wider scope:** Consult critical reviews of Baym that took up similar questions. • ▲)

Adams and Darwin

Adams' being troubled about the role of accident and blind forces in human life sounds as if he's been prompted by the writings of Charles Darwin. Check on the extent of the influence. • ▲

The Literary Classics of Science and Engineering

In the past few generations, critics have studied the literary value of the classics of science (e.g., J. M. Drachman's *Studies in the Literature of the Natural Sciences*) and of engineering (e.g., Walter James Miller and Leo E. A. Saidla's *Engineers as Writers: Growth of a Literature*). According to the scope of your assignment, select one or more of these writers: Darwin the naturalist, John Loudon McAdam the road-builder, O. H. Ammann the bridge builder. How do you and/or the critics rate them as writers? in their use of description? of metaphor? in their argumentation techniques? in their tone and style? • ▲

Engineers—Blind and Sighted— Write Their Autobiographies

John Metcalf, blind since childhood, still became a combat soldier and a great road-builder; he dictated his *Life* in 1795, when he had more than 90 living descendants! Such exhilarating careers are recounted in Samuel Smiles' classic *Lives of the Engineers*. If you are interested in such questions as "The Engineering Personality" or "The Type of Person Who Goes into Engineering" or "Are Engineers Different from the Rest of Us?," read selected chapters in Smiles and/or Ivor B. Hart's *The Great Engineers*, and/or study as many of these autobiographies as the scope of your assignment suggests:

- *Life of Thomas Telford, Civil Engineer, Written by Himself*
- Sir Henry Bessemer, *An Autobiography* (inventor of steel-making process)
- Michael L. Pupin, *From Immigrant to Inventor*
- Benjamin Garver Lamme, *An Autobiography* (electrical engineering genius)
- *Memoirs of Herbert Hoover* (mining engineer, later Secretary of Commerce and President) • ▲

How Are Atolls Formed? 115-Year Wait for Proof

Charles Darwin figured out the answer in 1837: A barrier reef and an atoll are simply stages in the same natural process. But it could not be proved until 1952! What theory of atolls was prevalent before Darwin's? Since he had to refute it, you'll find both theories discussed in his *The Structure and Distribution of Coral Reefs* (1842). Read also his letters on the subject—quoted in biographies? published separately?—including his 1881 letter to the American zoologist Alexander Agassiz; *The New York Times* accounts of the U.S. Navy borings made at Eniwetok Atoll in 1952; and other accounts in the scientific literature of the borings and seismic studies that proved Darwin right. • ▲

(**Wider scope or independent topic:** Write an appraisal of Darwin's excellent expository prose: his structure, his use of succinct examples, his simple syntax. • ▲)

The Third-Person Point of View in Autobiographical Writings

Occasionally a writer writes about him/herself in the third person (not about *me* but about *him*! or *her*!). What are the advantages/disadvantages of this approach? (1) Report on two outstanding examples of this point of view: Henry Adams' *The Education of Henry Adams,* and Norman Mailer's *Armies of the Night* and/or *Of a Fire on the Moon.* (2) Compare several of Mailer's first-person pieces in *Advertisements for Myself* with several of the third-person chapters of *Armies* or *Moon.* In which person is he more self-critical? more candid? more likeable? • ▲

The Compleat Angler—His Competition Today

One of the great "how to" books of all time is Izaak Walton's *The Compleat Angler* (the second edition is better: 1655). How does this classic stand up to the fishing manuals you go by? • ★

How Five Famous Engineers Structure Their Reports

"Unfortunately, most engineers think in terms of details. And so most engineering reports are cluttered with meaningless particulars." So the builder of the George Washington Bridge, O. H. Ammann, told your present writer.

"Actually what the reader needs most is a good general view of the situation. In my reports I usually start off with a summary and a statement of conclusions. Then I use logical subdivisions of the subject, and try to develop my basic material in language the layman can understand."

In other words, engineers design not only physical structures but also written communications. Compare the ways the following engineers have structured their reports: Sextus Julius Frontinus, *The Water Supply of Rome* (also translated as *The Aqueducts of Rome* in the Loeb Classical Library edition of Frontinus); John A. Smeaton, "Report of John Smeaton, Engineer; concerning the state and condition of the Edystone Lighthouse . . . 10th August, 1766," in *Reports of John Smeaton*; John Loudon McAdam, "To the Right Honorable the President and the Board of Agriculture" (his 1820 report published as an appendix in the revised editions of his book *Remarks on the Present System of Road Making*); Herbert Hoover, Secretary of Commerce, "Report on the Mississippi Flood"; O. H. Ammann, "Tentative Report on the Hudson River Bridge."

Tracking down these reports to their original publications will yield you other materials for a broader study; but for your use with this particular Idea, you will find all five reports in the critical anthology *Engineers as Writers* edited by Walter James Miller and Leo E. A. Saidla (from which the quote from the Ammann interview has been taken: p. 252).

Important questions for analysis of the structure of a report: How does the engineer introduce his subject (e.g., his aim, scope, history of the problem, and method of attack)? What use does he make of introductory summary? How does he thereafter relate generalizations to particulars and details? How does he subdivide his subject? How does he conclude? How do the Roman Frontinus, the Englishman Smeaton, the Scotsman McAdam, and the Americans Hoover and Ammann *differ* in their organization of a report? • ▲

Engineers as Poets: Their Use of Metaphor

Report on the way the engineer uses metaphor and analogy to help his reader visualize his subject matter. (INDEX: Metaphor.) Start with Vitruvius' discussion of "the holy ground of architecture" (in his *Ten Books on Architecture*); include a report by another ancient Roman, Frontinus (cited above in "Use of Metaphor in Nonfiction Writing"); note how in his *Narrative of the Building of the Edystone Lighthouse,* John Smeaton develops the shape of his now-classic structure in a detailed analogy with a great tree; how in his *Remarks on the*

Present System of Road Making, John Loudon McAdam calls a McAdam road "a roof" and his competitors' roads "reservoirs for water"; for a great twentieth-century example, see how Arthur E. Raymond, in his paper "The Well-Tempered Aircraft" compares the design of this machine with that of J. S. Bach's "Well-Tempered Clavichord."

For those texts cited here not available to you, substitute the anthology cited above, *Engineers as Writers,* and/or "What Can the Technical Writer of the Past Teach the Technical Writer of Today?" in *IRE Transactions on Engineering Writing and Speech,* Volume EWS-4 No. 3, December 1961. • ▲

7

Ideas on Music, Art, Science, History, and Current Affairs

Know what? Ideas for papers, reports, and projects just *bombard* you every minute. But so very gently! You just have to slow down and say hello to them as they *im-pinge* on you . . . as they *in-sin-u-ate* themselves into your presence.

They come at you on your walkman radio. From comments you hear at bus stops, gas stations, the dinner table. Ideas like these:

- Another big scandal in sports. Should every athlete be forced to take a urine test? (A productive approach, always: What are the arguments *against* it? Posing a question like that turns up material fast, pro and con!)
- Another big "sting" operation. Is temptation, entrapment, use of the agent provocateur, legal? even ethical?
- Politicians accused of using religious appeals to gain votes. Just what do constitutional lawyers mean by "separation of church and state"? Why did such a concept arise?
- Genetic engineering. Is science opening up another Pandora's box? Triggering more monstrous events like Chernobyl? Or will they be more careful this time?
- Abortion. What do the partisans mean by "the right to life"? "the right to choose"?
- Jazz. Concert tonight. My friend Josephine says her grandfather was a jazz player. He got furious if you said that jazz was a "Negro invention." (Was it?)

• U-2. Coming to town next week. But it's not like the last time. Then I was so excited I stood outside the auditorium all night, just to be sure I got good seats. And now. . . .

We might as well start there, with your changing tastes in music, and then say hello to other ideas available to you—coming at you all the time—in science, art, history old and new.

IDEAS ABOUT MUSIC

Your Changing Tastes in Popular Music

Depth psychologist Carl Jung showed that we begin (and end) friendships according to our needs in each stage of our growth. Can you draw a parallel with your tastes in music? Which rock (country, jazz, fusion, folk) group or star did you prefer three years ago? Which ones now? Looking back, can you explain why you needed one star and/or one style then, a different one now? Interview your friends for their experiences along these lines. ("No, not really? You actually *liked* Duran Duran?!") Write or speak on: "The Psychology of Changing Tastes in Popular Music." • ▲ ♊

Your Changing Tastes in "Classical Music"

Have you had a similar experience in "classical" music (see above)? Have you gone through a "Pachelbel's Canon" stage? a Tchaikovsky or Chopin period? a sudden craze over Baroque opera? Why did you need each influence at that particular point in your growth? Do you know anyone who's trying to convert you to Beethoven's late quartets? Or the twelve-tone scale? Write or talk on "The Psychology of Changing Tastes in Classical Music." • ▲ ♊

(**Wider scope:** Do both of the above ideas. Are there any similarities in the psychologies of the two forms of music? • ▲ ♊)

U.S. Rock and South Africa Jive: Paul Simon's Album *Graceland*

You can discuss this major event in modern music under any or all of these headings:

- Two cultures meet and merge: U.S. rock and South African "township jive"; result: a totally new kind of sound
- Two stages of global consciousness in recent popular music—*We Are the World* and *Graceland*—contrasted; music's role in international relations (see later Ideas on jazz)
- The Elvis Presley Shrine as a metaphor in *Graceland*
- The Mexican-American element in *Graceland:* why Simon included it
- The basic Soweto trio of *Graceland:* what Chikapa "Ray" Phiri, Isaac Mthsli, Baghiti Khumalo contribute to Paul Simon's masterpiece
- A cappella in *Graceland:* Joseph Shabalala and Paul Simon
- The accordion: the American connection in *Graceland*
- The shifting rhythms of African music: their effect in *Graceland*
- African acoustic instruments and the electronic "shadow" of the Synclavier in *Graceland*
- Tracks first, songs later: Simon's composing tricks in *Graceland*
- Critical reaction to *Graceland:* from *Rolling Stone* to *The New York Times* • ▲ ♫

The Woodstock Festival: A Landmark in American Music

The Woodstock Musical Festival (1969) provides you with material for whatever scope you need: from how Jimi Hendrix distinguished himself (short oral report) to the unprecedented social phenomenon of such a gathering (Ph.D. dissertation). *Practical side:* With hundreds of thousands of people camped in such a small area, how were the problems of organization, conviviality, management, sanitation, etc., handled? Who were the organizational geniuses? What were their tricks? *Musical side:* The highlights? New techniques developed for mass audiences? New talents born? New reputations established? New associations formed? *Aftermath:* Influence on popularity of rock? Personality and production problems with the film *Woodstock*? Why have there not been many regular sequels on a similar scale? • ▲ ♫ □

The Beatles before and after Ringo Starr

How did the Beatles' music change after Ringo Starr took over on drums? How do these two phases show us that ensemble music is a blend of individual statement and group collaboration? That it succeeds most when the "me" and

the "us" both thrive? When each player plays both against and with the others?
● ▲ ♫

(**Wider scope:** Include the next Idea too.)

The Roches, Two and Three: Before and After Suzzy

Originally there were only two Roches. How did their music—especially the dynamics and sonority—change when Suzzy joined them as the third singer? In what ways do these two phases show that musical quality is a blend of individual contribution and collaboration? ● ▲ ♫

New Wave and Punk Rock: American and European Novel

In our Ideas on the novel, we noted that American fiction tends to be less political than European and South American fiction, that actually political fiction is discouraged in the U.S. What parallels do you find in rock? Compare the first English wave (The Rolling Stones, The Beatles) and the second English wave (the punk rockers) with the American rock of the same periods. How do you and/or the rock critics/historians explain the differences? ● ▲ ♫

Musical Openers: Curtain Raisers

In our Ideas on drama we noted that Jules Verne, Anton Chekhov, and other nineteenth-century writers got their start by composing one-act plays to serve as "curtain raisers" for the main event of the evening. In today's popular-music concerts the equivalent is the "opener"—for example, in the 1960s the Lovin' Spoonful "opened" for the Supremes. Complete the parallels in the terms suggested for the "curtain raiser" (see INDEX). ● ▲ ♫

Mississippi John Hurt and the Lovin' Spoonful

Zal Yanovsky and John Sebastian, who played more than 100 sets with 'Sippi John, got more than the name of their group from him. Discuss the influence of Hurt on the Spoonful's style and subject matter, and on Sebastian's later (solo) career. ● ▲ ♫

History of a Rock Band:
The Lovin' Spoonful, or_____?

Write a critical history of a rock group, preferably a band that has disbanded (so you can do a complete beginning-to-end study). With its short history (1965–1967), the Lovin' Spoonful might serve your purposes perfectly. What distinguished this group founded by John Sebastian and Zal Yanovsky? How did it get its "folk rock punch"? Why were they asked to provide the score for movies by Francis Ford Coppola and Woody Allen? How did the Spoon prepare Sebastian for a solo career? • ▲ ♐ ☐

Rock 'n' Roll: The English Influence

From the sophisticated lyricism of the Beatles and the Rolling Stones to the aggressive social discontent of punk rock, trace the influence (positive and negative?) of British rock on American rock. Does the influence sometimes manifest itself in the form of a reaction? • ▲ ♐

Popular Composer-Musicians as Writers of TV/Film Scores

Carly Simon provided the score for *Heartburn,* the Lovin' Spoonful for *What's Up, Tiger Lily,* and *You're a Big Boy Now,* and John Sebastian the theme song of the TV comedy *Welcome Back, Kotter.* How much of the recognizable public-performer's style (Simon, Sebastian? your favorite?) comes across in their background music? How do they adapt to the medium? to the particular movie? to the invisibility and anonymity? • ▲ ♐ ☐

Rock 'n' Roll to Rock, Period: History and Development

Report on one, a series, or all of the following stages in the history of rock 'n' roll (now rock):

- Rock as a hybrid of blues, rhythm and blues, gospel, country and western, and harmony group music. How did the cross-fertilizations occur?
- Bill Haley's "Rock Around the Clock" as a catalyst
- Chuck Berry, Buddy Holley, Bill Haley, Elvis Presley: adolescent concerns
- Motown: its catering to the stars; Diana Ross; Temptations; Supremes
- Beatles, Rolling Stones: the first English wave

- Bob Dylan: folk-rock synthesis
- Jefferson Airplane: rebellion and acid
- *Hair, Jesus Christ Superstar, Tommy:* rock opera/musicals
- The Woodstock Festival (see Idea above)
- Country rock: a fusion. . . ?
- Disco: the mystique of repetitiveness
- English punk rock and the American new wave

In each case, try to isolate the characteristics, the nature, and the motivation of each new style or stage. Give individuals their due but don't minimize the magical effects of group collaboration, reactions, and interactions. • ▲ ⅀ ☐

Mozart and Beethoven: What Their Letters Reveal

For example, their letters indicate that their definitions of music, their methods of composition, their political orientations, their experience in love, indeed their very personalities were drastically different. Biographies contain samples of crucial correspondence and help you put an exchange of letters into its context; there are also paperback editions of selected letters available. • ▲ ⅀

(**Wider scope:** How great is the correlation between the personalities, as revealed in their letters, and the two types of music known as Viennese Classical and Early Romantic? • ▲ ⅀)

The Sonata-Allegro Form in Instrumental Works

What do we mean by "the sonata-allegro form" in instrumental music? How does it resemble dramatic form? How does it exploit contrasts? How does it develop? What is the overall emotional and intellectual effect of a work composed in sonata form? For a simple example, use the first movement of W. A. Mozart's *Eine Kleine Nachtmusik*. For a more complex example, and to show variations within the form, use the last movement of F. J. Haydn's *String Quartet in G Minor*. For guidance in your analysis, consult at least two standard histories of western music. • ▲ ⅀

(**Wider scope:** Explain what form in instrumental music was like before the sonata-allegro form was developed; it is helpful to contrast Baroque form and sonata form as, respectively, architectural and dramatic in their nature. • ▲ ⅀)

Voltaire's *Candide* as Music Criticism

In chapter 25 of Voltaire's novel *Candide,* read Lord Pococurante's criticism of "music today" (the novel was composed in 1759). Consider his remarks either on opera or on instrumental music or both. In what ways are his criticisms an accurate estimate of aristocratic Baroque style and an accurate forecast of the reasons for its sudden decline, soon after J. S. Bach's death? Include in your report on "Voltaire as a Music Critic" a biographical summary of his broad cultural concern and influence on European thought. • ★ ♋

Brahms' First Symphony or Beethoven's Tenth?

Why have some critics/historians referred to Johannes Brahms' first symphony as "Beethoven's Tenth"? In what ways is this a compliment to both composers? • ▲ ♋

Two Kinds of Genius: Innovative, Summational

In music, as in all arts and sciences, there are two kinds of geniuses: those who bring known styles, techniques, approaches to their highest degree of perfection (e.g., W. A. Mozart, Johannes Brahms, Giuseppe Verdi) and those who innovate and revolutionize (e.g., Ludwig van Beethoven, Richard Wagner, Arnold Schoenberg). Using one or more composers of each type, compare and contrast them in terms of their philosophy of music, their techniques, the nature of their improvement or innovation. • ▲ ♋

Composers Oriented or Not to the Piano

Before Hector Berlioz, most composers worked at the piano, even if they were composing an oratorio or a symphony. Berlioz could not play the piano and so, he complained, could not go "hunting for chords." Paul Simon, early in his career, composed on the guitar; later, at the electronic equipment. Using any two or more works of these or other composers, discuss the relationship between their primary instrumental affinity and the method and result of their composition. ○ ▲ ♋

Giants of Counterpoint: J. S. Bach and J. Brahms

Although counterpoint was not the usual means of harmonization in Johannes Brahms' day, he included this technique in his symphonies, using it so well that he is rated as surpassed in contrapuntal composition only by the master himself, J. S. Bach. Take one or more contrapuntal passages by each, compare them for design, sonority, overall emotional effect. What has Brahms added to the repertoire of counterpoint? ○ ▲ ♋

The Étude: Before and after Chopin

What was the étude before Chopin took it up? What did he develop it into? Who has continued to use the étude for similar purposes? For an oral report, tape and play back examples; for a written report, photocopy the passages you discuss and "quote" them in your text. ○ ▲ ♋

Why Did Paris Riot over a Ballet?

Igor Stravinsky's ballet music *Le Sacre du printemps* (*The Rite of Spring*) is now the most famous composition of the early twentieth century. But when it was first performed in Paris, it provoked a (now also famous!) riot. Why? • ★ ♋

Three Arts Involved in *The Rake's Progress*

William Hogarth did a series of paintings called *The Rake's Progress* (ca. 1734). More than two centuries later, these inspired the composer Igor Stravinsky to compose an opera based on Hogarth's pictorial narrative. He asked the poet W. H. Auden to supply the libretto; the English expatriate enlisted the aid of his friend, the Brooklyn-born poet Chester Kallman. Consider this unusual three-way collaboration of literature, music, and art. How much did the poets have to invent to fill in enough details for an opera? How did they achieve a poetic equivalent, and Stravinsky a musical equivalent, of Hogarth's scenes, themes, and moral? • ▲ ♋

Goodman, Springsteen and Mass Audiences

On 6 A.M. on a freezing day in January 1937, 3,000 girls and boys had already lined up outside New York's Paramount Theater for a Benny Goodman concert.

Later 2,000 others tied up traffic outside. Explore this historic occasion as setting a precedent for later concerts by rock stars. • ▲ ♋

(**Wider scope:** Compare and contrast the Goodman concert with Bruce Springsteen's record-shattering performances in January 1986. • ▲ ♋)

Influence of the Blues

Discuss and illustrate the influence of the blues on jazz, rhythm and blues, and rock 'n' roll. Start with Bruce Cook's *Listen to the Blues,* Samuel Charters' *Roots of the Blues,* and Paul Oliver's *The Story of the Blues* (Oliver's book is illustrated by the Columbia LP G30008 with the same title and with sleeve commentary by him). • ▲ ♋

Is the Blues a Native American Invention?

According to some historians, the blues—unlike other forms of American popular music—has no direct, obvious European or African antecedents. In both its verse form and its vocal effects, they say, the blues seems to be completely American in its origins. Other researchers disagree. Get your start with the books and the record album cited in the Idea above. • ▲ ♋

Louis Armstrong's Influence on "Serious" Trumpet Music

Explore the way Louis Armstrong's innovations in trumpet techniques have influenced composers and performers of classical music. ○ ▲ ♋

Benny Goodman's Bands and Racial Integration

In his role as leader of various ensembles, the great jazz clarinetist Benny Goodman selected top musicians regardless of their racial or religious background. Explore these early efforts at integration in American culture: their immediate impact, their long-range results. • ▲

Louis Armstrong and Efforts to Define "Swing"

The word "swing" originated as a way of describing Armstrong's rhythmic momentum. Discuss some of the critical efforts to *define* swing in words, as opposed to the ease of illustrating it with any of his recordings; explore the use of the word in such phrases as "swing era," "swing style," and "It don't mean a thing if it ain't got that swing." ○ ▲ ௸

Sociology of Jazz

How can we explain the fact that jazz, Afro-American in its origin, nevertheless is popular with Americans of all ethnic backgrounds? Include in your basic reading such classics as David Ewen's *Men of Popular Music,* Bruce Cook's *Listen to the Blues* (his jazz-musician father denied its Negro origin!), Alan Rich's *The Simon and Schuster Listener's Guide to Jazz,* Len Lyons' *The 101 Best Jazz Albums: A History of Jazz;* listen at the library to the Smithsonian *Collection,* read the accompanying literature. ● ▲ ௸

The Appeal of Jazz: The First Global Music

Why has American jazz become the first form of popular music to be enjoyed on all five continents? How much of this global appeal is a result of the intrinsic worth of the music, how much a result of American marketing and distribution techniques? Start with the sources listed in Idea above. ● ▲

Influence of Jazz On_____Native Music

Musicologists have noted that native music in many parts of the world has absorbed some characteristics of American jazz. During World War II, for example, soldiers returning from Bali reported that a new art form was developing there: a blend of American jazz and Balinese ritualistic music. Why and how do jazz techniques, formats, and instrumentation appeal to musicians of (the nation of your choice)? ● ▲ ௸

Budapest String Quartet and Benny Goodman

When the famous Budapest String Quartet toured America, they held auditions to find a clarinetist good enough to join them in playing W. A. Mozart's *Quintet in A Major for Clarinet and Strings.* Although many leading "classical" music performers tried out, it was the jazz clarinetist Benny Goodman who was chosen. How did journalists and music critics explain this? ● ▲ ௸

A Success Story: Benny Goodman or_____?

Jazz and rock have given many people from poor families a chance to reach fame as well as financial success. What factors in the history of popular music, combined with the "upward mobility" of American society, make these "rags to riches" lives possible? Limit the number of performers you consider so that you can go into convincing detail. • ▲ ♋

The Death of Bessie Smith

Our literature—biographies, histories, even a play by Edward Albee—contains many efforts to explain the tragic death of the great blues singer and composer. Explore the story as an instance of the effect of racism on American life. • ▲

Bessie Smith's Poetry

In her famous blues compositions, Smith used a hauntingly simple poetry. Discuss the requirements of the blues verse-form and what she contributed to its development. • ▲ ♋

Duke Ellington: The Art of Orchestration

Billy Strayhorn, frequent collaborator of Duke Ellington, said that "He plays piano but his real instrument is the orchestra." Explain, illustrate, discuss Ellington's contribution to the art of orchestration—e.g., his scoring of individual chords, his variety of sonorities, his originality in harmonies. • ▲ ♋

The Cowherd's Melody in Beethoven, Berlioz, *et al.*

Every district of the Swiss Alps has its own version of the *ranz des vaches,* a melody the cowherds sing or play on the alphorn to call in the cows. Why were Romantic composers fond of using variations of it? Compare and contrast its appearances in three or more of these works: Ludwig van Beethoven's *Sixth (pastoral) Symphony,* G. A. Rossini's *William Tell Overture,* Hector Berlioz' *Symphonie Fantastique,* R. A. Schumann's *Manfred,* Richard Strauss' *Don Quixote* and *Ein Heldenleben.* Why does Sir William Walton's masterpiece *Façade* contain a parody of the *ranz des vaches?* • ▲ ♋

The Pianist's Bible: Bach and Beethoven

The 48 preludes and fugues in J. S. Bach's *Well-Tempered Clavier* have been called the pianist's Old Testament, and the 32 piano sonatas of Ludwig van Beethoven the pianist's New Testament. Why? ○ ▲ ♫

Ballad Opera, Grand Opera

How do they differ? From histories of music establish good working definitions of both genres. Perhaps the best comparison can be made in terms of (a) an Italian opera fashionable in the 1720s and (b) John Gay's *The Beggar's Opera* (1728), which satirizes all Italian opera. You could start with Steven H. Gale's Monarch Note, *John Gay's "The Beggar's Opera."* ○ ▲ ♫

Modern Adaptations of *The Beggar's Opera*

In the two-and-a-half centuries since it premiered, John Gay's *The Beggar's Opera* has enjoyed tens of thousands of performances, including one run of 1463 performances in London starting in 1920. It has also enjoyed modern adaptations by eminent arists: playwright Bertolt Brecht and composer Kurt Weill created *The Threepenny Opera,* and Duke Ellington wrote the score for the Broadway musical *The Beggar's Holiday.* What do you and/or the critics see as the relative values of one or both of these adaptations compared to the original? To what extent are Gay's themes still valid today? Do the modern adaptations do justice to Gay's social criticisms? ● ▲ ♫

Aria and Recitative: Components of Opera

Report on the difference between the aria and the recitative: their structure and function in grand opera. For an oral report, play a passage (on tape or record) that goes from one of these components to the other; for a paper, photocopy such a passage from the score and libretto. In either case, offer a running commentary that shows how your passage typifies the differences under discussion. Get your bearings with classics like Donald Jay Grout's *A History of Western Music* (third edition), or Joseph Machlis' *The Enjoyment of Music* (fourth edition); a helpful handbook is Alan Rich's *The Simon & Schuster Listener's Guide to Opera.* ● ★ ♫

Schoenberg's *Survivor*, Stockhausen's *Young Ones*

Compare and contrast Arnold Schoenberg's *A Survivor from Warsaw* with Karlheinz Stockhausen's *Gesang der Jünglinge* (*Canticle of the Hebrew Children in the Fiery Furnace*) for their (a) themes, their (b) use of radical techniques (in Schoenberg, atonal idiom, the 12-tone row; in Stockhausen, tape recording, use of electronic generators, serial treatment, and the technique used for conclusion) and their (c) overall impact and effects. • ▲ ♫

Electronic "Classical" Music: History and Advantages

How has electronic engineering changed the nature of music and of the act of composition? Report on the three main stages in the development of electronic music: use of magnetic tape recording; evolution of synthesizers; use of electronic computers. Select three or more of these works to illustrate your main points: Karlheinz Stockhausen, *Electronic Composition #1, Hymen, Opus 1970;* Edgard Varèse, *Poème Électronique;* Milton Babbitt, *Philomel, Vision and Prayer;* John Cage, *Fontana Mix;* Mario Davidovsky, *Synchronisms #1.* • ★ ♫

Electronic Techniques in Popular Music

Apply the questions in the Idea above to recent popular music. Use three or more compositions, starting with Bill Haley's (preelectronic *The Comets*) in "Rock around the Clock"; use any Rolling Stone piece strong on "electric reincarnations"; Alan Parsons' "The Traveller"; Van Halen's "Why Can't This Be Love?"; The Roches' "Older Girls"; your own favorite for ingenious tape engineering, and/or synthesizer performance and/or computer composition; culminating perhaps in a really daring passage from Paul Simon's *Graceland.* • ★ ♫

Modal, Tonal, Atonal Music: Mysteries of the Scales

We are conditioned to *feel* that the scale we learned in childhood (do-re-mi-fa-sol-la-ti-DOHHH!) is natural, universal, of all time. Actually, our major-minor scale system—built into the bugle, harmonica, accordion, and piano—represents a narrow and arbitrary selection of all the sounds available to musicians.

It has been dominant only in Western culture, and even there only from about 1600 to 1900.

Ideas here: (1) Report on the scale development in Western culture: medieval *modal scales;* the Renaissance transition; the *tonal scales* developed in the Baroque period; and the *variety of scales* now available to western composers, including *atonal scales,* the *dodecaphonic scale*(s), and *the pitch continuum.* (2) Report on Oriental scales: *Javanese, Arabic,* and *Indian.* For an oral report, use taped samples; for a written paper, use photocopied pages of notations. • ★ ♒

What Would You Do If I Sang out of Tune?

In what sense is our modern diatonic scale ''off tune''? Report on the reasons we make this sacrifice. Compare the tuning of the Renaissance harpsichord with that of today's piano. Read up on J. S. Bach and his *Well-Tempered Clavier* (or *Clavichord*, as it is sometimes translated). • ▲ ♒

What Did They Sing and Play Before Notes Were Noted Down?

We *do* know that in ancient Greece the rhapsodes sang Homer, the lyric poets Sappho and Pindar sang their odes while playing their lyres, the theater choruses sang their strophes to instrumental accompaniment. But exactly what *notes,* what *melodies* or chords they played, we do not know. For musical notation, apparently, had not yet been invented. Report on what archaeologists and historians of music and drama have been able to reconstruct of (or hypothesize about) ancient Greek music. • ▲

Pythagoras' String Theory and the Music of the Spheres

Report on the ancient Greek philosopher Pythagoras' experiments with sounds produced by a plucked string. To what point were his discoveries accurate? At what point were his theoretical extrapolations wrong? What remains today of both his theory and his practice? (Could you build a simple apparatus like his? and pluck it?) • ★

The Weavers: A Study in the Effect of Blacklisting

In 1980, after an absence of several decades, the Weavers, one of the all-time great country-music groups, staged a two-night revival-and-farewell stand at

Carnegie Hall. They had been "absent" as a group because they had been "blacklisted" during the McCarthy period. Start your research with *The New York Times Index* for (1) their own direct coverage of those two nights and (2) their coverage of the premiere broadcast of the PBS documentary of the Weavers' preparation for, and performance in, those revival concerts. Listen to some Weavers' songs, including classics like "Irene, Goodnight" and their "Hammer Song." How did the Weavers and the public feel about this conclusion to a major problem created by the "blacklist"? (The documentary is often rerun. Perhaps WNET-TV, 356 West 58th St., New York, NY 10019, can guide you in finding out about the time and place of the next reruns in your area.)• ★ ♋

(**Wider scope:** How did the individual members of the Weavers—Pete Seeger, Lee Hayes, Veronica ["Ronnie"] Gilbert, Fred Hellerman—fare during the time their group was banned, as a group, from the entertainment world? • ▲)

A Shrine for Elvis Presley, A Shrine for Wagner

In the 1870s Richard Wagner built a Festspielhaus in Bayreuth, Bavaria, a theater suitable for performance of his music dramas. It has become virtually a shrine for Wagner aficionados who attend annual summer performances there. A shrine to the memory of rock star Elvis Presley has been established in Tennessee. What effects do such shrines have on popular taste? on musical composition after the shrines have been set up? on national and cultural pride? In what ways are they more commercial than artistic ventures? • ★

(**Wider scope:** Include the Westminster Abbey shrines in your report, especially as a contrast to the art/commerce question. • ★)

Music Not about Heroes but about the Victims (1)

Like all twentieth-century arts, music often tends to suspect the hero (as depicted in Beethoven's *Eroica* or Richard Strauss' *Ein Heldenleben* [*A Hero's Life*] and rather to concentrate on the victims of power, often heroic power. Report on two or more of these works, especially on the avant-garde techniques they use to explore their nontraditional themes: Krzysztof Penderecki, *Threnody for the Victims of Hiroshima;* Arnold Schoenberg, *A Survivor from Warsaw;* Karlheinz Stockhausen, *Gesang der Jünglinge* (*Canticle of the Hebrew Children*); Alban Berg, *Wozzeck.* • ▲ ♋

Music about Heroes and Victims Compared (2)

Compare two or more examples of music about heroic greatness with two or more examples of music about the victims of power. Emphasize tone, sonority, emotional intention of the composer, techniques employed to gain desired effects, overall impression about the condition of humanity as seen from these points of view. For heroic music, select from Richard Strauss' *Don Juan* and *Ein Heldenleben* (*A Hero's Life*), Hector Berlioz' *Harold in Italy* and *King Lear,* Richard Wagner's *Parsifal* (Prelude to Act III and/or Act III). For "victim" music, select from the compositions cited in Idea (1) above. ● ▲ ♋

Fragments of Ancient Music Preserved in Manuscript

Notation was invented (apparently) and developed in the Hellenistic period of ancient (Graeco-Roman) culture. But of the music noted down by the third century A.D. not more than a dozen fragments and pieces (including one Christian hymn) remain. Report on this tiny legacy of ancient Greek music. How did notation then differ from later notation? from today's? ○ ▲

Rousseau's System of Musical Notation

The great philosopher, Romantic author, and opera composer Jean-Jacques Rousseau invented a new system of notation. What were its advantages, as he saw them? Why did the French Academy reject his system? Include in your report a passage of music notated in both the traditional way and in Rousseau's way. ○ ▲

Contemporary Notation: John Cage, Earle Brown, *et al.*

Compare the notation in such works as Earle Brown's *Available Forms I,* or John Cage's *Aria* with traditional notation. How does this new kind of instruction for performers allow them to share with the composer in creating the work? In what sense is there here an analogy to jazz improvisation? If you cannot find scores in your library to photocopy, use samples in books like D. G. Grout's *A History of Western Music* (third edition), Joseph Machlis' *The Enjoyment of Music* (fourth edition), etc. N. B. There's an Index to Musical Notation at the Library of the Performing Arts of the New York Public Library. ○ ▲

IDEAS ABOUT ART

An Architect's Contribution to Drawing and Painting

Report on the discovery of scientific perspective by architect Filippo Brunelleschi; how it changed the artist's approach to his subject and materials; its effect on drawing and painting; compare a pre-Brunelleschi painting with a post-Brunelleschi painting (the earliest known use of the theory is in *The Holy Trinity* by Masaccio; for an oral presentation, use also a slide of Albrecht Dürer's *Demonstration of Perspective*. ● ▲ ☐

Scientific Perspective and the Tonal System

Compare the development of scientific perspective in drawing and painting with the development of the tonal system in music. In what sense is the painter's *vanishing point* analogous to the composer's *tonic triad?* Show how the systems of perspective and tonality proved to be valuable means of organizing, respectively, a canvas and a score. ○ ▲ ☐

David, Goliath-Killer, as Theme and Symbol in Italian Art

Review the story of David and Goliath in the Bible (*First Book of Samuel,* chapter 17). Assemble as many photographs/reproductions as you need to reflect well on these four major Italian works, all titled *David* (say *Dah*-veed): Donatello's bronze statue (1425?); Andrea del Castagno's painted leather shield (ca. 1455—this one you might be able to reflect on in person: it's in the National Gallery in Washington, DC; Michelangelo's marble statue (1504); and Gianlorenzo Bernini's work, also marble (1623).

Ideas: (1) Compare the four works for (a) their fidelity to the Bible story and (b) their interpretations. What is the significance of details added by each artist? (2) Consider how the four works represent not only four different artists, four different temperaments meeting the demands of four different patrons, but also four different periods in history, each with its own cultural (and military) climate, each with its own conception of the function of art, its own emphasis in technique, so that the same Bible story can have many different meanings! (3) Consider what different emotional effects result from each artist's *choice of moment in the story:* Donatello and Castagno chose success and its aftermath, but a different mood in each case; Michelangelo and Bernini chose moments before the crucial moment, but again with a different mood in each case. (4) Consider at least *three levels of symbolism:* (a) *General, overt symbolism:* the underdog, the citizen unarmored except in righteousness, versus the armored bully, the oppressor; (b) *General, subliminal symbolism:* the psychoanalytic, Freudian and Frommian undertones, the young boy becoming an adult by measuring himself against the seasoned, older male; notice that Donatello's David is a mere adolescent, his musculature still a promise; that Castagno's looks tragic, as though victory catapults him into new responsibilities; Michelangelo's has a touch of the young wiseguy in his attitude (his way of showing anxiety? by overcompensating for it?); and Bernini's certainly looks as if this is the crucial rite of passage. (c) *Topical, local symbolism:* Consider the historical connections: *Between* Donatello's conception (boy in a civilian hat, militarist in an elaborate helmet) and the young *republic* of Florence then at war with the arrogant *Duchy* of Milan. *Between* Castagno's David, even in victory seemingly poised for more trouble, and the situation his patron was in: was Castagno warning his patron's enemies? *Between* Michelangelo's calm, seemingly composed, David and the Neo-Platonist philosophy dominant in the Florence of his day. *Between* Bernini's David and the Church Militant in the Thirty Years War. • ▲ □

Bible Themes and Symbols in Painting and Sculpture

The procedure suggested above for doing comparative studies of works of art on the David theme can easily be adapted for—and applied to—any other persistent theme in Western art. Here, for example, is a list of the Bible subjects that have been most popular with the fine arts. If you check these or similar titles in the index of any history of art, you can in a few minutes discover which artists have handled which themes or subjects, check the illustrations and the text, and decide whether you have a subject suitable to your tastes and needs. Of course, it is important in this search to go beyond the one-volume history of world or western art and check into the period histories (Medieval, Renaissance, High Renaissance, Baroque and Neoclassical, Romanticist, Realist, Impressionist, Postimpressionist, Modern, Postmodern). They will give you more examples of works on the themes of:

Adam and Eve
Adoration of the Magi
Annunciation

Assumption of the Virgin
Christ Entering Jerusalem
Creation of Adam
Crucifixion
Descent from the Cross
Expulsion from Paradise (or Garden of Eden)
Flight into Egypt
Jacob Wrestling with the Angel
Last Judgment
Last Supper
Madonna Enthroned
Nativity
Pieta
Saint Mark
Saint Matthew

Once you have selected your subject for a comparative study, you will (1) Review the stories in the Hebrew Bible (Old Testament) or in the Christian New Testament, and then compare the works on your list for (a) their fidelity to the Biblical account and (b) their interpretation, including addition or modification of details; (2) Consider how the works differ and to what extent this is a matter of the attitudes of the period in which they were conceived, and of the originality of the individual artists; (3) Consider what special effects result from each artist's choice of moment in the Bible story; (4) Analyze the works for symbols that they employ on any or all of these levels: (a) general, overt symbolism; (b) general, subliminal symbolism; and (c) topical, local symbolism or connotation.
● ▲ □

Allusions in Caravaggio's *Calling of St. Matthew*

Comment on the arm and hand of Jesus in Caravaggio's masterpiece (1597?), as an allusion to the arm and hand of the Lord in Michelangelo's *The Creation of Adam*. Could we say that as Adam is called to life, so Matthew is created? Invited by this connection between the Old and New Testaments to see other allusions, would you see the shaft of light, also pointing at Matthew, as a visual equivalent of *Genesis* I: 4 ("Let there be light") and I:18 ("separate light from darkness")? Symbolism: As the Christian painter sees it, in what sense has Matthew been "in the dark" until this moment? being separated now from darkness? What does clothing symbolize here—the colorful suits and shoes of Matthew and his men, the simple clothes and unshod feet of Jesus and his companion? the plumes on some heads, the halo on another? • ▲ ☐

Catholic Caravaggio's Influence on Protestant Painters

Research and report on the explanations that art historians give for the profound influence of Caravaggio, a passionate proponent of the Catholic Reformation, on the Protestant artists of the North, especially Rembrandt. • ▲ ☐

Caravaggian Light and Renaissance Light

Compare Caravaggio's use of light with the light of the Renaissance painters. What are the effects of these two approaches? • ▲ ☐

Caravaggio's Aim and Tragic Fate

Report on Caravaggio's short and tragic life. It was his aim to bring Christianity to the common people by representing sacred subjects in realistic, everyday terms: for example, he sets *The Calling of St. Matthew* in a common tavern and pictures the divine figures as poor people. It was his fate, however, to be rejected by the man in the street (why?) and to become, instead, a painter's painter: one of the most influential of all time (why?). • ★ ☐

Comparison of Two Versions of the *Calling of St. Matthew*

In what ways does Hendrick Terbrugghen's version reflect Caravaggio's conception? In what ways is the Dutch painter's rendition original? In what sense is Terbrugghen a link between the Caravaggio style and the Dutch masters? • ▲ ☐

St. Theresa's *Life*, Bernini's *Ecstasy*

Elsewhere we consider St. Theresa of Ávila's place in literature and in the history of mysticism (see INDEX). Here we are concerned with her place in art. In her autobiography (*Life*) she tells how an angel pierced her heart with a golden arrow. "It was so painful," she recalls, "that I screamed out loud. But I felt, too, such infinite sweetness that I wanted the pain to go on forever. It was not physical pain but mental. Still it affected my body in some way. It was the sweetest caressing of my soul by God.'' Report on the way Gianlorenzo Bernini developed this account into three statue-groups in the Cornaro family chapel (Rome). As you work from slides (or large reproductions) of photographs of the chapel interior, consider how Bernini created the miraculous illusion that Theresa and the angel are rising toward heaven. What do you and/or the critics see as Bernini's success in catching the essence of Theresa's account? • ▲ ☐

Bernini's *Ecstasy of St. Theresa*, Shakespeare's Play-within-a-Play

Notice (Idea above) that Bernini placed his statue-group of Theresa and the angel over the chapel altar; in balconies on the sides of the chapel, he placed statues of the Cornaro family in rapt attention to the *Ecstasy*. The live audience sits between the marble worshipers. What is the effect on the live audience? In what ways is Bernini's effect comparable to one achieved by Shakespeare's use of a play-within-a-play in *Hamlet?* In what ways is Bernini's effect greater? Include in your appreciation the way Bernini is saying (1) come join us in contemplating this event and (2) this miracle is eternal: it can be observed as long as there are people to observe. • ▲ ☐

The Great Chain of Being in Bach, Pope, and Rubens

According to Alexander Pope's *Essay on Man*, every link in the Great Chain of Being must be occupied. Compare (1) the teeming life represented in his Epistle I with (2) that in the crowded canvas of *Marie Landing in Marseilles* by Peter Paul Rubens and the complex interweaving of multiple lines of sound in the Sanctus section of the *Mass in B Minor* by J. S. Bach. If you're making this an oral report to the class, don't just show a slide of the Rubens and play the Bach but also hand out photocopies of the Chain passages from Pope. • ▲ ☐ ♫

Poussinisme vs. Rubenisme: Factions in the French Academy

From standard histories of art, establish the principles of Nicolas Poussin which Charles Lebrun converted into the ''rules'' of the French Academy, and then the principles of the opposing Faction, the followers of the painter Peter Paul Rubens. Why did the Academy's admission of Antoine Watteau in 1717 signal the triumph of the Rubenistes? Stress the conflict over color (as emotional) and contour (as rational) as you use two works by each of the three principals to explain the controversy: e.g., for Poussin, *The Rape of the Sabine Women, The Funeral of Phocis;* for Rubens, *The Garden of Love, The Raising of the Cross;* for Watteau, *A Pilgrimage to Cythera, L'Enseigne de Gersaint.* • ★ □

Rembrandt's *Night Watch* Really a Daytime Picture

Once Rembrandt's *Night Watch* was given a scientific cleaning, its name had to be changed to *Captain Cocq's Company* (in the daytime!). Report on the strange history of this painting, including its alleged role in the decline of the painter's fortunes. If you see it that way, you could consider as the underlying question: Why must art be at the mercy of economics? • ★ □

Use of the Diagonal as a Baroque Device

Explore and comment on these two contrasting observations: (1) In neoclassicist French painting, no matter how much turbulence or emotion is represented, long-range stability is reasserted by strong horizontal and vertical contours that "contain" the turbulence; but (2) in many Baroque paintings, an imbalance, a kind of momentum or tipping, is deliberately created by the use of strong diagonals. For your examples use standard works easily found in most histories of art or most slide collections: e.g., (1) Nicolas Poussin's *The Rape of the Sabine Women*, J. L. David's *The Death of Socrates;* (2) P. P. Rubens' *The Raising of the Cross*, Rembrandt's *The Blinding of Samson*. What contrasting social attitudes are reflected here? • ★ □

Velazquez's Use of Light in *The Maids of Honor*

"For Velazquez, light creates the visible world," says H. W. Janson in his *History of Art*. Study and report on the ambiguities, mysteries, and varieties of light in the Spanish master's *The Maids of Honor.* • ★ □

Velazquez and Goya: Painters and Royalty

Compare and contrast F. J. Goya's *The Family of Charles V* with Diego Velazquez' *The Maids of Honor*. What deliberate allusions does Goya make to the Velazquez work? In what ways are the artists' studios similar? their use of light? their brushwork (most art books and slide collections give you a detail of the Princess Margarita showing that the brushwork is almost Impressionist)? the postures in which the two artists catch the central female figure? How do the two artists differ in their attitudes toward the royal family? How stupid did Charles and his family have to be not to know that they had been painted as stupid? ● ★ ☐

Rembrandt's Sympathy for the Dutch Jews

Discuss Rembrandt's interest in Hebrew themes and in the suffering of the Jews, an interest revealed in such works as the painting *Jacob Blessing the Sons of Joseph* and the etching *Christ Preaching* (the latter is assumed to be set in a corner of the Amsterdam ghetto). ● ★ ☐

Two Neoclassicist Periods, Two Political Purposes

Show that in Nicolas Poussin's day, French artists exploited classical models for absolute (monarchist) purposes, but in Jacques-Louis David's day they exploited the same themes for republican purposes. Start with the Poussin and David paintings cited above, and add David's *The Oath of the Horatii*. ● ★ ☐

Baroque and Rococo Styles: Similarities, Contrasts

The Rococo style grew out of the Baroque style. Rococo includes both similarities and contrasts to the Baroque. Illustrate these points with slides, or reproductions from art books or museums. Why was Rococo created? to meet what needs? ● ★ ☐

Reynolds and LeBrun: Their Rules for Artists

Sir Joshua Reynolds, first president of the Royal Academy, offered in his *Discourses* what he regarded as the basic principles for artists to follow. To what extent is Reynolds' thinking a rehash of Nicolas Poussin's and Charles LeBrun's "rules"? To what extent are the *Discourses* original? still valuable to painters? ● ▲

Mrs. Siddons as Painted by Reynolds and Gainsborough

In 1784 Joshua Reynolds painted *Mrs. Siddons as the Tragic Muse*. A year later Thomas Gainsborough painted *Mrs. Siddons* as Mrs. Siddons. Demonstrate the ways in which Gainsborough has deliberately opposed Reynolds' official Academy theory and practice (see Idea above). ● ▲

(**Wider scope:** How does Gainsborough's *Blue Boy* also gainsay Reynolds? ● ★ ☐)

Two Hogarths Compared in Use of Pictorial Fiction

William Hogarth introduced (in the 1730s) a new kind of picture: series of paintings (made into etchings for popular sale) that told fictitious but typical stories of, e.g., *The Rake's Progress* or *Marriage à la Mode*. They were typical stories in this sense: it was common for a rich country squire's son to go to London and squander his (father's) money in immoral living, and for an impoverished nobleman to marry the daughter of a rich middle-class family and to squander her fortune.

Two-and-a-half centuries later, William's American namesake, Burne Hogarth, introduced a more developed kind of narrative art in his books *Tarzan of the Apes* and *Jungle Tales of Tarzan*. *Marriage à la Mode* and the two Tarzan series are now available in critical editions that are rich in background detail and interpretation.

Ideas here: The general concept of narrative art or pictorial fiction: its value and viability. The use of symbolic details by the two Hogarths. The differences in themes in their respective works (Burne Hogarth seems more interested in an ideal character valuable in any period; William Hogarth, in social problems of his own day). Is Burne Hogarth more "Baroque" in his style than William Hogarth? ● ▲ ☐

Burne Hogarth's Influence on Comic Strip Art

Burne Hogarth has been hailed by French critics as "the Michelangelo of the comic strip" (he inaugurated the Sunday Tarzan page). See T. Durwood's essay "Burne Hogarth" in *Crimmer's: The Harvard Journal of Pictorial Fiction* (Winter 1975) and the present author's "Introduction" to Hogarth's book *Jungle Tales of Tarzan*. Report on Hogarth's influence on the growth and scope of the comic strip and on narrative art. ● ▲ ☐

West's *Death of General Wolfe* as a Romanticist Painting

Benjamin West, American-born painter who became the second president of the Royal Academy, was pressured to paint his *Death of Wolfe* in neoclassical, i.e., Poussiniste, style. In what way is his finished masterpiece at once indebted to Poussinism yet an original move toward Romanticism? • ★ ☐

Copley's American and European Periods

John Singleton Copley established himself as a Boston artist before he went to England and switched to a European style. In the opinion of some art critics/historians, what originality did Copley's American work display that was lost to us after his reorientation in Europe? • ▲ ☐

President Thomas Jefferson as Inventor and Architect

Thomas Jefferson was a statesman, ambassador, President, the main author of the Declaration of Independence. He was also a highly artistic architect and inventor. Report on his virtuosity and on his specific building designs (Monticello and others) and inventions (e.g., storm windows, dumbwaiters). • ▲ ☐

Red Man and Black Man as Romantic Symbols

Compare the role of the Indian figures in Benjamin West's *Death of General Wolfe* with that of the Black man in John Singleton Copley's *Watson and the Shark* (on view in the National Gallery in Washington, DC). • ★ ☐

Greuze's Symbolism of Irreversible Breakage

Discuss the symbolism and moral in J. B. Greuze's use of broken pitcher, broken egg, broken mirror in his paintings. What do you and/or the critics think he meant to symbolize? Why did Denis Diderot (editor of the *Encyclopedia*) praise these works? What part did they play in Diderot's war with the aristocracy? • ★ ☐

John Constable's Letters and His Credo of Art

Study John Constable's correspondence as a guide to his aims as a painter, especially his letter about the sky as "the key note, the standard scale, and the chief organ of sentiment.'.' Choose several of his landscapes (use slides or reproductions) to illustrate his ideas in practice. • ▲ ☐

Socrates and Jesus, Caravaggio and David

Discuss J. L. David's painting *The Death of Socrates* and the symbolism of twelve disciples; the use of Caravaggian light; the careful use of horizontal and vertical (as opposed to diagonal and curve) to restore balance and equilibrium in the midst of tragedy. • ★ ☐

Delacroix and Reynolds: Emotions in the Face

Joshua Reynolds (see Ideas above) advised artists to paint the face in classic repose because the face in emotion is not beautiful! How does Eugene Delacroix's portrait of Frederic Chopin gainsay Reynolds? Use this difference as indicative of Neoclassicist versus Romanticist approaches to art. • ★ ☐

How the Painter Can Influence History

Rarely does a painter have a measurable effect on political history. An outstanding exception is Jacques-Louis David. His *Oath of the Horatii* and *Death of Socrates* are credited with helping to create the climate of ideas for the French Revolution. Report on "David's Political Impact." • ▲ ☐

(**Wider scope:** See Ideas on "How the Fiction Writer Can Influence History." Compare painter David's impact with that of fiction writer Harriet Beecher Stowe or Upton Sinclair or Ivan Turgenev. • ▲ ☐)

David and Beethoven: Attitudes toward Napoleon

An admirer of the French Revolution, Beethoven is believed originally to have dedicated the Eroica Symphony to Napoleon. Then, at a certain point in Napoleon's doings, so the story goes, Beethoven struck Napoleon's name from the manuscript. Why? But the painter Jacques-Louis David, an actual partisan of the Revolution, still remained loyal to Napoleon. Again, why? Make Beethoven and David a means of (1) evaluating attitudes toward Napoleon and/or (2) commenting on the relation between art and politics. • ★

Bingham's Historic Frontier Pictures

Discuss the way in which George Caleb Bingham's paintings and drawings of American frontier life give us valuable clues to the actual appearance of frontier persons and situations (before cameras came into general use). • ▲ ☐

Courbet's Faceless Stone Breakers

What effect does Gustave Courbet achieve by making it impossible for us to see the expressions on the faces of *The Stone Breakers*? by using an old man and a young boy? by painting a huge mansion in the background and a torn shirt in the foreground? Why did Courbet's friend, the socialist P. J. Proudhon, liken this painting to a parable from the Gospels? • ▲ ☐

Baroque Caravaggio and Realist Courbet: Biographical and Artistic Parallels

Gustave Courbet saw his realist style as related to the style of Caravaggio, whom he had reached through his study of the works of Louis Le Nain and Rembrandt. Explore the parallels in the painting and the critical fate of the sixteenth-century Catholic and the nineteenth-century socialist. • ★ ☐

Bathers, Odalisques, and Ulterior Motives

Report on the themes of ''The Bathers,'' ''Odalisque,'' and ''The Harem'' as excuses employed by artists of the past for painting (e.g., J. A. D. Ingres) and sculpting (e.g., J. A. Houdon) the nude female figure. • ▲ ☐

Manet's *Luncheon on the Grass*

Renaissance and Baroque painters had often included nude figures in outdoor scenes along with clothed figures. Why then did Edouard Manet's *Luncheon on the Grass* raise such an outcry? Consult such books as Howard Greenfield's *The Impressionist Revolution*, George Heard Hamilton's *Manet and his Critics*, John Rewald's *History of Impressionism*, and Emile Zola's essay on Manet. Why is the *Luncheon* considered a manifesto of artistic freedom? • ▲ ☐

Whistler's Lawsuit Against Ruskin

Report on the American painter James McNeill Whistler's libel suit against the British critic John Ruskin. What is its importance in the history of art? In what way does the trial look back to William Turner's *Slave Ship* and ahead to American abstract expressionism? For your own enjoyment, as well as for the added pleasure of your readers/listeners, include Whistler's book *The Gentle Art of Making Enemies* in your report. • ▲ □

The Artist's Mother: Whistler's and Cassatt's

Two great modern American painters—Mary Cassatt and James McNeill Whistler—spent most of their adult life in Europe, both became disciples of Manet and the Impressionists, and both are well known for portraits of *The Artist's Mother*. Compare and contrast the two portraits, both Impressionist, yet—? • ★ □

Postimpressionist Artists as Seen by Novelists

Read Irving Stone's *Lust for Life* and W. Somerset Maugham's *The Moon and Sixpence*. Compare the novelists' characterizations of Vincent Van Gogh and Paul Gauguin with standard nonfiction biographies of these painters. How well have the novelists caught the spirit of the Postimpressionist world? • ★ □

Chardin, Cezanne, and Everyday Objects

Compare the still lifes of Jean-Baptiste Chardin (1699–1779) and Paul Cezanne (1839–1906) for their approach to everyday objects, their concern with the formal problems inherent in them, the symbolic value they invested in them. • ★ □

Theory and Practice of Seurat's Pointillism

Art, according to the Postimpressionist artist Georges Seurat, must be based on a system. (Did he have the great revolution of scientific perspective in mind?) Study his theory of Divisionism (or Pointillism). Is the theory borne out by his paintings? What does happen when you look at a Seurat pointillist painting? Why are the paintings famous and successful anyhow? • ★ □

Critics Attack, Defend Cezanne's Fruit Bowl

Study the critical reputation of Paul Cezanne's *Fruit Bowl, Glass, and Apples,* especially the critics' reactions to the off-center stem of the bowl. • ▲ ☐

Van Gogh's Equivalent of the Christian Halo

Vincent Van Gogh wrote to his brother: ''I want to paint men and women with that something of the eternal that the halo used to symbolize.'' Study several of his portraits. What does he do to achieve his own equivalent of the halo effect? Is it, in his case, a symbol just of the spiritual excellence or is it also—? • ★ ☐

A Picture Is—A View Through A Window? A Tray? A Playing Card?

The painter Maurice Denis said, ''A picture—before being a war horse, a female nude, or some anecdote—is essentially a flat surface covered with colors in a particular order.'' Apply this observation to three or more modern paintings, e.g., Edouard Manet's *Fifer,* James McNeill Whistler's *The Artist's Mother,* Henri Rousseau's *The Dream,* Pablo Picasso's *Les Demoiselles d'Avignon* and *Three Dancers,* Joseph Stella's *Brooklyn Bridge,* Marcel Duchamp's *Nude Descending a Staircase,* Jackson Pollock's *One,* one of Tom Wesselman's Great American Nudes.

In what sense is Denis's statement true even of premodernist paintings that purported to provide three-dimensional views through a window-frame? Consider any three or more you have studied so far, e.g., Peter Paul Rubens' *The Raising of the Cross,* Rembrandt's *The Polish Rider,* J.-L. David's *Death of Marat,* Jean-Auguste Ingres' *Odalisque,* William Turner's *Slave Ship.* Explore this implication in Denis's statement: It reminds painters that they are free, once again, to interpret reality in two dimensions, to stress the flat patterns they had been subordinating or even bypassing during the heyday of scientific perspective. • ▲ ☐

Effect of Photography on Painters and Painting

When the camera was perfected, many artists found themselves without commissions to do portraits and other realistic subjects. Other artists felt liberated at last from the need to be rigidly representational, from the responsibility to leave behind an objective pictorial history of the *outer* reality of their times. After all, writers and composers had long been free to depict *inner* reality as well!

Ideas here: (1) Explore the alternatives that were open to fine artists. For example, some artists, like Pablo Picasso and Paul Cezanne, took the opportunity to *interpret* outer reality without ever departing from it entirely. Other artists, like Marc Chagall and Salvador Dali, went entirely into *inner* reality. Still others, like Jackson Pollock and Mark Rothko, ventured into realms of the abstract. Exemplify, detail, explain these alternatives. Do the historians/critics include others we have neglected? (2) But what has happened with those artists who *persisted in, or later returned to,* realistic representation of outer reality? Is Philip Pearlstein's realism like Gustave Courbet's? Is Harvey Dinnerstein's realism like the nineteenth-century brand? What has happened even to "realism"? What does the new, contemporary representational art now reflect (and include?) of the decades of experimentation—of Impressionism, Expressionism, Postimpressionism, Cubism, Dadaism, Surrealism, etc.? ○ ▲ ☐

Picasso's Political Freedom, Doctorow's Complaints

Consider Francisco Goya's *The Third of May, 1808* and its powerful (anti-Napoleonic) political message; William Turner's *Slave Ship* for its propaganda value; Pablo Picasso's *Guernica* and its clear anti-Franco, anti-fascist message. Then consider in this light the complaints of E. L. Doctorow (see INDEX) that American novelists are discouraged from writing on political themes. ● ★ ☐

Why Did Giorgio de Chirico Repudiate His Dream World?

The Italian painter Giorgio de Chirico produced a series of moody fantasy paintings of arcades by moonlight, railroad locomotives on pitiless deserts, furniture vans locked or wide open and empty and deserted, paintings with dream titles like *Mystery and Melancholy of a Street.* He could himself not explain these works. Then suddenly he repudiated these masterpieces (now hanging in leading museums the world over) and became a conventional painter. Why? Why should he have felt obliged to "explain" his works in words, since his was a visual medium? Would Beethoven feel embarrassed at being unable to translate the Fifth Symphony into sentences? See de Chirico's memoirs and studies by J. T. Soby, Isabella Far, others. ● ▲ ☐

Claes Oldenburg's Giant Ice Bags

What are the psychological, esthetic, and social effects on viewers of Claes Oldenburg's gigantic *Sculpture in the Form of a Trowel Stuck in the Ground*, his *Giant Ice Bag* (fifteen feet high), and his design for a skyscraper shaped like a clothespin? Consult the critics/art historians if your responses need nudging. What does Oldenburg's still life have in common with Jean-Baptiste Chardin's? ● ★ ☐

Romare Bearden's Art about the Jazz Experience

Report on the techniques that artist Romare Bearden uses to represent jazz players and their instruments. In *One Night Stand, 1974,* for example, how do his cubist and collage effects actually simulate a jazz tempo? In *Jamming at the Savoy, 1981* note how his flat planes of color are so related that they give us a visual equivalent of the rhythm the players are working to produce. Perhaps his *Music Stand with Woodwinds* deserves comparison with J. B. Chardin for the way he can bring out the beauty of man-made objects. But Chardin's objects are true *still* life, passive, while Bearden's seem alive, active. How does he manage to make these idle, unplayed instruments seem eager to dance with each other? How much of their bizarre excitement is created by a clever juxtaposition of Freudian symbols? ● ▲ ☐

Cassatt and Bearden: Outside History?

As late as 1977—when the second edition of H. W. Janson's famous and best-selling *History of Art* appeared—well-established artists like Mary Cassatt and Romare Bearden were not represented in most standard, layman's art histories. Both had already made it into the 1975 edition of *The New Columbia Encyclopedia*. What accounts for such disparities? ● ★

How do Soviet Émigré Artists Fare in America?

How has self-imposed exile changed their lives? their art? How do they respond to the highly competitive world of American art? Do they find themselves exhibited more or less often than they were in the U.S.S.R? Reviewed, recognized? How has their Soviet art education prepared them for practice here? Get your start with Marilyn Rueschemeyer *et al., Soviet Émigré Artists*. In review-

ing this short and compact work, critics—especially for the art periodicals—
have doubtless added more details about Soviet émigré careers in the U.S. • ★

Was Abstract Expressionism
Used to Bury "Social Painting"?

When David Sutherland's film *Jack Levine: Feast of Pure Reason* premiered at
the Museum of Modern Art (late 1986), it represented a major comeback for this
social realist. A professional artist at 17 (in 1932), Levine had had a one-man
retrospective at the Whitney in 1955. But in the film and in other interviews,
Levine has said it would have been impossible for him to be so exhibited
(Whitney, etc.) again after 1960. Why?

According to Levine and critics who share his views, a few wealthy Americans in effect suppressed "social painting" by pouring millions into Abstract
Expressionism. Schools, dealers, galleries, museums allegedly turned away
from realism because abstract art was "where the money was" and—it was
"safe"! It had no "social content," like Levine's work (see *Feast of Pure
Reason, Ways and Means, Election Night*).

Ideas here: (1) Compare the critical reactions to the 1955 retrospective with
those to the 1986 film. (2) In what ways do Levine's complaints (that art of
social protest was suppressed) resemble those of novelist E. L. Doctorow (that
fiction dealing with politics is discouraged)? What makes a painter like Levine
(or other realists: Ben Shahn, Raphael Soyer, Philip Evergood, Harvey
Dinnerstein, Edward Hopper) suddenly "go out of fashion" and then "come
back"? Do all the historians/critics agree with Levine's explanations? This is a
good time to remember what Montaigne would say: we must know all points of
view before we can know any. Start with Serge Guilbaut, *How New York Stole
the Idea of Modern Art;* the Greenwich Village periodical *The New Common
Good,* September and October issues, 1986; and Frances Frascina, ed., *Pollock
and Afterward: The Critical Debate,* especially Eva Cockcroft's essay "Abstract Expressionism: Weapon of the Cold War" (published originally in
Artforum, May 1974). • ▲ ☐

• average difficulty	○ previous knowledge	★ most libraries
▲ larger library	☐ visual component	♫ audio component

IDEAS ABOUT SCIENCE

Two Conceptions of Science: Faustians vs. Baconians

Two opposing attitudes toward the uses of science have played major roles in modern history. The legendary Doctor Faust(us) typified medieval science in that his discoveries were *his* secrets, not to be shared but to increase his personal power and to die with him. But in *New Atlantis*, Francis Bacon promulgated the modern doctrine: Scientists should publish and thus share their results so that they can benefit by each other's work and science can advance that much faster.

Trace the history of these two doctrines, including developments like these: uses of alchemy and astrology, policies of the Royal Society, international aspects of the publication of Ben Franklin's kite experiments, Robert Fulton's destruction of his submarine, Matthew Maury's internationally-shared data, secrecy of the Wright Brothers, sudden discontinuation of international sharing in physics during World War II, what Professor J. Z. Young says about the secrecy of naval research on whales (*New York Review of Books*, July 12, 1975), etc. Report on "Humanity's Gains and Losses under the Faustian and Baconian Systems of Science." ● ▲

Can Your Face Be Read Like an Open Book?

"After 40, every man is responsible for his own face," wrote Albert Camus, Nobel Prize-winning novelist. But does that mean that we can judge character from a person's facial features? For example, can we identify "criminal types" by their appearance alone? Every generation produces its new physiognomists: e.g., Johann Kaspar Lavater (1741–1801), Cesare Lombroso (1836–1909), Eric Berne (contemporary). Why have many authors—Johann Wolfgang von Goethe, Jules Verne, Walt Whitman—been seriously interested in physiognomy? What is the status of physiognomy in the scientific community today? Report on these efforts to establish a reliable typology of facial expression. ● ★

Two Stages in the Growth of the Submarine

General George Washington commissioned a submarine in 1776. Its crew, Sergeant Ezra Lee, actually made underwater contact with the British flagship in New York Harbor. For almost two centuries thereafter, almost every submarine was built for military purposes. Today, there are huge fleets of armed submarines prowling under the seven seas. But in the twentieth century, many submarines have been designed, built, and operated for scientific purposes: to enable scientists to observe sea-bottom conditions and life. How do these two vastly different purposes—military and scientific—affect the design of a submarine? What scientific discoveries have been made aboard submarines that would have been impossible without them? Report on the history of submersible craft for either military or civilian purposes, or for both, depending on the scope your assignment permits. • ★

Human Beings under Water (I): History of Scuba Gear

Human beings can now live under water if they carry with them—or are otherwise provided with—a sufficient supply of breathable air. But they could not descend very far until scientists had realized—and solved—the problem of equalizing the pressure. Trace the fascinating history of what we now call scuba gear. Start with early diving helmets, and why they were ineffective; the breakthrough with use of compressed air; the gear invented by two Frenchmen, mining engineer Benoit Rouquarol and naval officer Auguste Denayrouze; the closed helmet with check valves developed by the German Augustus Siebe; work toward the American refinements and the effects that today's scuba gear have on our practical and recreational life. Strive for absolute clarity in your step-by-step explanations of the technical problems involved. • ★

Human Beings under Water (II): How Are Sea Colors Determined?

One of the mysteries of the sea is how its colors are determined. For example, at a depth of 30 feet, scuba divers report that solar rays dissipate all color and tints darken into fine gradations of ultramarine. At lower depths, skin divers report that red blood from fish appears to be green. Report on yesterday's and today's theories that explain how human beings experience colors at various depths. • ★

Human Beings under Water (III): Finding Best Rates of Ascent

What happens when a diver descends more than 30 feet? 100 to 300 feet? below 400? when she ascends? Report on the exciting history of research into the proper conditions for descent and ascent. Start with Paul Bert's research into proper rates of ascent (1875), and include the compilation of U.S. Navy standard decompression tables. Why does a diver who has spent 150 minutes at 300 feet need 1165 minutes of ascent time? • ★

Human Beings under Water (IV): Villages on the Ocean Floor

Did you know that whole communities can now live in submerged, pressurized housing projects? Start your research with the 1969 experiments off the Island of St. John in the Virgin Islands and the 1971 Soviet expedition in the Baltic Sea; include the development of artificial gills that undersea dwellers can strap on when they want to take a stroll "out-of-doors." Explain how they will become the most adaptable specimens of *Homo sapiens,* able to live on land, in outer space, and under sea. • ★

Why Have Great Submarines Been Named *Nautilus?*

What is there in the ancestry claimed for an atomic submarine named *Nautilus?* Trace the genealogy back to Robert Fulton's *Nautilus* (1801), named after a mollusk that can ascend or descend at will by adjusting the amount of gas in its chambers; include Verne's fictitious submarine in *Twenty Thousand Leagues Under the Sea*; The World War II submersible *Nautilus*; note the ways the nuclear-powered *Nautilus* has earned its name: e.g., it was the first submarine to sail "across" the North Pole by traveling *under* the ice pack there (an exploit predicted by Verne's craft). If the mollusk *nautilus,* whose genus has survived for hundreds of millions of years, is one of nature's most extraordinary creatures, what is the current *Nautilus* among man-made mechanisms? • ★

Submarines without Periscopes: The Problem and Its Solution

It's hard to imagine, but all early submarines were blind, operating without periscopes. Simon Lake, for example, did not include one in his designs until 1893, and John Philip Holland did not use one at all, even on his 1900 model. Report on the reasons the periscope was useless until twentieth-century German physicists hit upon an ingenious *combination of both ends of the telescope with the periscope!* Start with books by A. M. Low and Herbert S. Zinn. • ★

Darwin's Captain: Scientist Overshadowed by Darwin

The fame of Charles Darwin overshadows that of Robert Fitzroy, his captain on the H. M. S. *Beagle*. Report on (a) Fitzroy's own outstanding accomplishments and (b) his tragic death as a result of his personal religious conflict over Darwin's theories. • ▲

Commander Maury (1): Not a Fighter of Other Nations but a Uniter

A carriage accident that lamed naval officer Matthew Maury in 1839 removed him from the ranks of sailors training to *fight* other nations and put him rather in the unique position of being able to *unite* nations. Starting with the *Dictionary of American Biography* and histories of the U.S. Navy, outline the story of his services to mankind: his *Wind and Current Charts* that made available to any navigator the cumulative experience of "a thousand vessels that had preceded him on the same voyage"; his organizing the International Maritime Conference held at Brussels in 1853; the international acclaim for his *Explanations and Sailing Directions* which cut trips from England to Australia by 20 days, for example, New York to California by 48 days; his (the first) depth map of the North Atlantic. Read his classic *Physical Geography of the Sea and Its Meteorology*. Report on the massive benefits to world shipping of his practical methods and data. • ▲

(**Wider scope:** Include the following and give examples: While his theoretical contributions are far less valuable than his practical information, his theoretical excursions have stimulated valuable discussions in meteorology and oceanography. • ▲)

But Maury (II) Turns Fighter for the Confederacy

However, when the southern states seceded from the Union in 1861, Maury, a native Virginian, accepted command of the South's coastal, harbor, and river defenses. He invented an electric torpedo and a harbor mine that wrought havoc on Northern warships. Report on Maury's career as scientist in the service of defensive warfare. • ★

Commander Maury (III) as Educator: Professor, Textbook Writer

After the South lost, Maury tried to found a colony of Virginians in Mexico, but by 1868 he settled down as professor of meteorology at Virginia Military Institute. His textbooks were widely read on all levels; *Maury's Elementary Geography* prevailed in primary and intermediate classes as late as 1901. Report on "Maury's Third Career." • ★

General Lee, Commander Maury: The Warrior as Educator (I)

In the opinion of Paxton Davis, Virginia novelist and columnist, Robert E. Lee's greatness flowered not in his career as general (see Davis' novel *Three Days* about Lee's failures at the Battle of Gettysburg), but in his years as educator: he became president of Washington and Lee University. Did Maury also find his real place in the academic world? Report on "The South's Military Leaders as Educators." • ★

Lee, Maury, Eisenhower: The Warrior as Educator (II)

After his long military career, including command of Allied forces in Europe in World War II, General Dwight Eisenhower became president of Columbia University. Some of the (tenured) faculty spoke ironically of him as "Doctor Eisenhower." How did the warrior, who had only to command, never to persuade, function in that role? How had the role of college president changed between Lee's presidency of Washington and Lee and "Ike's" at Columbia? Report on "U.S. Military Leaders as Educators." • ★

The Military as Sponsors of Scientific Research

The British Navy's sponsorship of Darwin's research, and the U.S. Navy's of Maury's work, exemplify the good side of relations between the military and science. For allegedly bad aspects of this relationship, start with E. H. Shenton's *Diving for Science* (especially passages on troubles Auguste and Jacques Piccard had with the U.S. Navy over their *Trieste* dive into the Challenger deep); J. Z. Young's July 17, 1975 article, "Save the Whales!" in *The New York Review of Books;* and Kurt Vonnegut's famous 1969 speech to the American Physical Society (reprinted in *Wampeters, Foma, and Granfalloons*) in which he discussed the moral dilemma of physicists who cannot get proper research facilities without working under the military. He defined "virtuous physicists" as "those who don't work on new weapons"; some physicists, he added, "are so virtuous that they don't go into physics at all." • ▲

What Causes Ocean Currents?
Theories of Franklin, Maury, *et al.*

The debate has raged for centuries. Benjamin Franklin's hypothesis was succeeded by Matthew Maury's and revived by James Croll; then the Franklin-Croll explanation was merged with Maury's as Vilhelm Bjerknes and Walfrid Ekman extended them into what is known now as the Coriolis Effect. Why, at a depth of 200-to-500 feet, will currents flow in a direction opposite to that of the wind on the surface? • ▲

Near Extinction, Then Total Recovery of Sea Otters

By 1900 it was believed that the sea otter, web-footed member of the weasel family, had become extinct. Why had hunters killed them? How had fishermen indirectly helped destroy them? How did conservationists accomplish the revival of one of the few animals that can use tools? • ▲

Oceans and Earth's Crust:
Neptunists, Vulcanists, and _____?

Trace the history of ideas about the relationship between the ocean and the formation of rocks. Include (1) the theory of the German geologist A. G. Wermer and his followers, the Neptunists; (2) the theories of opposing schools, especially the Vulcanists or Plutonists; (3) subsequent theories, including today's. • ★

The Kraken: A Sea Beast or a Floating Island?

In his *Natural History of Norway* (1755), Bishop Erik Pontoppidan described the kraken as the "largest . . . of all the animal creation," sometimes measuring a mile and a half in circumference. From more credible details that he offered, it seems the kraken was probably a giant squid. This creature has frequently appeared in the records, been denied, reappeared. When a French sea-captain reported an encounter with one in 1861, the French Academy said his crew had really grappled with a sea plant and then become hysterical! However, the captain was right. Report on ''The Giant Squid: Legend and Fact.'' • ▲

(**Wider scope:** Include the giant squid's appearance in fiction, as in Victor Hugo's *Toilers of the Sea* and Jules Verne's *Twenty Thousand Leagues under the Sea.* • ▲)

What Happens When Sailors "Heave the Log"?

''We heaved the log,'' says a character in that very Verne novel (see Idea above), ''and calculated that the *Abraham Lincoln* was going at the rate of 18½ miles an hour.'' What is this device that mariners trail from a ship to ascertain their speed? How does it work? How accurate is it? When was it invented? Report on it in a spirit of admiration for the ingenious, simple technology of premodern times. How do mariners perform this calculation today? • ★

The Space Program: Its Everyday Benefits to Humanity

How have research and development in the space effort benefitted the average person? Include spinoffs in medicine, engineering, metallurgy, as well as improved knowledge about the universe. • ▲

Channels or Canals on Mars?
Mistranslation and Science (Fiction)

An Italian astronomer, G. V. Schiaparelli, observed in 1877 a network of lines or grooves on the surface of Mars. He reported them as *canali,* meaning, in that context, *channels.* Alas, *canali* was mistranslated as *canals.* The English-speaking world, assuming canals could be created only by quasi-human creatures, became excited about ''intelligent life on Mars.'' What were the results in astronomy? in science fiction? of photographs sent back by space probes? Report on ''The Effects in Science and Science Fiction When a Word is Mistranslated.'' • ▲

Tunnels through a Mountain: Would They Ever Meet?

In 152 A.D., the Roman engineer Nonius Datus supposedly wrote a famous memorandum-report to the magistrates of Saldae, Algeria. They had asked him to inspect the work on a water tunnel he had designed: the contractors had excavated from both sides of a mountain but the two excavation parties had failed to meet in the middle! What does this report reveal about Roman engineering methods and engineering writing? Have modern engineers faced a similar problem—e.g., in the driving of the Holland Tunnel between New York and New Jersey? Why have some historians challenged the authenticity of the Datus report? Start with James Kip Finch's *Engineering and Western Civilization,* including his bibliography; later histories and encyclopedia articles; W. J. Miller and L. E. A. Saidla's *Engineers as Writers.* What would have been the point of a forgery? • ▲

McAdam, Engineering Genius: A Refugee from the U.S.A.

Unwelcome in New York after the Americans won their independence, John Loudon McAdam, 27-year-old Tory, returned to his native Scotland. There he conducted experiments to determine the most scientific methods of building a road; his famous results are built into the English language with such words as "macadamize," "macadam," and "macadam road." Were his ideas welcome in America then, if his person was not? Yes, his *Remarks on the Present System of Road Making* was avidly read and utilized even among McAdam's ex-fellow-Americans. Write a report on "McAdam's Relations with the U.S.A.: A Study in Irony." • ▲

Macadamize, Telfordize: Engineers Immortalized

John Loudon McAdam's road-building became so famous that in the early nineteenth-century world, "macadamize" was coined to mean "make progress in a scientific manner." McAdam's contemporary, Thomas Telford, builder of canals and bridges as well as of roads, was similarly honored with the coinage "telfordize." Look up both words, as well as "macadam road" and "telford," in an unabridged dictionary. How has "macadamize" taken on a narrower meaning today? What is the difference in the meanings of "macadamize" and "telfordize"? Report on "How Two Engineers Have Been Immortalized in Language." • ★

(**Wider scope:** Check different forms of both "macadam" and "telford" in unabridged dictionaries of several foreign languages. Report on "How Two Engineers Have Been Immortalized Internationally." • ▲)

Engineers' Conceptions of Engineering Science

How do engineers themselves see their profession? For three classic descriptions/definitions, report on: Georgius Agricola's defense of the metallic arts in his *De Re Metallica* (translated by Herbert Clark Hoover and Lou Henry Hoover); Arthur Mellen Wellington's preface and introduction to his *The Economic Theory of the Location of Railways*; and Herbert Hoover's *Memoirs*, Volume I, Chapter 11. Why is it that descriptions of engineering seem inevitably to lead to some social criticism? or at least to social questions? • ▲

(**Wider scope:** Write to the editors of the journals that serve the engineering societies and ask them to recommend published descriptions of their branch of engineering that are held in high esteem by the profession. Apply the same questions about mission and social value. • ▲)

Theoreticians Remembered only for Practical Gifts

Matthew Maury's contributions to science (see Ideas above) reflect a familiar pattern in history; that of the researcher whose theories prove wrong but whose practical contributions still make him famous. Compare the reputations of Pythagoras, Archimedes, and Matthew Maury in this respect. Why would all three have preferred to be remembered as theoretical scientists? Can your science teachers provide you with any other examples? • ★

The Book of Exodus and Modern Science

In their flight from Egypt, the Israelites crossed not the Red Sea but the Sea of Reeds. This new biblical interpretation, based on archaeological discoveries, made page one of *The New York Times* of October 12, 1962. Later research by Johns Hopkins University Egyptologist Hans Goedicke has helped make it possible to show when, why, and how the events of the biblical story actually took place. Start your research with *The New York Times Index* for 1962 and include in your bibliography *Exodus: The True Story* by Ian Wilson. • ★

Einstein = Space and Time
Edelman   Memory, Perception

In his essay-review "Neural Darwinism: A New Approach to Memory Perception" (*New York Review of Books*, October 9, 1986), Israel Rosenfield declares that Gerald M. Edelman's new theories may well be as important to psychology as Alfred Einstein's were to our views of space and time. Rosenfield's essay comprises a popularization for laymen, and his own interpretation, of nine papers by Edelman. *Ideas here:* (1) Can you prepare an outline and a practical condensation of Rosenfield's essay that will serve as an information report for students—on the student level? (2) To increase the value of your information report, follow through on critical reaction to Rosenfield's article; *New York Review of Books* itself has published some of these reactions; what have *Psychology Today* and the professional psychological journals had to say on these momentous developments? • ★

Scientific Management and "Taylorism"

When Frederick W. Taylor published his *The Principles of Scientific Management* (1909), a new branch of engineering was born: industrial engineering. "Efficiency experts," as industrial engineers came to be known, make time-motion studies of each job and reeducate workers on how to increase their output without, presumably, increasing their *physical* burden. Production at Midvale Steel Works, where Taylor was chief engineer, rose almost 300 percent, while wages rose about 100 percent. But while scientific management was enthusiastically adopted by industry, it was resented by organized labor. "Taylorism," as labor called it, became a dirty word. Why? Does it denote a *psychological* burden? In its present usage, the word seems to connote excessive, detailed control over workers' lives. That is clearly its meaning as it is used in *The Progressive,* also founded in 1909 (by Senator Robert M. La Follette, Sr.). In an article about President Ronald Reagan's advocacy of urine tests to weed out drug addicts from the workplace, *The Progressive* said: "Management can now oversee the work force beyond the wildest dreams of Taylorism, and many employees are powerless to defend themselves" (October 1986). Report on both sides of the question. • ▲

What is the Radon Danger in Your House? Your School?

Stanley Watras, a Pennsylvania engineer, repeatedly set off radiation alarms when he entered the nuclear-power plant where he worked. Trying to find the reason for his high radioactivity, officials followed him home. In his house they found concentrations of radon gas to be 2700 picocuries per liter of air. Radon is an invisible, odorless gas produced by the decay of uranium in soil and stone.

The average house supposedly has one picocurie per liter; the U.S. crucial level is four, which, it is believed, would cause lung cancer in one out of every hundred people. A picocurie (one trillionth of a curie) represents the decay of two radon atoms per minute. A conservative estimate is that this naturally formed gas, which accumulates indoors, causes about 10,000 of the country's annual lung-cancer deaths.

Ideas here: (1) These scary developments are so new that even a simple background-information report would be of great value. Start with *The New York Times Index* (1986 especially, the eighties generally). What do the scientific journals say? What does your local board of health say? For example, a toll-free call to Virginia's Radiological Health Office (1-800-468-0138) gets you a free booklet, "Indoor Radon," which suggests ways to reduce radon exposure. (2) More advanced questions: Suppose there's a smoker in a house whose air is tested out for a mere four picocuries per liter. How much does that increase the occupants' chances of lung cancer? How much radioactivity does every nuclear test or disaster add to our soil and stone? What happened to Mr. Watras? • ★

IDEAS ABOUT HISTORY AND CURRENT AFFAIRS

Your Account of One Day in the History of World War II

"Stauffenberg won an assured place in history by his remarkable exploit in placing a time bomb under Adolf Hitler's map table," says the *Simon & Schuster Encyclopedia of World War II*. Get oriented with a few such summaries and then get as close to the primary sources as you can. *Exercise in nonfiction writing*: By using flashbacks of Stauffenberg's life and of the assassination plot, weave the whole story into the action of that one day, July 20, 1944. • ★

Why Vietnam? Colonel Patti *et al.*

In World War II, Colonel Archimedes Patti worked closely with the Vietnamese rebels fighting Japan. After the war, they hoped to gain their freedom from France. They modeled their Declaration of Independence on the classic American document, and they hoped for U.S. help. But the White House ignored Patti's advice, turned its back on the Vietnamese, and helped the French return to power over Vietnam. Patti sees these as the tragic beginnings of American blunders in Southeast Asia, leading to U.S. military involvement in Vietnam. The colonel was officially discouraged for decades from publishing his book *Why Vietnam?* How did the critics, especially the contemporary historians, receive Patti's revelations? Compare Patti's answers to *Why Vietnam?* with those of at least two other writers on the subject. • ▲

Unexpected Strategic Benefit of Doolittle's Raid on Japan

Colonel J. H. Doolittle's daring raid on Tokyo, just five months after Pearl Harbor, was intended mainly as a booster-shot for American morale. However, the fringe benefits were fantastic. Report on the way the raid triggered events that led to the defeat of the Japanese at Midway. Get your bearings by reading "First Special Aviation Project" in the *Simon & Schuster Encyclopedia of World War II* and the piece on Doolittle in the *Historical Encyclopedia of World War II* (Facts on File). Aim to get as close as you can to wartime accounts by both sides, but also use later accounts that put the war in better perspective. • ★

Deism as a Major Faith among the Founding Fathers

Why did so many prominent figures of the Age of Reason regard deism as their faith? Establish a working definition of deism so that you can identify its doctrines when you investigate the religious beliefs of the American Founding Fathers. Be careful to distinguish among deism, theism, and atheism. Keep in mind that Crane Brinton, Harvard expert on that period, said that "deism was . . . the belief of the 'intellectuals.' It was held not infrequently by men who never formally gave up conventional Christianity." He gives as a good example the poet Alexander Pope, "whose *Essay on Man* is a neat summary of deist commonplaces," who "was born into the English Catholic minority and remained a kind of Catholic" all his life. Limit your research to several of the American intellectuals, e.g., Thomas Jefferson, Benjamin Franklin, George Washington, Alexander Hamilton, Samuel Adams. • ★

Freak Naval War Maneuver: Towing Yourself to Safety

Report on the way the U.S.S. *Constitution* was saved from destruction by a British fleet on July 18, 1812. • ▲

The Ram as a Weapon in Naval Warfare

It does not surprise us that the ram was a powerful weapon in ancient warfare, before the invention of guns, mines, torpedoes, and armor plate. But why was it revived in modern times? Consider its value in the American Civil War; its decisive role in the Battle of Vis between the Austrians and Italians in 1866; its self-destructiveness in British Royal Navy maneuvers in 1893; its virtual disappearance by 1900. ● ▲

Author? Cartoonist? Photographer? Balloonist? Nadar Was All

One of the most remarkable men of the nineteenth century was Gaspard-Félix Tournachon, who operated in all these fields—and others—under the name of Nadar. In all his endeavors, he combined technical inventiveness with romantic imagination. He pioneered in aerial photography (from a balloon), in long-distance balloon trips, in military ballooning (he was a hero in the Franco-Prussian War). *Ideas here:* The psychological and creative advantages of being not a specialist but a generalist; creativity vs. specialization; Nadar's contribution to one of his four fields as it was influenced by the other three; how Nadar's eccentric life style fostered his virtuosity; Nadar as the model for Jules Verne's character Ardan in *From the Earth to the Moon*; Nadar as depicted by biographers compared with Ardan as portrayed by Verne; critical reaction to showings of Nadar's photography (*The New York Times Index*, 1970–1980s). ● ▲ □

Role of Breadfruit in World History

Why did Captain James Cook recommend that the Pacific islands' breadfruit be transplanted to the Americas? How did Captain William Bligh of H. M. S. *Bounty* become involved? Why does breadfruit now flourish from Mexico to Brazil? ● ★

"The Soldier's Disease": Post-Bellum Drug Addiction

Why was drug addiction called "the soldier's disease" after the American Civil War? What drugs were involved? How were they obtained? What were the state and federal governments' attitudes toward the "disease"? ● ▲

Drug Addiction in the Vietnam War

Report on the use of "controlled substances" by members of the U.S. armed forces during the war in Vietnam. What were the penalties? How widespread was the practice? Had the servicepeople brought the habit with them, or acquired it in the service? After checking *The New York Times Index* and guides to periodical literature, look up books about the war in the library catalogs. • ★

(**Wider scope:** What was the relation, if any, between drug addiction and the alleged practice of "fragging"? • ▲)

"Fragging" in Vietnam; "90-Day Wonders" in WWI

There were widespread rumors, after World War I, that many second lieutenants (graduates of 90-day training camps) had been shot in the back. Your present writer, for example, was warned (*sotto voce*) not to go to officer candidate school by a member of his draft board who claimed the rumors were true! Similarly, during and after the Vietnam War, there were allegations that many U.S. officers had been "fragged"—i.e., targets of grenades tossed by their own men. *Ideas here:* How many of these rumors and allegations have been verified? How much opportunity does war provide for the safe murder of one's personal (as distinguished from national) enemies? Why does such violence against soldiers on one's own side figure throughout our literature, from the David and Bathsheba story in the Bible to novels like Normal Mailer's *The Naked and the Dead* and William Gaddis' *Carpenter's Gothic*? • ▲

(**Narrower scope:** Concentrate only on the alleged "fragging" in Vietnam OR alleged "shooting in the back" in France. • ▲)

A Study in U.S. Attitudes toward Wartime Atrocities (I)

The worst European atrocity of World War II committed against American troops occurred on December 17, 1944, when a Nazi task force murdered about 86 captured Americans in a field at Malmédy, Belgium. The worst atrocity committed by American ground forces occurred in the South Vietnam hamlet of My Lai on March 16, 1968, when Lieutenant W. L. Calley's men murdered 347 unarmed civilian men, women, and children. Report on American public opinion toward these two incidents. • ★

A Study in U.S. Attitudes toward Wartime Atrocities (II)

Compare the American public's reactions to (1) the Nazi bombing of undefended Rotterdam that resulted in 20,000 civilian deaths and (2) the Anglo-American bombing of undefended Dresden five years later that wiped out 120,000 civilians in one night. Why was Kurt Vonnegut—when, after the war, he wrote to the U.S. Air Force asking for details about the Dresden massacre—told "that the information was top secret still"? How much does the official USAF history of World War II tell about the raid? Read Kurt Vonnegut's *Slaughterhouse-Five*, his novel based on his experiences as an American prisoner of war in Dresden. (He and about 100 other American servicemen survived the fire-bombing because they and their guards had taken shelter in the underground chambers of Slaughterhouse-Five.) What was the public's reaction when Vonnegut's novel focused belated attention on "the largest massacre in European history"? Some of it you can pick up from critics who reviewed *Slaughterhouse-Five*. You will find a bibliography of major criticism of the novel in the Monarch Note *Kurt Vonnegut's "Slaughterhouse-Five."* Be sure to read the Alfred Kazin review as one clue to public opinion on the Dresden affair and on government suppression of it. Also check *The New York Times Index* and other guides to periodical literature for articles about public response to Vonnegut's revelations. • ▲

A Study of U.S. and U.S.S.R. Attitudes toward Wartime Atrocities (III)

During World War II thousands of Jews were murdered at Babi Yar by Nazi troops. Check the histories and encyclopedias of the war for the basic facts; read in translation the Russian poet Yevgeny Yevtushenko's poem "Babi Yar"; follow through in the guides to periodical literature and *The New York Times Index* for (a) American public opinion toward the massacre itself and (b) the Soviet people's changing attitudes toward the massacre and towards Yevtushenko's poem when it was first published and today. • ▲

Who Did It, the Rough Riders or the Negro Tenth Cavalry?

Who took San Juan Hill in Cuba in the Spanish-American War? Teddy Roosevelt and his Rough Riders, right? Well, yes, "TR" and his men took all the credit, but the real heroes of the battle were the Negro Tenth Cavalry. If you start your research with standard reference books, you're likely to hear once again all about the Riders and nothing about the Tenth, but such distortion of the facts is part of your story. You'll really get under way when you find a copy of Edward Wakin's *Black Fighting Men in United States History;* also read P. T. Drotning's *A Guide to Negro History* and *Black Heroes in our National History*. Check also general histories of the Spanish-American War, of the Cavalry, biographies of Roosevelt, his own writings. • ▲

(**Wider scope:** When "TR" became President, he had to make the final decision in the case of a Negro unit that had been accused of misconduct. Follow through on the history of the case until its final disposition in the eighties. • ▲)

Black Fighting Men in American History

How many black soldiers served in General Washington's army? What were they assigned to do? How did they acquit themselves? in the Mexican War? the Civil War? Indian Wars? Spanish-American War (see Idea above)? World War I? (How did General John "Blackjack" Pershing get that nickname?) Were black soldiers still segregated in World War II, the war against fascism and racism? Why was the percentage of black casualties in the Korean and Vietnam Wars greater than the percentage of blacks in the total population?

Limit yourself to one war, or one period, or, as the Idea above would suggest, one campaign or one battle, or one unit. Once you've established the numerical identity of the black units—e.g., the 99th Pursuit Squadron of World War II—try for special unit histories and rosters, some available from state and national governments, some published by the veterans associations of the units themselves. Again, you can get your bearings with the Wakin and Drotning books (above). For specific wars, try Bertram Hawthorne Groene's *Tracing Your Civil War Ancestor;* Thomas Wentworth Higginson's *Army Life in a Black Regiment* (he was the white colonel of the first Negro regiment in the Civil War); Florette Henri's *Bitter Victory: A History of Black Soldiers in World War I;* and A. E. Barbeau's and Florette Henri's *The Unknown Soldier: Black American Soldiers in World War I.* • ▲

"The Lonely Eagles"

Their nickname was an ironic twist on the sobriquet "The Lone Eagle" given to Charles Lindbergh. Report on the indignities suffered by these black officers who trained at Tuskegee Army Airfield (Alabama) in World War II. • ★

Davis and the Black 99th

Report on the record of the first black aviation unit to see combat in World War II, the 99th Pursuit Squadron, commanded by Colonel B. O. Davis. • ★

Davis and the Black 332nd

Report on Colonel Davis and the all-black 332nd Fighter Group (the 99th, 100th, 301st, 302nd Squadrons) which he commanded. • ★

Parrish and Racial Integration

Report on the work of Colonel N. F. Parrish, a white officer who took command of Tuskegee Army Airfield in 1942. How did he help the U.S. Air Force to achieve racial integration (after World War II)? • ★

Generals Senior and Junior

Report on the famous father-son combination in the U.S. military. Benjamin Oliver Davis, Sr. became the first black general in the U.S. Army (1940–1948). His son, B. O. Davis, Jr., one of the "Lonely Eagles," became the first black Air Force general and the first black to achieve three-star rank in the services at large. • ★

Japanese-Americans and Pearl Harbor (II)

After Japan attacked Pearl Harbor in 1941, the American government decided to move all Japanese-Americans (even native-born Americans) to War Relocation Camps inland. Do an historical account of the reasons advanced by the government in 1942, the ruptures caused in personal lives and careers, the conditions in the camps, the racist (and fascist) aspects of the camps in the midst of an anti-fascist war, the legal efforts of the Japanese-Americans to gain some rectification (40 or more years later!) of the injustices perpetrated on them. *Start* with *The New York Times Index* and standard histories and encyclopedias of World War II. • ★

(**Wider scope:** Include a summary of the part that Japanese-American draftees and volunteers played in actual naval, ground, and aerial combat. • ★)

Writers in Uniform

Many writers and editors (e.g., Merrill Miller, Louis Rubin) got their start in the literary world by serving on the staff of one or more of the World War II periodicals of the Army of the United States: *Yank, Army Times, Fort Benning* (Ga.) *Bayonet, Spirit of the 176th, Academic Regiment Mirror*, etc. After doing an initial survey, pick one periodical and show how it developed young writers who became professional authors after the war. • ▲

An International Language: Artificial or Natural?

On a cruise aboard Jules Verne's yacht, Raoul Duval, French politician, made a passionate, impromptu speech to the Pillars of Hercules—in Volapük! This was an artificial language, created in 1879; eight years later, Esperanto was invented; in our time, Interlingua. Why do we seek an artificial tongue? Why have Volapük and Esperanto proved unsuitable? Why does Interlingua have a better chance? Will English become so widely used that no artificial language could compete? In your study, give examples of how words are created for these artificial languages and how the principle used in each case has affected that "tongue's" viability. • ★

Five Women Become Heads of State:
India, Israel, Britain, Iceland, The Philippines

Since World War II, five nations have chosen women as their heads of state. To date, no woman has been elected to the U.S. Presidency, nor have any been nominated for it by a national party. How do the political scientists, and the feminists, account for this disparity in opportunities for women in world politics? • ★

Loss of Two Nationally Elected Leaders in One Term

The U.S. has only two officers elected by the people at large—the President and the Vice-President. In the mid-1970s we lost both officers during one presidential term, and Congress had to replace them with politicians *not* elected by

• average difficulty	○ previous knowledge	★ most libraries
▲ larger library	☐ visual component	♫ audio component

popular vote. Report on (1) the history of the Constitutional predicament, why it occurred; (2) the necessary element of compromise which resulted in the choice of relatively weak officials at the very time strong ones were needed; (3) the likelihood of the country's often being headed by officials not popularly elected; (4) the long-range problems that remain unsolved; (5) proposals for solutions offered by political scientists and constitutional lawyers. • ★

The Electoral College vs. Popular Elections

We spoke loosely, in the Idea above, about the "popular vote." In actual practice, Americans don't vote directly for their President and Vice-President but for electors "pledged" to vote for certain candidates. What are the liabilities? What threats have been made (e.g., during a presidential campaign by Governor George Wallace) to use the electoral-college situation to get into office a man who did not have the popular vote? Why is the electoral college maintained in the face of these liabilities? • ★

Function and Power of the Book Reviewer

What do the reviewers/critics think of a recent book of fiction or nonfiction (but no self-help or how-to books) that *you* have enjoyed? Check the book review digests in your library for leads, then read at least five reviews in the chronological order in which they appeared. Probably *Publishers Weekly* reviewed it first, months *before* publication; followed rather closely by the *American Library Association Journal, Booklist, Choice;* and around or soon after its "pub date," *The New York Times Book Review* or the daily *Times* book pages, *The Washington Post, The Christian Science Monitor* and other prominent newspapers might have reviewed it. Was it reviewed in your local papers? Was it, eventually, reviewed in the intellectual journals, e.g., *The New York Review of Books, The New Yorker, The Nation, The New Republic, Atlantic, Harper's*? Publications of the "right" (*National Review, Insight*)? of the "left" (*In These Times, Daily World*)?

Consider some or all of these *Ideas:* How do the reviewers compare in their emphasis? their judgment of the content? the style? the effectiveness and value of the book? Which reviews contained original thinking, and which followed the lead of the jacket copy or of the earlier reviewers (*PW, ALAJ*)? How have the reviews deepened your appreciation of the book? What had you missed that they have shown you to be there? What, in your opinion, did some of the reviewers miss (or deliberately overlook)? Which reviews do you see as the most important in deciding the fate of a book? • ▲

Canada, Unknown Neighbor?

Is it true that most citizens of the United States know virtually nothing about Canada and the Canadians? Is this true of Uncle Sam's people living along the border? How do Canadians feel about their neighbors to the south? *A research project:* Subscribe for one month to a major Canadian newspaper, a major newspaper of a U.S. border city (see the reference librarian's guides to periodicals, like *Ayer's*), and to the newspaper most widely read in your area. (If you live near the Canadian border, make that third newspaper one published 200 miles south of you.) What events important to an understanding of Canada are ignored by your local paper? What coverage does the U.S. border-city offer of Canadian affairs? Why? What does the Canadian paper reveal about coverage of, attitudes toward, the U.S.? • ★

(**Wider scope:** Get leads for your project by reading *The Canadians* by Andrew Malcolm, a *New York Times* reporter whose beat is north of the border. • ★)

(**Wider still:** Include in your background research your reading of a history of Canada, by a Canadian, published in Canada. • ▲)

A Major World Court Case (I): Nicaragua vs. United States

In the mid-eighties, Nicaragua took the U.S. to court because the CIA and/or other U.S. agencies had mined Nicaraguan waters in violation of international law. Report on: the function and aim of the World Court; U.S. participation in earlier cases; the U.S. position on the Nicaraguan case; how and why Nicaragua won its case; the effect on world opinion of U.S. refusal to accept the Court's decision; opinions of international lawyers on the U.S. position and its effect on U.S. credibility and World Court prestige. • ★

A Major World Court Case (II): Nicaragua vs. Costa Rica

In 1986 Nicaragua sued Costa Rica in the World Court for permitting its territory to be used by Nicaraguan rebel forces. Pick up the trail of events in *The New York Times Index* and the reader's guides. Note that *The New York Times* reported (September 29, 1986) that Americans had supervised the building of a "military-sized airstrip" in Costa Rica near its border with Nicaragua; that the following month a plane originating in El Salvador flew over Costa Rican air space to drop rebel supplies in Nicaragua (where it was shot down by a single teen-age soldier); that the airstrip is six miles from an American-built base where Green Berets have trained Costa Rican border patrolmen. What did the World Court decide about Costa Rica's alleged violation of its neutrality? What was the reaction in Congress and the American press about U.S. involvement in Costa Rican affairs? See Idea above: what will be the effect on the prestige of the World Court? on efforts to enforce international law? • ★

A Working Glossary of Political Terminology

Are you confused, as you read and/or listen to the world news, by the large number of unfamiliar labels used in identifying people prominent in political life? Can you distinguish easily among a neo-Stalinist, a Leninist, a Trotskyist? a Christian Socialist and a Social Democrat? a conservative, a rightist, and a fascist? Have you been influenced to think of *capitalism* and *democracy* as automatic synonyms, *socialism* and *dictatorship* as synonyms too, and of an anticommunist as automatically pro-democracy? Your friends are probably just as confused as you are. Why not compile a list of political terms you read in the next two weeks, check carefully on their distinctions and differentiae, try these words out on 15 or so young people (or parents?!), and report on the results: "How Knowledgeable Are Americans about Distinctions among Political Labels?" • ★

U.S. "Leak" of "Disinformation": What Would Machiavelli Say?

In fall 1986, the press questioned Secretary of State George Schultz about reports that the U.S. had "leaked" false information to the press. The Secretary, according to *The New York Times,* said the Administration was free to take whatever actions might cause trouble for Colonel Muammar el-Qaddafi, Libyan head of state. The *Times* reported that while the Administration was manipulating the press by using it to release "disinformation" in a psychological war with Libya, the White House was also threatening to punish reporters who sought the *correct* information. *Ideas here:* (1) Some observers see such developments as Presidential efforts to control the press. Opinions pro and con?

(2) Other observers say the government is simply following normal "corporate public relations policy." What does this mean about corporation "PR"? After briefing yourself with the October 3, 1986 *Times,* be sure to see: the August 25, 1986, *Wall Street Journal,* in which some of the White House "disinformation" was allegedly planted; the August 27, 1986, *New York Times,* which made the allegation; issues of the *Washington Times,* a conservative organ, for its coverage of the summer-fall '86 controversy. Include in your research the weekly newsmagazines. Present all the views supporting (1), then those behind (2), and then write your own conclusions on (3) What the lesson is here for government, press, and citizenry. • ★

(**Wider scope:** Put the issue in a larger context. What would Niccolò Machiavelli say? What does history say about the struggle for a free press in colonial America? What does the U.S. Constitution say? Has the U.S. government ever before made legal efforts to curb the press? Put the "disinformation" issue in the light of democracy's chronic anxiety about anything that can develop into attacks on its freedoms. • ★)

National Health Insurance: The Story of Its Nonexistence

The gruesome story goes that if an American family is hit by a fatal disease, they should move to Canada. Canada would care for them under national health insurance; in the U.S., however, they might go into debt for hundreds of thousands of dollars, probably bequeathing such debts to their children/grandchildren. Another story: an American student in Sweden gets free medical and dental care; a Swedish student in the U.S. does not. Canada and Sweden are far more typical of the average "advanced" nation in this respect. Why was it that when most countries were adopting national health insurance in the nineteenth century, the U.S. instead opted for the Community Chest? *Ideas here:* (1) History of the national health insurance movement in Europe and North America. (2) The movement in the U.S. today for national health insurance: history; who is for it? who against it? alleged advantages? alleged disadvantages? • ★

Social Security Problems for Today's Young and Old

Social security deductions from paychecks are required by law. All their working lives, millions of people have had large portions of their income collected at the source so that—they were assured—they could get it back when they retired. Now, as they see it, they almost have to beg to get their money back;

they are on the defensive, insecure about their future. Meanwhile, young people are angry that they have to suffer big payroll deductions to help meet the demands on the government for retirement benefits for the elderly. What went wrong? What happened to a system that was supposed to make young and old both feel more secure? Report on the history of the problem. • ★

(**Wider scope:** Include a survey of proposals that have been advanced to find a fair solution for all ages. • ★)

Political Action Committees—Legalized Corruption?

The Wall Street Journal reported that Jay Rockefeller spent $10 million "from his own deep pockets" to win a West Virginia Senate seat. Nelson Rockefeller was reported to have spent $5 million of Rockefeller money for *each* of his four successful campaigns for the New York State governorship. In one election, his Democratic Party opponent could raise only $250,000! After NR won, he taunted his opponent for not having put up a fight.

"Increasingly, candidates who aren't rich as Rockefeller," says *Wall Street Journal* writer Brooks Jackson, "must turn to wealthy donors and special-interest groups to raise the kind of money required for a modern, capital-intensive campaign." These groups include the Political Action Committees which, in return for campaign donations, expect to influence the way the office-holder votes/speaks out. With PACs, according to former Congressman John Cavanaugh, "we've institutionalized corruption."

If election depends on the amount of money a candidate can raise, he is then not a servant of the people but of his "donors." Review the reasons PACs were legalized; criticisms of the system from business, labor, and citizens' groups; alternatives suggested for raising campaign funds. Start with Jackson's series "The Influence Peddlers" (*Wall Street Journal*, July 1986), then check *The New York Times Index* and the guides to periodicals. • ★

• average difficulty	○ previous knowledge	★ most libraries
▲ larger library	□ visual component	♑ audio component

8

Suggestions for Further Reading

So you've met the first of the "three big challenges" we anticipated in our Introduction. You've found your (1) "writable Idea (or a speakable one)." You're warming up, then, for (2) researching that Idea and for (3) the writing up, or oral presentation, of your findings. Here are a few suggestions for basic books that you'll find helpful in those latter two stages of your project.

American Psychological Association. *Publication Manual of the American Psychological Association*. Washington: American Psychological Association, 1983.

Barzun, Jacques, and Henry F. Graff. *The Modern Researcher*. 4th ed. New York: Harcourt, Brace, Jovanovich, 1985.

Brohaugh, William, ed. *Writer's Resource Guide*. Cincinnati, OH: Writer's Digest Books, 1979.

Cottam, Keith M., and Robert W. Pelton. *Writer's Research Handbook*. New York: Barnes & Noble, 1978.

Downs, Robert B., and Clara D. Keller. *How to Do Library Research*. Urbana, IL: University of Illinois Press, 1975.

Gates, Jean Key. *Guide to the Use of Books and Libraries*. 3rd ed. New York: McGraw-Hill, 1973.

Keyworth, Cynthia. *How to Write a Term Paper*. New York: Arco, 1985.

Lenmark-Ellis, Barbara. *How to Write Themes and Term Papers*. Woodbury, NY: Barron's, 1981.

Miller, Walter James, and Elizabeth Morse-Cluley. *How to Write Book Reports*. New York: Arco, 1984.

McCoy, F. N. *Researching and Writing in History: A Practical Handbook for Students*. Berkeley, CA: University of California Press, 1974.

Rivers, William L. *Finding Facts: Interviewing, Observing, Using Reference Sources*. Englewood Cliffs, NJ: Prentice-Hall, 1975.

Todd, Alden. *Finding Facts Fast*. 2nd ed. Berkeley, CA: Ten Speed Press, 1979.

Turabian, Kate L. *A Manual for Writers of Term Papers, Theses, and Dissertations*. 4th ed. Chicago, IL: University of Chicago Press, 1973.

Index to Persons, Titles, Subjects, Ideas

compiled by J. B. Miller

263

LET ARCO HELP YOU
PREPARE FOR COLLEGE ENTRANCE

  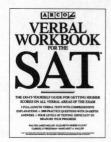

*SAT**

PRELIMINARY SCHOLASTIC APTITUDE TEST/
NATIONAL MERIT SCHOLARSHIP QUALIFYING TEST
65-06100 $7.95

Complete preparation for the PSAT/NMSQT, which can lead to scholarship consideration
and higher SAT scores.

PREPARATION FOR THE SAT
67-70086 $8.95

Revised and expanded version of Arco's acclaimed SAT prep book with eight full-length
exams and explanations for all questions.

MATHEMATICS WORKBOOK FOR THE SAT
65-06138 $7.95

The most thorough SAT math refresher available. Includes extensive learning aids for
review and three full-length math exams.

VOCABULARY BUILDER FOR THE SAT
65-06369 $5.95

Master 600 new words to increase your SAT score and enrich your word-power skills.
Includes word quizzes and a comprehensive final exam.

VERBAL WORKBOOK FOR THE SAT
65-06135 $7.95

An intensive review for the Verbal Ability and Test of Standard Written English sections
of the SAT, with five full-length verbal exams.

CBAT

COLLEGE BOARD ACHIEVEMENT TEST IN
AMERICAN HISTORY AND SOCIAL STUDIES
65-05746 $6.95

COLLEGE BOARD ACHIEVEMENT TEST IN BIOLOGY
65-05861 $7.95

COLLEGE BOARD ACHIEVEMENT TEST IN CHEMISTRY
65-06168 $7.95

COLLEGE BOARD ACHIEVEMENT TEST
IN ENGLISH COMPOSITION
65-05728 $6.95

COLLEGE BOARD ACHIEVEMENT TEST
IN MATHEMATICS: LEVEL I
65-06595 $7.95

COLLEGE BOARD ACHIEVEMENT TEST
IN MATHEMATICS: LEVEL II
65-05646 $5.95

COLLEGE BOARD ACHIEVEMENT TEST IN SPANISH
65-06547 $8.95

AP

ADVANCED PLACEMENT EXAMINATION
IN AMERICAN HISTORY
65-06484 $8.95

ADVANCED PLACEMENT EXAMINATION IN BIOLOGY
65-06472 $8.95

ADVANCED PLACEMENT TEST
IN COMPUTER SCIENCE (PASCAL)
65-06095 $8.95

ADVANCED PLACEMENT EXAMINATION IN ENGLISH:
COMPOSITION AND LITERATURE
65-06467 $8.95

ADVANCED PLACEMENT EXAMINATIONS IN MATHEMATICS:
CALCULUS AB AND CALCULUS BC
65-06477 $8.95

 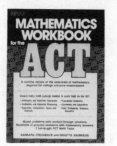 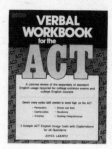

ACT

AMERICAN COLLEGE TESTING PROGRAM
65-05957 $7.95

Increase your chances of acceptance at the college of your choice with Arco's complete ACT preparation guide. Includes four full-length model exams with explanatory answers and test-taking tips.

MATHEMATICS WORKBOOK FOR THE ACT
65-05443 $6.95

This invaluable study aid reviews and reinforces all the mathematical concepts you need to score high on the ACT Mathematics Test. Includes three sample ACT math exams with detailed solutions for all questions.

VERBAL WORKBOOK FOR THE ACT
65-05348 $6.95

In-depth preparation for the English Usage and Reading Comprehension sections of the ACT with three full-length English Usage Tests and explanations for all answers.

ORDER THE BOOKS DESCRIBED ON THE PREVIOUS PAGES FROM YOUR BOOKSELLER OR DIRECTLY FROM:

PRENTICE HALL PRESS
c/o SIMON & SCHUSTER MAIL ORDER BILLING
Route 59 at Brook Hill Drive
West Nyack, NY 10994

To order directly, complete the coupon below. Enclose a check or money order for the total amount or include credit card information. No C.O.D.s accepted.

To order by phone, call 201-767-5937.

MAIL THIS COUPON TODAY!

Mail to: **Prentice Hall Press, c/o Simon & Schuster Mail Order Billing, Route 59 at Brook Hill Drive, West Nyack, NY 10994.**
Please rush the following books:

NO. OF COPIES	TITLE #	TITLE	UNIT PRICE	TOTAL
		SUB-TOTAL		
		SALES TAX FOR YOUR STATE		
		12% PACKING & MAILING		
		TOTAL		

I enclose check ☐, M.O. ☐, for $_____ or charge my ☐ VISA ☐ MASTERCARD

Account # _____ Exp. Date _____

Signature _____

NAME _____

ADDRESS _____

CITY _____ STATE _____ ZIP _____

Every Arco book is guaranteed. Return for full refund within ten days if not completely satisfied.

NOT RESPONSIBLE FOR CASH SENT THROUGH THE MAILS